Counselling Pupils in Schools

D1370122

Counselling Pupils in Schools is a comprehensive guide to the effective use of counselling in schools. It provides practical guidance for teachers and those responsible for pastoral care on how to develop counselling skills and intervention strategies. The book combines theory and research with practical classroom strategies designed to focus on the social and emotional development of students and their teachers.

Topics covered include:

- a model for counselling in school
- skills and intervention strategies for teachers
- cross-cultural and sensitive issues
- peer counselling and support
- empowering pupils and parents
- classroom-based activities

The ethics of teacher–student relationships are also discussed and teachers are provided with ideas for collaboration and managing their own stress in order to be more effective in counselling and guidance.

This book is relevant to all professionals who work with young people: Teachers, PSHE co-ordinators, SENCos, Education Welfare Officers and Educational Psychologists will find it particularly useful.

Garry Hornby is Professor of Education at the University of Canterbury in Christchurch, New Zealand. His previous publications include *The Special Educational Needs Co-ordinator's Handbook* (Routledge, 1995) and *A Mental Health Handbook for Schools* (RoutledgeFalmer, 2002).

Carol Hall is Head of the School of Education and Director of the Centre for the Study of Human Relations at the University of Nottingham.

Eric Hall is a Chartered Counselling Psychologist. He was formally a Senior Lecturer in the School of Education and Director of the Centre for the Study of Human Relations at the University of Nottingham.

Carol and **Eric** have co-authored *Human Relations in Education* (1988) and *Scripted Fantasy in the Classroom* (1991), both published by Routledge.

Counselling Pupils in Schools

Skills and strategies for teachers

Garry Hornby, Carol Hall
and Eric Hall

RoutledgeFalmer
Taylor & Francis Group

LONDON AND NEW YORK

First published 2003
by RoutledgeFalmer
11 New Fetter Lane, London EC4P 4EE

Simultaneously published in the USA and Canada
by RoutledgeFalmer
29 West 35th Street, New York, NY 10001

RoutledgeFalmer is an imprint of the Taylor & Francis Group

Typeset in Goudy by
Newgen Imaging Systems (P) Ltd, Chennai, India
Printed and bound in Great Britain by
T J International Ltd, Padstow, Cornwall

British Library Cataloguing in Publication Data
A catalogue record for this book is available from the British Library

Library of Congress Cataloging in Publication Data
A catalog record for this book has been requested

ISBN 0-415-15834-6

To all the children and young people in schools who can benefit from counselling and guidance

Contents

Figures

Contributors

Margaret Nelson Agee lectures in counselling in the School of Education at the University of Auckland. A former secondary school teacher, she has extensive experience as a counsellor in a range of settings, including secondary schools. She teaches and writes about professional ethics, and is a member of the Ethics Committee of the New Zealand Association of Counsellors.

Max Biddulph is a lecturer in the Centre for the Study of Human Relations at the University of Nottingham and has also worked as a senior manager and teacher of Personal, Social, Health Education in four UK secondary schools. He has an on-going interest in the area of Sex and Relationships Education, particularly in terms of the pastoral implications for educators and young people.

Mariana Chadwick is a Chilean psychologist who holds a PhD in Education from the University of Caen, France. She has been lecturer and researcher at the universities of Chile, Italy, Guatemala and Brazil. She has developed a systems approach to help families deal with emotional and learning problems. From the 1970s up to now, she has been author and co-author of several learning disabilities publications in Chile, Spain and Brazil.

Hans Everts is Senior Lecturer and Coordinator of Counsellor Education at the University of Auckland in New Zealand. He is a trained clinical and educational psychologist and has long been interested in family relationships, couple resilience, adolescent issues, and multi-cultural counselling. The chapter on peer counselling and support is related to current research he is conducting into the development of peer support to better meet the needs of overseas-born students in New Zealand high schools.

Carol Hall is Head of the School of Education and Director of the Centre for the Study of Human Relations at the University of Nottingham. She has worked as a teacher, lecturer and consultant on aspects of human relations in education and business in the UK and abroad. Her books include *Human Relations in Education*, *Scripted Fantasy in the Classroom* and *Developing Leadership in the Primary School*.

Eric Hall recently retired from the Centre for the Study of Human Relations in the School of Education at the University of Nottingham and is now a freelance writer, facilitator and Human Relations consultant. A counselling psychologist and former teacher, he has written widely on the areas of education, counselling and experiential learning, and recently on Buddhism and counselling.

Belinda Harris is a member of the Centre for the Study of Human Relations at the University of Nottingham and lectures in the areas of Counselling, Human Relations, Special Needs and Educational Leadership. As a teacher and senior manager of an inner city, multi-racial community college, she has extensive experience of teaching and counselling children. She was a founder member of the BACP's RACE division.

Garry Hornby is Professor of Education at the University of Canterbury in Christchurch, New Zealand. He worked as a secondary school teacher and educational psychologist before lecturing in England, New Zealand and Barbados. He is a chartered counselling psychologist and has published several books including, *Counselling in Child Disability*, *Improving Parental Involvement*, and *Mental Health Handbook for Schools*.

Bob Manthei trained as a counselling psychologist and has gained wide experience in counselling and counsellor education in the US and New Zealand. He is Associated Professor in Counsellor Education at the University of Canterbury, New Zealand, where his teaching and research interests include counselling processes, outcomes, supervision, and the client's view of counselling. His latest book is *Counselling: The Skills of Finding Solutions to Problems*.

1 Teachers and counselling

Garry Hornby

First toad was nursed by his friends. Then they encouraged him. Then they told him, quite sternly, to pull himself together. Finally, they spelled out the drab and dismal future facing him unless he 'got a grip of himself'... But none of this had any effect on Toad.... Finally, Badger could stand it no longer ... 'There is only one thing left. You must have counselling!'

(de Board, 1998, p. 3)

Various authors estimate that between 10 and 20 per cent of school-age children exhibit emotional and behavioural problems (Kottler and Kottler, 1993; Vernon, 1993; Mental Health Foundation, 1999; Thompson and Rudolph, 2000). This reinforces the importance of teachers being able to use basic counselling skills in order to help a substantial number of their students. In fact, Mosley (1993, p. 105) firmly believes that 'personal counselling is an essential activity which should be included in all schools'. In order to fulfil their pastoral duties and play their part in the teaching of personal and social education (PSE), all teachers need to have basic counselling skills, and at least one teacher in each school needs to have developed specialist expertise in counselling (McGuiness, 1998). The purpose of this book is to help classroom teachers, and those in schools responsible for pastoral care and PSE, to develop effective counselling skills and intervention strategies.

What is counselling?

Counselling is the skilled and principled use of a relationship to facilitate self-knowledge, emotional acceptance and growth, and the optimal development of personal resources. The overall aim is to provide an opportunity to work towards living more satisfyingly and resourcefully.

(British Association of Counselling, 1991, p. 1)

This definition is in accord with the way counselling is viewed in this book as being used in schools. The goals identified in the definition are ones which are encompassed by the overall aims of education. Schools aim to facilitate their students' self-knowledge and emotional acceptance. They also aim to promote personal growth and optimal development of each student's potential, the ultimate aim of education being to produce contented, productive and resourceful citizens. In schools, the relationship referred to in the definition is typically not one of counsellor to client but that of teacher to pupil. As suggested, this relationship needs to be based on certain theoretical principles and to involve the use of specific counselling skills.

Rationale for developing counselling skills

Teachers are in an ideal position to help children with their social and emotional development (McLaughlin, 1999). Since they see pupils regularly over a long period of time and
have extensive experience of children's development they are able to identify those children who are experiencing difficulties. They can then mobilise the school's pastoral care or
guidance network to deal with these difficulties, either by helping the students themselves,
referring them on to others, or by using the school's personal and social education programme. Teachers are also in an ideal position to bring their concerns to the attention of
parents and offer guidance on different strategies and sources of help which may be needed.

In order to optimise the help they can provide to children and to their parents, teachers
need to develop their knowledge and skills in the areas of counselling and consultation.
Support for the idea of teachers being able to use basic counselling skills comes from publications in the field of pastoral care (e.g. Hamblin, 1993; Lang, 1993) as well as from
Government reports on the topic of guidance in schools. For example, one of the recommendations of the Elton Report (1989) on discipline in schools was that training in basic
counselling skills should be included in initial teacher training and be provided to staff
involved in pastoral care who are already in schools by means of in-service training.

Over the past thirty years, increasing emphasis has been placed on the provision of pastoral care at all levels of the education service. There is now a greater realisation that there
is a sizeable proportion of troubled and troublesome children in schools and a greater understanding of the kinds of needs they have. Incidents such as the murder of a toddler by two
primary school children in Liverpool and the spate of shootings of school children by adolescents in the US have further emphasised the importance of the school's role in promoting
healthy social and emotional development.

Also, teachers are now expected to work more closely with parents and other professionals
such as psychologists and social workers. In addition, senior teachers are expected to be able
to support and appraise other teachers. To fulfil their roles in each of these areas teachers
need to possess basic counselling skills.

Difficulties for teachers in fulfilling their counselling and guidance role

The current emphasis on reforming school curricula and promoting academic success, which
is evident in many countries around the world, has focused attention away from the broader
function of schools which is to produce productive, fulfilled citizens. When schools are
mainly concerned with 'delivering' an academic curriculum, other aspects of the school's role,
such as providing personal and social education, tend to be overlooked. This leads to insufficient attention being paid to the needs of children for counselling and guidance and therefore
also to a lack of appreciation for the key role which teachers can play in meeting these needs.

Lane (1996) notes that British schools do not have trained counsellors on their staff and
that few of the teachers in senior positions in the pastoral network are trained in the use of
counselling skills. She, therefore, expresses concern about the general lack of counselling
expertise available to help children or their parents. A further problem concerns what
teachers generally understand counselling to be. Lane (1996) suggests that there is a continuum of helping strategies typically used in schools which ranges from directing, advising,
informing, teaching and supporting through to counselling. She comments that when
teachers use the term counselling they are, in fact, referring to some or all of the approaches
within the continuum of strategies listed above. Furthermore, she suggests that teachers

tend to use more helping strategies at the directing and advising end of the continuum rather than at the supporting and counselling end.

Regardless of the above difficulties it is inescapable that many children are in desperate need of counselling and guidance and that teachers are ideally placed to provide this. In fact, it is often the case that pupils are more likely to open up with teachers they know well than with others in the education system, such as guidance counsellors and educational psychologists, who are usually more qualified in counselling and have more time to do it, but do not have the rapport with pupils which comes from day-to-day contact. So it seems that, difficulties or not, teachers have a vital role to play in the school's pastoral care system or guidance network.

The place of counselling in the provision of pastoral care

The position taken in this book is that counselling should be an essential element of the pastoral care which schools provide for their students. Pastoral care is taken to be that part of the educational process which is concerned with providing help in the areas of personal, social and moral development, educational guidance and vocational guidance. Pastoral care is considered to be a central feature of the education offered to all young people.

As illustrated in Figure 1.1, counselling is seen as one strategy for dispensing pastoral care which should be available alongside the other major *pastoral strategies* of guidance and PSE.

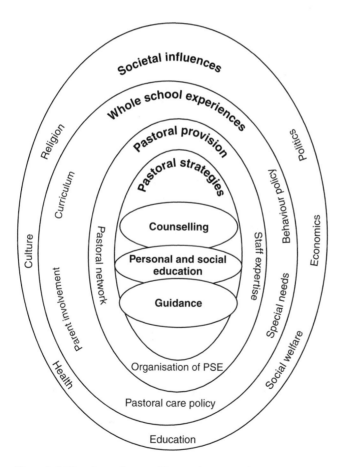

Figure 1.1 The place of counselling in the pastoral system.

These pastoral strategies are at the centre of the school's pastoral care provision. The school's *pastoral provision* encompasses the structure of the pastoral network, staff expertise and the different methods through which PSE is provided. This pastoral provision is set within the context of the *whole school experience* which has an impact through school policies on such things as curriculum, discipline, special needs and parental involvement. The whole school experience is impacted by *societal influences* which include the organisation of the education system, the economic, legal and political systems and the cultural and religious values of the society.

Pastoral strategies

These are the means by which the pastoral care provided by the school is dispensed to students. There are three major pastoral strategies: counselling, guidance and PSE.

Counselling

Counselling in schools involves helping students individually or in small groups to deal with the concerns or difficulties they are experiencing. It is considered that four levels of counselling need to be in evidence in schools (Hamblin, 1993; Lang, 1993).

- Level (1) is the use of counselling skills in the classroom in order to provide a positive learning environment and promote high levels of pupil self-esteem.
- Level (2) is the use of counselling skills by the form tutor in order to help pupils solve day-to-day problems, as well as the use of counselling skills to facilitate group activities as part of the school's PSE programme.
- Level (3) is the individual or small group counselling available from a trained specialist within the school. This could be a school counsellor or guidance counsellor, head of year or house, or a senior teacher who has a pastoral leadership role within the school.
- Level (4) involves referral procedures to help pupils access professionals outside the school, such as psychologists and psychiatrists, for specialist counselling help.

All teachers need to develop basic counselling skills, sufficient to fulfil their roles as classroom teachers and form tutors at levels (1) and (2). In addition, at least one member of the staff should have had further training in counselling in order to provide intensive counselling at level (3) and to know when and where to refer pupils for specialist help outside the school at level (4). This member of the staff should also provide training, supervision and support to teachers in their work at levels (1) and (2).

Guidance

Guidance involves helping students individually or in small groups with making personal, educational or vocational choices. It is considered that four levels of guidance need to be in evidence in schools.

- Level (1) is the provision of information by classroom teachers as part of a wide range of subjects in the curriculum in order to provide pupils with the knowledge needed to make personal, educational and vocational choices.
- Level (2) is the use of guidance by form tutors in order to help pupils make personal, educational and vocational choices. This can be provided individually or as part of the school's PSE programme.

- Level (3) is the individual or small group guidance available from a trained specialist within the school. This could be a careers officer or guidance counsellor, head of year or house, or a senior teacher who has a pastoral leadership role within the school.
- Level (4) involves referral procedures to help pupils access agencies outside the school, such as careers, services or job placement agencies.

All teachers need to have a basic knowledge of guidance, sufficient to fulfil their roles as classroom teachers and form tutors at levels (1) and (2). In addition, at least one member of the staff should have had further training in order to provide intensive guidance at level (3) and to know which agencies to refer pupils to outside the school at level (4). This member of staff should also act as a resource to other teachers in the school.

Personal and social education

A personal and social education programme, which also includes moral and vocational education, is an essential part of the pastoral care provision of every school. There are three ways in which PSE is carried out in schools.

- *PSE is infused into all subjects across the curriculum.* All teachers cover aspects of PSE as part of their subject teaching. For example, mathematics teachers will cover budgeting, social studies teachers will address the issue of discrimination and science teachers will cover sex education.
- *PSE is included in the tutorial work programme.* Form tutors teach it to their tutor groups, along with other activities, during form periods.
- *PSE is taught as a separate subject.* PSE is regarded as a specific subject on the school's curriculum. It is taught by form tutors or by specialists such as guidance counsellors or guidance teachers, or by some combination of these.

The content of PSE programmes varies from school to school. Many schools use published materials such as Active Tutorial Work (Baldwin and Wells, 1979) while others have developed and use their own materials or use a combination of their own and published materials. Both primary and secondary school programmes will address aspects of health education and moral education as well as personal and social development, which may be done in separate science or religious education lessons. In addition, secondary school PSE programmes also address vocational development and careers education.

Pastoral provision

The pastoral strategies described above are set in the school's overall pastoral care provision. The major elements of this provision are the pastoral network, staff expertise and training, and the organisation of PSE within the school.

Pastoral network

The pastoral or guidance network refers to the ways in which schools organise the lines of communication and support between staff involved in the pastoral care of pupils. The two major systems for this in secondary schools are the house system and the year system. The year system is the more widely used with a head of year and deputy head of year being assigned to each year group of pupils. However, there are many variations on how this is done and each school is likely to have its own variant.

Staff expertise

A key element of the school's pastoral provision is the expertise in the areas of counselling, guidance and PSE which is available. If the school does not have any specialists in counselling or careers education on its staff, there will clearly be significant gaps in the pastoral care it can provide. Similarly, if most teachers have not had any training in counselling skills or the skills needed for conducting the group activities used in PSE programmes they will be unable to effectively fulfil their roles as form tutors.

Organisation of PSE

As discussed above, there are three major ways in which PSE is taught in schools, as a separate subject, as part of the tutorial programme or infused into subjects across the curriculum. All schools use at least one of these methods, many use two of them and some use all three approaches. Although the actual organisation for the teaching of PSE will vary from school to school, all schools need to have an organisational structure within which PSE is taught.

Whole school experience

The provision of pastoral care within schools is set within the overall impact of the school on its pupils. Foremost in this will be the school's policy on pastoral care. What is the structure of the guidance network? How is PSE organised? What expertise and training should the staff have? But the impact of the school on its pupils will also be affected by its policies on various other issues. For example, if the school's policy on curriculum places great emphasis on academic subjects there will be little room for separate PSE programmes. Similarly, if the school's behaviour management policy focuses mainly on maintaining discipline, and disruptive pupils are viewed as problems to be got rid of rather than children in need of help, then the quality of pastoral care will be severely reduced.

Societal influences

The impact of schools on pupils is set within the overall impact of societal influences on schools. Foremost in this will be the organisation of the school system. For example, in Barbados, entry to secondary schools is based on students' performance in an 11 plus examination. This ensures that primary school curricula are closely geared to teaching the academic skills required to do well in this examination and there is little room for a broad curriculum which includes PSE.

Other societal influences are the political and economic systems operating in the society. For example, is there large scale unemployment and poverty or is it a society which attempts to ensure that all adults have jobs and all families have a reasonable standard of living?

Further influences are the cultural and religious values held by members of the society. For example, is it a society which emphasises collaborative relationships and values quality of life for all its citizens or is it one which considers that competition is the best way to motivate its members and thereby accepts that some people will have a much greater share of the society's resources than others.

The role of the form tutor

It is widely believed that form tutors are a key element in the provision of pastoral care within schools (Adams, 1989; Marland and Rogers, 1997). A few years ago, the National

Association for Pastoral Care in Education drew up a list of goals for the form tutor's role and proposed a list of competencies required to function effectively as a form tutor (NAPCE, 1986). The major goals and skills needed to fulfil these goals are listed below in order to consider the place of counselling in the role of the form tutor.

Form tutor goals include:

- providing continuing personal contact with each student;
- facilitating a caring climate within the tutor group;
- monitoring students' progress and achievement;
- communicating with pupils, parents and colleagues;
- providing 'first line' guidance and support to students.

Form tutor skills needed include:

- skills for listening to and counselling students;
- skills for providing information and guidance;
- skills for observation and analysis of students' behaviour and progress;
- skills for communicating with parents and colleagues;
- skills for leading group activities used in PSE or tutorial programmes.

It is clear from the above lists that counselling and communication skills are essential to the role of form tutors. The NAPCE (1986) also proposed that pastoral leaders, such as heads of year, require similar competencies as form tutors but at a more advanced level as well as additional skills such as managerial and team leadership skills.

Developmental needs and tasks of children at various ages

In order to understand the problems that students are likely to experience it is useful to consider their developmental needs and the developmental tasks they will encounter at primary school and secondary school levels. There are several models of children's developmental *needs*, including those by Erikson (1968) and Glasser (1986), which are well known to teachers. An alternative perspective, which is particularly useful in education, has been provided by Havinghurst (1974). He has suggested that there are certain developmental *tasks* which children must master at each stage of development in order to prepare for later life. Successful mastery of these tasks results in well adjusted children who are able to cope with the tasks they encounter in later developmental stages, whereas failure to master the tasks results in maladjustment and the inability to complete successfully future tasks. He has identified the following tasks for primary and secondary age children.

Developmental tasks of primary school-age children:

- learning the physical skills necessary for games, for example, throwing, kicking;
- building self-esteem and a wholesome attitude toward one's body;
- learning to get along with one's peers;
- learning appropriate masculine or feminine social roles;
- developing fundamental skills in reading, writing and arithmetic;
- developing concepts necessary for everyday living;
- developing conscience, morality and a core of values;
- achieving personal independence or autonomy;
- developing rational attitudes to social groups and institutions.

This list of tasks suggests that primary school-age children are likely to experience problems at school in areas related to learning difficulties, particularly with the 3Rs, as well as issues in personal development, such as independence and self-esteem, and also problems with peer relationships such as in conflicts with friends and classmates.

Developmental tasks of secondary school-age children:

- achieving new and more mature relations with peers of both sexes;
- achieving a masculine or feminine social role;
- accepting one's physique and using the body effectively;
- achieving emotional independence from parents and other adults;
- preparing for marriage and family life;
- preparing for making a living or career;
- acquiring a set of values, ethics or an ideology as a guide to behaviour;
- developing socially responsible behaviour.

This list of tasks suggests that secondary school-age children are likely to experience problems with identity and social relationships, particularly associated with relationships with peers and the opposite sex, as well as with issues related to autonomy and preparation for work and family life.

Problems exhibited by school-age children

Kottler and Kottler (1993) claim that one in five or 20 per cent of children have emotional problems over and above those expected in normal development. They go on to suggest that the majority of children's problems are overlooked by teachers because they have not been trained to identify them. A list of problems which children can experience and their identifying features, which has been adapted from Kottler and Kottler (1993), is outlined below.

Generalized anxiety. This is characterised by excessive worry or apprehension about things which are outside children's control. It is identified by: headaches, stomach aches, restlessness, dizziness, nausea, irritability and frequent urination.

Depressive disorder. This is a pervasive disorder of mood in which the child feels sad and withdrawn. It is identified by low self-esteem, poor concentration, loss of appetite, sleep disruption, listlessness, hopelessness and suicidal thoughts.

Phobic disorders. This is characterised by avoidant or anxious responses to specific situations such as spiders, high places, open spaces, everyday objects or places. It is identified by persistent fears and physical sensations such as sweating, trembling, nausea and dizziness.

Behaviour disorder. This is characterised by a persistent pattern of ignoring rules and abusing the rights of others or hostile, defiant or uncooperative behaviour. It is identified by frequent fighting, destructiveness, cruelty to others, aggressive behaviour, arguments, temper tantrums, swearing and annoying others.

Attention deficit hyperactivity disorder. This is defined as involving impulsivity, inattention and overactivity. Identifying features include fidgeting, restlessness, distractability and difficulty following instructions and completing assignments.

Eating disorders. These are characterised by obsession with food (anorexia nervosa), binging and forced vomiting (bulimia) and eating non-food substances (pica). Main identifiers are poor eating habits and weight loss.

Psychotic disorder. There is distortion of reality with hallucinations, delusions or bizarre behaviour. Symptoms include social withdrawal, incoherent speech, delusional beliefs and inappropriate emotional reactions.

Substance abuse. This refers to addiction to or habitual use of drugs, alcohol or other substances. Identifying signs include slurred speech, unsteady gait, sores around mouth or nose, bloodshot eyes, irritability or lethargy.

Effects of sexual abuse. This refers to inappropriate touching or sexual acts with children. Identifying signs include fear of adults, withdrawal, frequent nightmares, precocious behaviour and reluctance to go home.

Effects of physical abuse. This is characterised by non-accidental injuries such as bruises, burns or bite marks. Overcompliant, attention seeking or aggressive behaviour may be signs of physical abuse.

Obsessive-compulsive disorder. This is characterised by obsessive thoughts or repetitive behaviours apparently beyond the child's control. It is identified by observation of compulsive or repetitive behaviour or reports of recurrent thoughts.

Psychosomatic disorders. These are persistent physical complaints which are due to stress rather than physiological causes. Identifying signs include facial tics, headaches, back pain, stomach pain, wetting and soiling.

Personality disorders. This refers to enduring maladaptive or dysfunctional behaviour. Identifying features include persistent lying and stealing, irresponsibility, unpredictability, antisocial, bizarre or dependent behaviour.

Adjustment disorders. These are characterised by reactions to traumatic life events such as bereavement, moving house, illness and divorce of parents. Identifying features include anxiety, depression, withdrawal, physical complaints and deteriorating academic performance.

The benefits and difficulties of teachers using counselling skills

In order to help children who are experiencing any of the above problems teachers need to develop at least a basic level of counselling skills. They need to be able to listen attentively, use some basic counselling strategies and know when to refer on. Lane (1996) supports the idea of all teachers needing to have training in basic counselling skills. She suggests that, ideally, supervised practice in the use of these skills needs to be provided in the school context. She also asserts that, in order to use counselling skills effectively, teachers need to be aware of their personal boundaries and values, particularly those which are likely to interfere with their ability to help certain clients. Added to this must be the teachers' awareness of the limits of their competence and the importance of referring on to qualified counsellors when necessary.

Lane (1996) then goes on to discuss particular difficulties related to counselling in schools regarding confidentiality, training, supervision and personal boundaries and values. She considers that confidentiality is the most problematic issue for teachers. The most crucial aspect of this is the conflict between the need to maintain confidentiality in order to establish their students' trust and the need to pass on information to other people in some circumstances, such as in cases of physical or sexual abuse. These issues are discussed further in Chapter 15.

How teachers can develop counselling skills

In the past, teachers have had little opportunity to learn about counselling in either pre-service or in-service training. However, there is a rapidly growing interest from teachers in learning counselling skills. It is to address this need for information about counselling and the desire for learning counselling skills that this book has been written. Each of the authors has been involved in leading courses aimed at helping teachers to develop counselling skills for a number of years. Courses on counselling at various levels are now available in most parts of the world. Many of these courses are suitable for teachers to attend. In order to prepare themselve for using counselling skills with children, teachers should ideally enrol in a course teaching counselling skills alongside reading this book. In addition to training in specific skills an understanding of counselling theory will be helpful to the teacher. Whenever possible, it is also valuable for teachers to observe skilled counsellors in action as well as to have supervision from qualified counsellors when putting their counselling skills into practice.

However, it is recognised that most teachers will be unable to undertake extensive training in counselling theory and skills or to benefit from observation of, or supervision from, qualified counsellors. These things are not essential since it is not the intention of this book to transform teachers into counsellors, although it is recognised that most of the counselling and guidance which occurs in schools is already carried out by teachers. It is not a case of suggesting that teachers take on a new role so much as helping them to function more effectively in a role they are already fulfilling. If this book can assist teachers in improving their skills and knowledge about counselling in order to help them more effectively meet their students' counselling and guidance needs, then it will have met its intended aim.

References

Adams, S. (1989) *A Guide to Creative Tutoring*. London: Kogan Page.

Baldwin, J. and Wells, H. (1979) *Active Tutorial Work* (Books 1 to 5). Oxford: Blackwell.

British Association for Counselling (1991) *Code of Ethics and Practice for Counsellors*. Rugby: B.A.C.

de Board, R. (1998) *Counselling for Toads: A Psychological Adventure*. London: Routledge.

Elton, L. (1989) *Elton Report: Discipline in Schools*. London: HMSO.

Erikson, D. (1968) *Identity, Youth and Crisis*. New York: Norton.

Glasser, W. (1986) *Control Theory in the Classroom*. New York: Harper and Row.

Hamblin, D. (1993) *The Teacher and Counselling* (2nd edn). Hemel Hempstead: Simon and Schuster.

Havinghurst, R. J. (1974) *Developmental Tasks and Education* (3rd edn). New York: David McKay.

Hornby, G. (2000) *Improving Parental Involvement*. London: Cassell.

Kottler, J. and Kottler, E. (1993) *Teacher as Counselor*. Newbury Park, CA: Corwin Press.

Lane, J. (1996) Counselling issues in mainstream schools. *Emotional and Behavioural Difficulties*, 1(2): 46–51.

Lang, P. (1993) Counselling in the primary school: An integrated approach. In K. Bovair and C. McLaughlin (eds) *Counselling in Schools: A Reader*. London: David Fulton, pp. 21–35.

Marland, M. and Rogers, R. (1997) *The Art of the Tutor*. London: David Fulton.

McGuiness, J. (1998) *Counselling in Schools: New Perspectives*. London: Cassell.

McLaughlin, C. (1999) Counselling in schools: looking forward and looking back. *British Journal of Guidance and Counselling*, 27(1): 13–22.

Mental Health Foundation (1999) *Bright Futures: Promoting Children and Young People's Mental Health*. London: Mental Health Foundation.

Mosely, J. (1993) Is there a place for counselling in schools? *Counselling*, 4(2): 104–5.

National Association for Pastoral Care in Education (1986) *Preparing for Pastoral Care*. Coventry: N.A.P.C.E.

National Curriculum Council (1989) *The National Curriculum and Whole School Curriculum Planning; Preliminary Guidance – Circular Number 6*. York: N.C.C.

Thompson, C. L. and Rudolph, L. B. (2000) *Counseling Children* (5th edn). Belmont, CA: Brooks/Cole.

Vernon, A. (1993) *Counseling Children and Adolescents*. Denver: Love.

2 A model for counselling in schools

Garry Hornby

Counselling can be a tool for preventing 'normal' problems from becoming more serious and resulting in delinquency, school failure and emotional disturbance. It can be a method for creating a healthy environment to assist children in coping with the stresses and conflicts of their growth and development. Counselling can also be a major remedial force for helping children in trouble through appraisal, individual or group counselling, parent or teacher consultation, or environmental changes.

(Thompson and Rudolph, 1988, p. 9)

Why do we need a model for counselling in schools?

It is the contention of this book that a specific model is needed to guide the practice of counselling in schools because counselling in schools differs substantially from the way in which most counselling normally takes place. There are six ways in which counselling in schools differs from other forms of counselling.

First of all, what sets counselling in schools apart from counselling in other settings is that it has a broader focus than in most situations in which counselling is used. Most forms of counselling have a remedial focus, that is, they deal with specific problems which concern clients. Counselling in schools, in addition to focusing on remediation of students' problems, also has preventative and developmental focuses, as suggested by the above quotation. For example, counselling skills are used by teachers in providing guidance to students on topics such as drug education which are designed to prevent them from developing problems. In addition, counselling skills are used by teachers in order to facilitate students' personal, social, moral and vocational development.

Second, the counselling which takes place in schools is typically not like the formal counselling which is discussed in most books on counselling where a client seeking help arrives for a pre-arranged session of one hour with a trained counsellor in a room organised specifically for this purpose. In schools, the setting will often be an empty classroom or a senior teacher's office. The sessions will often be brief, sometimes conducted in the few minutes between lessons or in the slightly longer times available at break or at lunchtime. Much of the counselling in schools occurs spontaneously, for example, at the end of a lesson, when a student appears to need help. The student may approach the teacher or the teacher may initiate the counselling because of concern about the student.

This points up the third way in which counselling in schools is different. In contrast to most other settings, in which clients are self-referred, a large proportion of counselling contacts in schools are initiated by teachers or parents rather than children or young people themselves. A subject teacher may approach a child's form tutor or head of year with a concern about progress or behaviour and ask for the child to be seen. Alternatively, a parent may express a concern to a student's headteacher, head of year or form tutor and expect that someone would talk with the student. The fact that such interactions have not been initiated by the children themselves is likely to influence their willingness to accept guidance from teachers or participate in meaningful counselling.

The fourth way in which counselling in schools is different is that the people doing most of the counselling are not qualified counsellors, but teachers, many of whom have had little or no training in counselling. In schools which do not have counsellors, teachers do all of the counselling. Even in schools which do have counsellors, teachers tend to do much of the counselling. This is because most students find it easier to open up with teachers they know well rather than counselling or guidance staff who are less well known to them. It also happens because counsellors can only take on a few students with the greatest difficulty leaving teachers to deal with the majority of students' counselling needs.

The fifth way in which counselling in schools is different is that it is not a specific, isolated, helping strategy which is on offer but is part of a continuum of helping strategies, ranging from directing, and advising through to supporting and counselling, which are typically used in schools, as noted in Chapter 1. It is considered that teachers currently tend to use more helping strategies at the directing end of the continuum rather than at the counselling end (Lane, 1996). This book hopes to encourage teachers to use more strategies at the counselling end of the continuum and to use them more effectively.

The sixth way in which counselling in schools is different is that the clients are children or adolescents rather than adults, who are the focus of most counselling theories and counsellor training courses. Therefore, counselling theories and skills need to be adapted in order to be successful in schools. Counselling children is considered to present a special challenge since they are different from adults in their cognitive, emotional and social development (Erdman and Lampe, 1996). Children at earlier stages of development cannot think abstractly and therefore respond best to practical activities such as sand play, art therapy or storytelling. They may find it difficult to understand other people's points of view or have simplistic notions of basic concepts such as cause and effect. They may also have difficulty in accepting help from a counsellor if they view all adults as authority figures.

Children's counselling needs

When counselling children strategies need to be used which take account of children's cognitive level as well as their social and emotional development. A useful guide to the implications of children's cognitive level is provided by Piaget's model of cognitive development which suggests that children's cognitive development progresses through four stages: sensorimotor; pre-operational; concrete operations; and formal operations.

It has been found that, because of the wide range of abilities encountered in schools, children of primary school age (5–11 years) may be functioning at any one of three stages of cognitive development. For example, whereas the average child of nine years of age will be at the concrete operations stage, a child of low intellectual ability may still be at the pre-operational stage, while a child of high ability may be at the formal operations stage. So, for primary school children, thinking processes can be anything from lacking an understanding of cause and effect to an ability to solve problems using abstract thinking. Hence, the importance of taking into account primary school children's cognitive level when counselling them.

At secondary school level (11–18 years) Piaget's model suggests that all pupils will be at the formal operations stage, which is characterised by being able to think abstractly. However, recent research (Adey and Shayer, 1994) has suggested that around half of secondary age pupils have not reached the formal operations stage by the time they are sixteen years old, let alone twelve years which is the age that Piaget suggested. If this is the case, then it must be assumed that, although some secondary school pupils are at the stage of formal operations, most of them will be at the concrete operations stage and therefore cannot think abstractly to any great extent. This places severe limitations on their ability to solve the problems which they will encounter as adolescents and therefore has important implications for the counselling strategies which should be used.

In addition to their cognitive development, children's social and emotional development also need to be taken into account when considering which counselling strategies to use. For example, there are substantial differences between primary and secondary age children in their social relationships with peers and with adults. In addition, the ability to identify and express emotions differs markedly between young children and adolescents.

A suitable model for counselling in schools

Given the specific difficulties involved in counselling children and the other aspects of providing counselling in schools, which were discussed above, it is considered necessary to use a counselling model which takes all these factors into account. Specifically, the counselling model needs to be:

- able to be used preventatively, developmentally and to remediate problems;
- able to be adapted to suit children at different developmental levels;
- able to be implemented by teachers with minimal training in counselling;
- able to be used in brief helping interactions in non-ideal settings;
- congruent with the guidance strategies, personal and social education (PSE) and overall approach to pastoral care which are found in schools;
- easily understood by and acceptable to teachers and parents.

The counselling model presented in this chapter is designed to take into account the above factors. It is a *developmental* model of counselling, set in a *humanistic* framework and which is based on a *psycho-educational approach* to helping. These three major aspects of the model are explained below.

Humanistic framework

> … the counselling relationship is merely a means of tapping personal resources and developing human potential.
>
> (Thompson and Rudolph, 2000, p. 142)

The humanistic principles on which this model is based are mostly derived from the work of Rogers (1980) and Maslow (1970). The major assumptions of this perspective are that children are basically good and have an innate tendency toward growth and fulfilment of their potential, that is, toward self-actualisation. It is believed that, given love, respect, empathy and genuineness from the significant people in their lives children will develop into happy and productive citizens. They will become fully-functioning people who are able to live life to the full, be open to new experiences and maintain a high level of self-esteem. If these conditions are absent then their growth toward self-actualisation will be blocked, their self-esteem will be threatened and they are likely to develop psychological problems.

From the humanistic perspective a psychologically healthy person is one who is fully functioning in the process of self-actualising. Emphasis is placed on the uniqueness of the individual and the subjectivity with which reality is perceived. Respect, genuineness and empathy are the bases for healthy relationships. Everyone is regarded as having a responsibility to work towards improvement of the human condition particularly as regards the young, the old, the disadvantaged and the disabled. The difficulties for which people need counselling are regarded as being due to them experiencing problems in living rather than them being sick or mentally ill.

The key components of a psychologically healthy person (according to Cole, 1982) are:

- *High self-esteem*, the essential ingredients of which are considered to be: security, self-awareness, a feeling of belonging, a sense of purpose and a feeling of personal competence.
- *Internal locus of control*, that is, a belief that one's own actions are more influential than outside forces in achieving one's goals.
- *Self-management*, being able to plan, consider options and adapt to suit the different situations one encounters.
- *Intrinsic values*, having philosophical, religious or spiritual beliefs to guide one's behaviour.
- *Social responsibility*, feeling the need to contribute to the life of others.
- *Competence in life skills*, which encompasses personal, social, vocational, practical and leisure skills.

It is clear that the humanistic perspective is consistent with the aims of pastoral care and personal and social education in schools, as outlined in Chapter 1. In fact, humanistic principles provide much of the underpinning theoretical base for pastoral care or guidance and counselling in schools.

Developmental model

Helpers listen to the problem situations of their clients in terms of developmental stages, tasks and crises, in terms of interactions with the social settings of life, and in terms of the strengths, deficits, and unused potential in the area of life skills.

(Egan, 1984, p. 139)

The developmental approach to counselling is based on the idea that there are developmental stages through which children must progress if they are to lead effective lives as adults. Satisfactory progression through the stages depends on the successful accomplishment of the developmental tasks (Havinghurst, 1972) which are specific to the stages, as discussed in Chapter 1. Accomplishment of these developmental tasks is dependent on mastery of the life skills appropriate to each stage and task. Inadequate resolution of these developmental tasks leads to children experiencing psychological problems or crises in their lives.

The developmental approach also takes into account the extent to which the ecology of human development (Bronfenbrenner, 1979) impinges on the resolution of developmental tasks. As discussed in Chapter 8, children and families need to be viewed from this wider ecological perspective. They are seen as part of a dynamic system, the various levels of which will either facilitate or attenuate their learning of life skills and thereby their progress through the developmental stages. For example, at the microsystem level the absence of one parent through death or divorce will make progress more difficult. At the mesosystem level, support from teachers and extended family members may ameliorate this to some extent. At the exosystem level, an education system which emphasises PSE will help children cope with their loss and facilitate their progress while a school system obsessed with academic goals will tend to retard their progress. In addition, at the macrosystem level societal values and public attitudes regarding single parent families will play an important role in determining the level of support and resources made available to facilitate the healthy development of such children.

The overall goal of developmental counselling is facilitating children's self-actualisation by helping them address the various tasks associated with each developmental stage. Remediation of the immediate problem situation is the short-term goal. The long-term goal is to equip children with new skills so that they can solve their own problems and thereby live their lives more effectively. Since children's problems are considered to be due to deficits in the life skills necessary to deal with the developmental tasks they are facing, counselling involves teaching them the skills they need to be able to deal with their current situation. Developmental counselling also involves teaching children other life skills in which they are deficient in order to help them cope with future difficulties and thereby facilitate their self-actualisation.

Developmental counselling is therefore consistent with the role of teachers when providing personal and social education to their pupils. The teacher/counsellor facilitates children's exploration of the problem situation and then teaches them the life skills they need to deal with the problem through explanation, modelling, role-play and homework assignments. The teacher/counsellor also supports the changes which children make and acts as a coach in the development of further life skills.

Psycho-educational approach

> Every problem, whether it involves mastering a developmental task, resolving a life crisis, or deepening a human relationship, is conceptualised as involving specific skills that can be taught.
>
> (Larson, 1984, p. 5)

From the psycho-educational perspective, children's problems are viewed as skill deficits rather than abnormality or illness. This model differs from therapeutic approaches which are based on the medical model which can be summarised by the following paradigm:

illness $\Rightarrow$ diagnosis $\Rightarrow$ prescription $\Rightarrow$ therapy $\Rightarrow$ cure

In contrast, the psycho-educational model is based on the paradigm below:

problem/ambition $\Rightarrow$ goal setting $\Rightarrow$ skill teaching $\Rightarrow$ progress/achievement

That is, every problem or ambition which children have is dealt with by teaching them the skills needed to overcome their problem or achieve their ambition.

From this perspective, counselling is a process by which counsellors share their skills with children by means of facilitating, modelling or directly teaching the skills needed. In this way, children learn the skills needed to cope with the problems they face or achieve the ambitions they desire. In addition, children can be taught other skills which they need in order to live their lives more effectively. These skills are drawn from the pool of life skills which encompass a wide range of aspects of effective living. They include: problem-solving skills, communication skills, health and fitness skills, leisure skills, study skills, vocational skills and parenting skills (Gazda, 1984).

In the psycho-educational model of counselling, all interventions are viewed as means of training clients in the skills of effective living. Therefore, any life skill which can be taught to children can be included in the stock of interventions at the counsellor's disposal. This means that techniques from a wide range of theoretical approaches can be used as psycho-educational interventions. For example, children can be taught skills drawn from humanistic, behavioural, cognitive or psychodynamic theories of counselling. The psycho-educational model therefore provides the means for a systematic and integrative eclecticism, as suggested by Egan in the following quotation,

> Helpers need a conceptual framework that enables them to borrow ideas, methods and techniques systematically from all theories, schools and approaches and integrate them into their own theory and practice of helping.
>
> (Egan, 1986, p. 9)

The psycho-educational model provides a framework which allows for interventions from different theoretical approaches to be used within a skills-training paradigm. Interventions from widely differing theoretical approaches can be used as long as they can be formulated as skills which can be taught to children to help them live their lives more effectively. Since the majority of counselling techniques can be formulated in this way teachers using a psycho-educational model have a wide array of intervention strategies at their disposal.

Three-stage counselling model

The model proposed in this book for counselling in schools is a developmental counselling model, based on humanistic principles, set within a psycho-educational framework. This model has been influenced by previous models of counselling such as those proposed by Egan (1982, 1986) and Hornby (1990) but has been adapted to make it suitable for counselling in the school setting. The model is summarised in Figure 2.1.

Exploration	*Intervention*	*Empowering*
Three aspects	Examples	Three aspects
Establishing therapeutic relationship	Problem solving	Supporting action programmes
	Cognitive therapy	
Exploring concerns	Play therapy	Consolidating changes
	Solution-focused therapy	
Assessing situation	Writing therapy	Enabling self-actualisation

Figure 2.1 Three-stage counselling model for schools.

The three stages of the model focus on *Exploration, Intervention* and *Empowering*. Briefly, teachers use listening skills to help pupils' *explore* their concerns and feelings, then select and implement strategies from a range of possible *interventions* in order to help pupils move forward. Finally, teachers *empower* pupils by focusing on the development of their full potential and helping them to build on strengths and overcome weaknesses.

It is considered that the three-stage counselling model fits well with what teachers who are skilled in helping typically already do. First, they use listening skills in order to *explore* what pupils have to say about their problems, concerns, ideas or ambitions. Second, they come up with *interventions* designed to help pupils. For example, the use of problem-solving techniques to help pupils work out for themselves the course of action which appears best. Third, effective teachers typically do not leave it there, wherever possible they seek to *empower* pupils they have tried to help in a variety of ways. For example, they may talk to the pupil about how they can build on their strengths, perhaps by joining a particular group or club or by reading a certain book or by talking with another person who is an expert in the area.

The key features of the three stages of the counselling model are outlined below.

Exploration

There are three aspects of the first stage of the model: establishing a therapeutic relationship; exploring concerns; and assessing the problem situation.

Therapeutic relationship. Teachers must first develop sufficient rapport with students for them to be willing to open up. This is often referred to as a therapeutic alliance which is mostly based on the teacher's ability to communicate empathy, genuineness and respect to the student. Use of the listening skills discussed in Chapter 3 is crucial to establishing this relationship.

Exploring concerns. Listening skills are also essential for facilitating the exploration of students' concerns. By getting students to talk about their problems or ambitions and express feelings teachers can help them to clarify their concerns or desires.

Assessing the situation. Helping students to clarify their concerns also enables teachers to assess the problem situation as well as the unresolved developmental tasks and deficits in life skills which have led to the situation. As well as considering students as individuals teachers need to focus on their interactions with others and the broader aspects of school, family and community which have an impact on their lives. This assessment helps teachers to decide on the types of intervention which are most appropriate.

Intervention

In the second stage of the model various intervention strategies are used in order to teach students the life skills they need to deal with their current problem situation or ambition. There are two aspects of this second stage: the types of intervention strategies available; and the methods used to implement them.

Types of intervention strategies. As discussed earlier, a wide range of intervention strategies are able to be used within this psycho-educational model of counselling. A selection of these, which are able to be used by teachers without extensive training in counselling, is presented in Chapter 4. Intervention strategies range from use of the 'empty-chair' technique to help students express unresolved emotion, through cognitive restructuring in order to develop positive self-statements and build self-esteem, to the use of problem-solving techniques to help students decide on their best course of action.

Implementation methods. There are three ways in which the intervention strategies are implemented. First, teachers act as a model demonstrating skills such as 'active listening' and assertion skills in their interaction with students. Second, teachers act directly, guiding students through activities or exercises designed to help students develop the life skills they need. Examples are the use of the 'two-chair' technique to enable students to become aware of disparate parts of themselves or the use of 'guided fantasy' to enable students to get in touch with repressed thoughts and feelings. Third, teachers provide direct instruction to students to teach them the life skills they need. Examples are, the teaching of relaxation skills to reduce anxiety, or the teaching of focusing to develop experiential awareness, or the teaching of behaviour modification techniques to facilitate the development of self-management skills (see Chapters 4–6 for details of these skills).

Empowering

There are three aspects of the third stage of the model: supporting action programmes; consolidating changes; and enabling self-actualisation.

Supporting action programmes. Teachers need to support students in carrying out the action programmes they have developed in order to deal with their problem situations or make progress toward their ambitions. This support can range from simple praise and encouragement to teaching students how to be more assertive in order to achieve their goals.

Consolidating changes. An important aspect of this stage is helping students to maintain and consolidate the changes they have made. Teachers can help with this by reminding students of the progress they have made and by encouraging them to persevere in spite of the difficulties they will face in maintaining the changes.

Enabling self-actualisation. The major aim of stage three is to enable students' self-actualisation. That is, to facilitate students' growth and fulfilment of their potential to the fullest possible extent. Teachers need to help students to become aware of the life skill areas in which they have strengths and those in which they have weaknesses. Students can then be taught life skills which may be unrelated to their current concerns but which need to be developed to facilitate their progress towards self-actualisation. For example, students can be helped to improve their study skills in order to achieve higher levels of academic achievement. A variety of strategies for empowering students are discussed in Chapters 5 and 6.

Flexibility within the model

While it is seen as useful for teachers to work within the framework of the three-stage model this does not mean that all three stages would be used with all students who are counselled. For some students, stage one will be sufficient to help them to clarify their problem or ambition and initiate their own exploration of possible courses of action. Other students will need to progress through stage one to stage two in order to benefit from one or more interventions implemented by the teacher. Having learned the requisite life skills to cope with their immediate concern some students will have no further contact with the teacher. Other students need to move on to stage three in which teachers help students consolidate changes and empower their further development toward self-actualisation.

Attitudes, knowledge and skills needed to implement the model in schools

In order to be able to use this model for counselling in schools, teachers need to possess certain attitudes, skills and knowledge. It is the intention of this book to provide teachers with the requisite knowledge and help them develop the skills and attitudes needed for effective counselling in schools. These are outlined below.

Attitudes

The attitudes which teachers need in order to counsel effectively in schools are the basic underlying attitudes of genuineness, respect and empathy suggested by Rogers (1980). They must be *genuine* in their relationships with pupils, their parents and colleagues. That is, they must come across as real people with their own strengths and weaknesses. For example, they should always be prepared to say that they 'don't know' when this is the case. Teachers should also show *respect* for the views of pupils, their parents and colleagues. For example, children's or their parents' opinions and requests should always be given the utmost consideration. Most importantly, teachers should develop *empathy* with children and their parents. They should try to see the child's and family's situation from the point of view of the parents and pupils. If teachers can develop an empathic understanding of their pupils' and parents' perspectives then it is likely that productive relationships will evolve. In addition, there are several core beliefs that are useful in becoming an effective teacher/counsellor (Manthei, 1997):

- as much as possible, counselling should focus on the students' competence rather than their deficits, their possibilities rather than limitations;
- counselling should focus on bringing about a better future rather than focus on past difficulties;
- students should be regarded as competent, capable and responsible;
- simple interventions should be tried before moving on to more complicated ones;
- bringing about small changes can lead to larger changes, in a sort of ripple effect.

Skills

In order to provide effective counselling and guidance to pupils and their parents, teachers need to have good interpersonal communication skills. An essential part of this is the possession of basic listening skills discussed in Chapter 3 and the counselling skills discussed in Chapters 4 and 5. Briefly, teachers need to be able to use listening skills to help pupils *explore* their concerns and feelings. They also need the skills to implement a range of possible *counselling interventions* to deal with these concerns. Finally, they need the skills to *empower* pupils by helping them to build on strengths and overcome weaknesses. Possessing the skills required to implement this three-stage model of counselling will contribute enormously to the ability of teachers to provide effective counselling and guidance to pupils and their parents.

Other interpersonal skills required by teachers include the skills needed for communicating effectively with parents and for collaborating with colleagues which are discussed in Chapters 12 and 13. They also need to develop the stress management skills which are discussed in Chapter 14. In addition, teachers need to have group leadership skills, discussed in Chapter 5, so that they can facilitate various group experiences with pupils and parents.

Knowledge

The knowledge which teachers need in order to effectively counsel is extensive but much of it will already be possessed by most teachers. First, teachers need to have a good knowledge of child development, including the various stages and tasks which were described in Chapter 1. Second, they need an understanding of the typical emotional and behavioural problems which children experience, such as conduct disorders and phobias, as outlined in Chapter 1. Third, they also need to have an understanding of children's reactions to loss and trauma, and other sensitive issues as discussed in Chapters 10 and 11.

Fourth, teachers need to have good knowledge of the school's pastoral care system and of the outside agencies which can also provide guidance and counselling to students and their parents, as outlined in Chapter 1. Fifth, they also need to know about their students' backgrounds, particularly those from different cultural groups, as discussed in Chapter 9. Sixth, they need a thorough knowledge of the school's Personal and Social Education curriculum, as discussed in Chapters 1 and 6. Seventh, they need to know about a variety of intervention strategies, as discussed in Chapter 4. Finally, teachers need an understanding of the ethical and professional issues raised by counselling in schools, such as confidentiality and supervision, which are discussed in Chapter 15.

Practical considerations for counselling in schools

Counsellors and teachers need to adapt their approach and skills in order to effectively counsel children and adolescents (Thompson and Rudolph, 2000). First of all, an appropriate place for counselling children needs to be found. Ideally, a comfortable room, free from distractions and with seating suitable for children should be used. Children should be allowed to choose where they will sit. Teachers should then seat themselves at eye level with the child.

Building trust in the relationship may take longer with children than adults so teachers need to be patient. Listening skills are particularly important but non-threatening questions, such as about the child's age and family members may help to initiate discussion. Asking the child for help often enables the teacher to be seen as less of an authority figure, for example, 'Tell me how I can help you with this problem'.

Maintaining a facilitative attitude is essential, in particular avoiding blocks to communication such as advising, moralising, consoling or kidding, which are often unwittingly used by teachers. Using questions appropriately is also important. Open-ended questions and clarifying questions can be useful but the use of too many questions, closed questions, or 'why' questions should be avoided. The use of questions and other intervention strategies is discussed in Chapter 4.

Conclusion

This chapter has presented a rationale for using a three-stage model for counselling in schools, which focuses on exploration, intervention and empowering. These three stages of the model are described in detail in the following four chapters, as follows: stage one in Chapter 3; stage two in Chapter 4; and, stage three in Chapters 5 and 6.

References

Adey, P. and Shayer, M. (1994) *Really Raising Standards: Cognitive Intervention and Academic Achievement.* London: Routledge.

Bronfenbrenner, U. (1979) *The Ecology of Human Development*. Cambridge, MA: Harvard University Press.

Cole, D. R. (1982) *Helping*. Toronto: Butterworths.

Egan, G. (1982) *The Skilled Helper* (2nd edn). Monterey, CA: Brooks/Cole.

Egan, G. (1984) Skilled helping: a problem-management framework for helping and helper training. In D. Larson (ed.) *Teaching Psychological Skills: Models for Giving Psychology Away*. Monterey, CA: Brooks/Cole, pp. 133–50.

Egan, G. (1986) *The Skilled Helper* (3rd edn). Monterey, CA: Brooks/Cole.

Erdman, P. and Lampe, R. (1996) Adapting basic skills to counsel children. *Journal of Counselling and Development*, 74(4): 374–7.

Gazda, G. M. (1984) Multiple impact training: a life skills approach. In D. Larson (ed.) *Teaching Psychological Skills*. Monterey, CA: Brooks/Cole, pp. 89–103.

Havinghurst, R. J. (1972) *Developmental Tasks and Education* (3rd edn). New York: David McKay.

Hornby, G. (1990) A humanistic developmental model of counselling: a psycho-educational approach. *Counselling Psychology Quarterly*, 3(2): 191–203.

Lane, J. (1996) Counselling issues in mainstream schools. *Emotional and Behavioural Difficulties*, 1(2): 46–51.

Larson, D. (1984) Giving psychology away: the skills training paradigm. In D. Larson (ed.) *Teaching Psychological Skills: Models for Giving Psychology Away*. Monterey, CA: Brooks/Cole, pp. 1–18.

Manthei, R. J. (1997) *Counselling: The Skills of Finding Solutions to Problems*. Auckland: Longman.

Maslow, A. (1970) *Motivation and Personality* (2nd edn). New York: Harper and Row.

Rogers, C. R. (1980) *A Way of Being*. Boston: Houghton Mifflin.

Thompson, C. L. and Rudolph, L. B. (1988) *Counseling Children* (2nd edn). Pacific Grove, CA: Brooks/Cole.

Thompson, C. L. and Rudolph, L. B. (2000) *Counseling Children* (5th edn). Belmont, CA: Brooks/Cole.

3 Exploration of concerns and feelings

Garry Hornby

Kids are so used to not being listened to that even ten minutes intense 'grunt therapy' is a luxury they respond to.

(Ellin, 1994, p. 160)

The importance of listening to children

The usefulness of listening skills for teachers was brought home to me following a two-hour workshop in which a colleague and I introduced a group of experienced teachers to active listening. In the follow-up session, two weeks later, we asked for feedback on the teachers' experiences with active listening. The first teacher to report back told how, soon after the workshop, one of his pupils, who was usually well-behaved, had been behaving so badly he was about to shout at him across the classroom. But then he thought he would try out active listening instead. He escorted the boy outside the classroom and asked him if there was a problem. The boy began to cry and explained how things at home were so tense and horrible that it was really upsetting him at school. The teacher reported that all he did was listen to what the boy had to say and told him just to do his best. Back in the classroom the boy got on with his work and his behaviour had not been a cause of concern since that day.

The teacher said that this incident had changed his views about the value of listening to pupils. He realised that if he had used his usual technique of shouting at the boy this would have probably made matters worse. The boy's poor behaviour may well have continued, creating more disruption in the classroom. But, more importantly, the boy would not have been encouraged to express his feelings and would have been left in emotional turmoil. By using active listening, the teacher had made the boy feel that his problems were acknowledged and that someone cared about him and understood what he was going through.

Attitudes required for effective listening

There are certain key attitudes which are required for effective listening to take place. According to Gordon (1970), listeners must:

- really want to hear what the other person has to say;
- sincerely want to help other people with their concerns;
- be able to respect the other person's opinions, feelings or values even though they may conflict with their own;
- realise that feelings are transitory and not be afraid when children or adults express strong feelings such as anger or sadness;
- have confidence in people's ability to solve their own problems;

- believe in the potency of listening in facilitating the helping process;
- exhibit the three attitudinal qualities which are considered essential in all helping relationships: genuineness; respect; and empathy (Rogers, 1980) which are described in Chapter 2.

Blocks to communication

In addition to possessing the above attitudes effective listeners must also avoid certain common barriers or blocks to communication (Gordon, 1970; Bolton, 1979). These are ways of interacting with children and adults which we have learned in order to cope with everyday situations. Their value is that they keep our involvement on a superficial level, which is necessary in order to survive day-to-day life at school and home. However, they are not appropriate when we are seeking to help children and adults deal with their problems. So we must be aware of and seek to avoid these blocks to communication when we are attempting to listen fully. Examples of these blocks are as follows (more details can be found in Hornby, 1994):

Reassurance: Don't worry, I'm sure it'll work out alright.
Denial of feelings: Cheer up and look on the bright side of things.
False acknowledgement of feelings: I know exactly how you feel.
Diverting: Let's not dwell on those problems. Tell me about something else.
Advice giving: I know just what you should do …
Logical argument: Yes, but …
Inappropriate questioning: But why did you do that?
Criticising: You should not have done that.
Being sarcastic: Yeh, in your dreams!
Labelling: You are a worrier.
Diagnosing: I know what your problem is.
Moralising: The 'right thing' for you to do is …
Ordering: What you must do is …
Threatening: If you don't … then …
Inappropriate self-disclosure: I know someone with that problem, what they do is … .

Self-listening. An important block to communication is created without having to utter a word. While you have been reading this chapter you are almost certain to have had various thoughts enter into your mind. Some of these thoughts will have been triggered by the content of this chapter or you may have thought back to what you were doing earlier in the day or thought ahead to what you will be doing later. This phenomenon has been termed 'self-listening' and is considered to be due to the fact that because our brain power is not fully utilised when we are processing written or oral communication, some of the brain's capacity is available for other activities (Bolton, 1979).

The drawback of self-listening is that when someone is listening to another person and begins to self-listen there is a likelihood that important aspects of what is said will be missed. The listener may then become confused and will be unable to respond effectively to the other person, who will therefore become aware of the inadequacy of the listening and tend to clam up. This is why it is very important that when teachers are listening to children or parents they are able to reduce self-listening to a minimum. The best ways of limiting self-listening are to use the techniques of attentiveness, passive listening, paraphrasing and active listening, which are discussed next.

Attentiveness

In addition to having appropriate attitudes and avoiding blocks to communication, effective listening requires a high level of attentiveness. This involves physically focusing one's attention on the person being listened to, and is often referred to as using attending skills (Egan, 1982). There are eight major components of attentiveness: maintaining good eye contact; facing the client squarely; adopting an open posture; leaning toward the other; remaining relaxed; appropriate body motion; non-distracting environment; and interpersonal distance. These components are described below.

Eye contact. The most important component of attentiveness is maintaining good eye contact. This involves looking directly at the other person's face and only shifting one's gaze to observe any gestures or body movements. In situations where eye contact is a problem for the listener it is usually satisfactory for him or her to look at the speakers' mouth or tip of the nose instead. Listeners most often cannot tell the difference.

In some cultures, it is not acceptable for certain members of the society to make eye contact with other members, except in certain situations. For example, in many Pacific Island countries like Samoa a younger person may not look an elder directly in the eyes. Also, in many Arab countries it is not permitted for women to look into the eyes of men they are not related to. When listening to someone from such cultures one must be sensitive to these constraints and attempt to communicate attentiveness through culturally appropriate means.

Facing squarely. To communicate attentiveness it is important for the listener to face the other person squarely. Turning one's body away from another person suggests that you are not totally with them. However, some people find that sitting squarely is too intense and can be somewhat intimidating to the other person, so they prefer to sit at a slight angle, which is quite acceptable.

Leaning forward. Leaning slightly forward, towards the person being listened to, communicates attentiveness. Alternatively, leaning backwards, worst of all in a slouch, gives the impression that you are not interested in what is being said.

Open posture. Having one's legs crossed and, even more so, one's arms crossed when listening gives the impression of a lack of openness, as if a barrier is being placed between the listener and the person talking. Attentiveness is communicated by the adoption of an open posture with both arms and legs uncrossed.

Remaining relaxed. An essential component of attentiveness is being relaxed while adopting an appropriate posture. If one is not comfortable with the posture adopted then it is not possible to concentrate fully on what is being said. Therefore, it is important to take up an attentive posture in which one feels relaxed, even if this doesn't exactly follow the guidelines discussed above. Most of these guidelines appear to have been based on the attentive posture used by Carl Rogers in counselling sessions which were recorded on film. While this posture was comfortable for Rogers, it does not suit everyone and should not be slavishly adhered to.

Appropriate body motion. There are two aspects of moving one's body appropriately when listening. First, it is important to avoid distracting movements such as looking at your watch, fiddling with something in your hand, fidgeting in your seat or constantly changing position. Secondly, it is important to move appropriately in response to the speaker, in a way mirroring the speaker's body motion. A listener who sits perfectly still, almost not blinking, can be quite unnerving and does not communicate attentiveness.

Non-distracting environment. One cannot expect to listen attentively in an environment in which there are distractions. The room used should be free from outside noise and the door should be kept closed. Telephone calls should be put on hold and if possible a 'Do not disturb' sign hung on the door. Within the room the chairs used should be comfortable and there should be no physical barrier such as a desk between the speaker and the listener.

Distance. The distance between the speaker and the listener has an impact on the level of attentiveness perceived by the speaker. If the distance is too great then it may seem that the listener does not want to get too involved in the interaction. If the distance is too small then the speaker will feel uncomfortable and this will impede the communication. Judging the optimal distance is complicated by the fact that this differs both between cultures and within each cultural group. In Western cultures, a distance of about three feet is recommended (Bolton, 1979) but it is best to always look for signs of discomfort or anxiety in the listener and adjust the distance accordingly.

Passive listening

Passive listening occurs when complete attention is given to the person being listened to. Listeners demonstrate through their non-verbal behaviour that they are fully with the person who is talking. They do not say anything which could act as a block to communication and mainly remain silent. This gives people the space to explore their thoughts in a situation where they feel supported. It is therefore extremely useful and is sometimes sufficient to meet the needs of people seeking help. The main aim of passive listening is to help people to open up and feel comfortable about talking about their concerns, feelings and ideas. It builds on the attentiveness discussed above with the use of four additional skills: door openers; minimal encouragers; open questions; and attentive silence (Bolton, 1979).

Door openers. A door opener is basically an invitation from the listener for the other person to talk about whatever is on his or her mind. Both children and adults who are troubled often show signs of this, either non-verbally through their facial expressions, voice tone or body posture, or verbally through what they say. The majority of people are not comfortable about getting troubled children or adults to open up and therefore react to such signs by using the blocks to communication described earlier, such as diverting or denial of feelings. In contrast, an effective listener uses an appropriate door opener. Door openers typically have four components:

> *First,* the listener feeds back the child's or adult's body language. For example, 'You look hassled' or 'You seem upset'.
> *Second,* the listener provides an invitation to talk. For example, 'Would you like to talk about it?'
> *Third,* the listener stays silent to give the other person time to open up and begin to talk.
> *Fourth,* the listener uses attentiveness skills to demonstrate that he or she is paying complete attention.

Finding the right words for the invitation to talk depends on who the talker and listener are and how well they know one another. With children, it is often useful to sit down with them or work alongside them. Being engaged in a joint activity often makes it easier for them to open up. With adults, inviting them to have a cup of tea or coffee can be the catalyst needed to enable them to open up. Children or adults will not always be ready to talk about their concerns. All the listener can do is provide an appropriate door opener and then leave it to them. No one likes to be coerced into talking about their concerns but if they know there is someone prepared to listen they can always take up the opportunity at a later time.

Minimal encouragers. Once someone has begun to talk, it is important to let them know that you are with them, in a way that does not interfere with the flow. Listeners may smile or nod their heads or use what are referred to as 'non-verbal grunts', such as 'Mm-mm', 'Yes', 'Right' and 'Go on', to encourage the speaker to continue. This is the source of the reference to the 'grunt therapy' in the quotation at the start of this chapter. The implication is that listening passively using minimal encouragers is appreciated by children even if teachers don't use the more advanced listening skills described later.

Other minimal encouragers are slightly more intrusive but still basically supportive, for example, 'Tell me more about ...', 'And?', 'So?', 'For instance?'. A further way of encouraging the speaker to continue is when the listener repeats the last word or a key word in the speaker's statement.

Open questions. Open questions are designed to help children or adults clarify their own concerns rather than provide information for the listener. In contrast to closed questions which typically require a one word answer such as 'yes' or 'no', open questions usually start with the words, 'How?' or 'What?' and encourage a longer response. In most instances, when one is using listening skills, it will be necessary to ask some open questions. For example, when the listener is confused about what the person is saying, or what he or she really means, it is important to use open questions to provide some clarification.

However, asking too many questions, particularly closed questions, acts as a block to effective communication. Avoiding asking questions is the biggest hurdle teachers face when attempting to improve their listening skills. Most teaching involves a question and answer mode of interacting with children and this proves very difficult for some teachers to get out of. Practice of the active listening skills discussed later in this chapter usually helps in this regard.

Attentive silence. Using silence appropriately is a very effective way of encouraging people to open up and continue exploring their thoughts and feelings. During silences, speakers are typically clarifying their thoughts and going deeper into their feelings. Therefore, good listeners tend to pause after each thing they say to give the speaker the opportunity to carry on talking or to remain silent.

There are three things that one can do during a silence in order to be able to use attentive silence and thereby become a better listener (Bolton, 1979). First, one should continue to demonstrate attentiveness, as discussed earlier. Second, one should observe the speaker's body language very carefully. Third, one should focus on the key message which the speaker is communicating.

However, silence can be taken too far. If, during a silence, the other person appears to be uncomfortable and looks at the listener for a comment, the silence should be ended, typically by using paraphrasing, which is discussed next.

Paraphrasing

If paraphrasing is used along with attentiveness and passive listening, the quality of listening overall will be improved. Paraphrasing is a skill which most people already use to some extent. When someone has told us something important and we want to be sure that we have understood correctly, we feed back the main points of the message to the person for confirmation. This is a crude form of paraphrasing which is similar to that used by competent listeners. An effective paraphrase has four components (Bolton, 1979):

First, the paraphrase feeds back the key points of the speaker's message. Less important parts of what the speaker has said are omitted, and no new ideas are added by the listener.

Second, the paraphrase focuses on the speaker's thoughts rather than his or her feelings. That is, paraphrasing is concerned with the factual content of the speaker's message.

Third, an effective paraphrase is short and to the point. It is a summary of the speaker's key message, not a summary of everything said.

Fourth, a paraphrase is made up of the listener's own words, not a repetition of the words the speaker has used. Also, effective paraphrases are stated in language which is familiar to the speaker. For example, colloquial expressions such as, 'fed up' are particularly effective.

Paraphrases are used when there are natural breaks in the interaction, such as when the speaker pauses and looks at the listener or when the speaker inflects his or her voice at the end of a sentence, clearly wanting some response from the listener. At this point the listener feeds back the essence of the speaker's message and then waits for a response. When the paraphrase hits the mark the speaker typically indicates that this is the case by saying, 'That's it' or 'Right' or 'Yes' or by some non-verbal means such as nodding his or her head.

If the paraphrase is not accurate or only partly accurate then the response will not be so positive and in most cases the speaker will correct the listener. In so doing, speakers are also clarifying for themselves exactly what is meant, so the paraphrase will still have been of value.

Sometimes the listener is not sure what the speaker's key message is and so does not know what to paraphrase. A suggestion in this situation is to paraphrase the last issue which the speaker has raised on the basis that people often finish with the issue that is of most importance to them.

There are five main reasons for using paraphrasing:

First, it shows you are really listening, because it is not possible to correctly paraphrase someone when you are not listening well.

Second, it is the best way of making sure you have understood correctly, and of letting speakers know you have understood them.

Third, the act of attempting to paraphrase actually helps to stop self-listening and reduce the risk of a communication block being used.

Fourth, it helps speakers to clarify their thoughts.

Fifth, it encourages speakers to go on exploring their concerns or ideas.

Many people are very unsure about using paraphrasing in this way when they first hear about it. Some are sceptical about whether it will work, while others consider it artificial and feel awkward using it. However, all new skills feel awkward at first and practice will make it become more natural and eventually automatic. Some teachers are so sceptical they are not prepared to try using paraphrasing. Unfortunately, this means that they are unlikely ever to realise its value and will miss out on learning a skill that could significantly improve the quality of their listening, teaching and possibly their personal lives. Lots of people learn to paraphrase well within a few hours of practice, including those who were initially sceptical.

Paraphrasing is a skill which superficially appears simple but in fact is quite difficult and takes considerable practice to do well. Fortunately, one does not have to be an expert to put it to good use. As long as people attempt to paraphrase, rather than use the usual blocks to communication they will see positive results. This is because, unless practically every paraphrase is off the mark, speakers will use the listeners' imperfect attempts at paraphrasing to clarify their thoughts and continue to explore their concerns. Paraphrases do not have to be perfect to be helpful.

Reflecting feelings

Since most children and adults who need to discuss their concerns have strong emotions associated with these, it is important to be able to listen to and reflect back their feelings. Reflecting feelings is less likely to be familiar to people than the reflection of thoughts or paraphrasing discussed above. In fact, listeners generally tend to focus on facts rather than feelings. This is because most societies constrain people to hide their emotions, which in turn makes it more difficult for others to tune into them. However, reflecting feelings helps people to understand their reactions to the situations with which they are faced and therefore move closer toward finding solutions to their concerns. So it is an essential component of the listening process (King, 1999).

Reflecting feelings involves listeners feeding back, as concisely as possible, the feelings communicated, either verbally or non-verbally, by speakers. The format, 'You feel ...' is usually used, for example, 'You feel angry' or 'You are annoyed' or 'You're furious'. In order to do this listeners must be able to identify feeling clues from what speakers say and from their body language. Since much of the emotional content of people's messages is communicated by their body language, it is sometimes more important to listen to what is *not* said than to what is said.

Reflection of feelings typically has four elements (Brammer, 1988):

First, the feeling which the speaker is communicating is identified.
Second, this feeling is reflected back to the speaker.
Third, the listener carefully observes the speaker's reaction.
Fourth, the listener judges the accuracy of the reflection from the reaction which it provokes.

As with paraphrasing, inaccurate reflection of feelings can have a facilitative effect, because the speaker corrects the listener and in so doing clarifies the emotions he or she is experiencing.

Probably the most difficult aspect of reflecting feelings is identifying the correct feeling. There are four things one can do to help with this (Bolton, 1979):

First, pick up on any words which are used to describe feelings. If these are congruent with the person's body language then they can be reflected directly. If they are not congruent then this contradiction can be fed back to the speaker. For example, 'You say you are pleased about what has happened but you don't look it'.
Second, the overall content of the message may be of help in identifying the likely feelings experienced. For example, if the person is speaking about a close friend who has just died then it is likely that feelings of sadness and loss will be to the fore.
Third, the speaker's body language will probably provide strong clues regarding the feelings experienced. The listener should pay close attention to facial expressions,

changes of body posture, tone of voice, breathing or speech, plus other aspects of body language.

Fourth, listeners should ask themselves, 'What would I be feeling if I were in this situation?' Although different people can react very differently to the same situation, the listeners' reactions may provide a useful clue to the speaker's feelings, which can be compared with the clues gathered from other sources before feeding them back.

Finding just the right words to reflect back the speaker's feelings is also very difficult. It is important to feed back the correct level of emotion as well as the type. For example, for a person expressing anger the emotional level can range from being 'slightly annoyed' to 'absolutely furious'. Once again, if the level of feeling is wrong, the speaker will correct it, thereby further clarifying the feelings involved.

Reflecting meanings

Reflection of meanings involves reflecting both thoughts and feelings back to the speaker. The speaker's key feeling is fed back along with the apparent reason for the feeling. Typically, the formula, *'You feel ... because ...'* is used. For example:

> You *feel* frustrated *because* you haven't finished the job.
> You *feel* delighted *because* she has done so well.

When someone has learnt to paraphrase (reflect thoughts) and to reflect feelings then it does not usually take too long for them to learn to reflect meanings using the, 'You feel ... because ...' formula. Although it is common to experience the artificiality of this formula, it is useful, in the early stages of practising the skill, as an aid to producing a concise response which includes both a feeling and the reason for the feeling. Once the skill has been mastered then other words can be used instead of 'feel' and 'because' so that it becomes more natural. Examples are:

> You *are* angry *about* the way you were treated.
> *You're* sad *that* it has come to an end.
> You *were* pleased *with* the result.
> You *were* annoyed *by* her manner.

Active listening

Active listening involves listeners being actively engaged in clarifying the thoughts and feelings of children or adults. This is done to provide a kind of 'sounding board' to facilitate exploration and clarification of the speaker's concerns or ideas. It is therefore the most useful form of listening when children or adults have a problem for which they are seeking help and is the key to competence in interpersonal communication. Active listening is generally considered to be, trying to understand what the speaker is feeling and what the key message is in what they are saying, then putting this understanding into your own words and feeding it back to them (Gordon, 1970).

Thus, active listening is taken to include all aspects of attentiveness and passive listening, plus paraphrasing, reflection of feelings and reflection of meanings. That is, active listening involves the use of everything that has been discussed in this chapter so far. It is the most advanced and facilitative form of listening and is useful in a wide variety of situations including counselling, interviews and times when one has to be assertive. It is a skill well worth practising because the potential benefits for improving interpersonal communication and quality of life are substantial. However, until one has experienced the benefits of active listening, both as a listener and as the person being listened to, it is difficult to fully appreciate its value.

A young trainee teacher on a course I once led was so uncertain about active listening that she refused to practise it in the training group. The following week she asked if she could say something to the group. During the week a close friend had telephoned her to say that her husband was terminally ill with cancer. She said that to her surprise she found herself using active listening. The various blocks to communication we had discussed seemed totally inappropriate and all that had felt comfortable was reflecting back her friend's thoughts and feelings. This real life experience had convinced her of the value of active listening.

However, learning to use active listening is not without its pitfalls. There are several typical errors which people make in the early stages of learning the skill (Brammer, 1988):

> *First*, there is a tendency to stereotype responses by beginning all responses with the same words, such as 'You feel ...', or 'I hear you saying ...', or 'I gather that ...' It is best to vary these and make your responses as natural as possible.
>
> *Second*, beginners often try to get in with a listening response after each thing which the speaker has said. This is unnecessary and breaks up the speaker's flow. It is best to wait until the speaker pauses and indicates to the listener that a response is wanted. However, some children and adults will go on and on unless you stop them, so it is important to interrupt such people occasionally so that active listening can be used to facilitate more meaningful exploration of their concerns and feelings.
>
> *Third*, beginners often find it difficult to gauge the correct depth of concern and intensity of feeling to feed back. It is usually better to err on the side of less drastic levels of concern and less intense feelings initially. The speaker will correct this if necessary.
>
> *Fourth*, a frequent mistake for beginners is to use language that is not commonly used by the speaker. The more listeners use the vocabulary typically used by the children or adults they are listening to the more effective their responses will be.

Summarising

A final listening skill is summarising. This encompasses all the skills which are discussed in this chapter. Summarising is used to help children or adults to focus on the major concerns and feelings they have expressed at a particular time. The summary need not include all the concerns and emotions expressed but will include the key concerns and strongest feelings. In this way, summarising helps children and adults to focus on the aspects of their lives which they would most like to change. Summarising therefore leads naturally into considering strategies to bring about such changes. That is, it provides a link between the first stage of the helping process, which involves the use of listening skills, and the next stage of the process which involves using various intervention strategies.

An example of the use of summarising is illustrated by the following incident. A student has asked to see her form teacher at lunch time and has talked about having problems at home, disagreements with other children, conflict with teachers and worries about the poor marks she is getting for her work. The teacher has been using paraphrasing and active listening to help the student express and explore her feelings and concerns and has reached the point when she seems to have said everything she wants to about her situation. Summarising can then be used to move the helping process along with a response such as, 'So you have been getting upset about all the hassles at home and your feelings have spilled over into school causing you to get into strife with teachers and your schoolmates, as well as interfering with your ability to produce your best work'.

Summarising enables listeners to confirm that they have understood the key concerns, feelings and ideas which have been expressed. Therefore, it is a skill which is useful at all stages of the helping process.

Value of listening skills

The value of learning listening skills was brought home to me by an incident which occurred when I was a trainee educational psychologist. I was asked to give a talk to parents at a pre-school playgroup about how to prepare children for going to school. After the talk, a mother came up and asked me what I could recommend for her two-year-old child who was 'throwing tantrums'. On the spot the only thing which came to my mind was the book *Parent Effectiveness Training* by Thomas Gordon (1970) which I had heard about and whose title suggested it might address this parent's problem. Later, when I had read the book and discovered that it focussed on active listening, and other interpersonal skills I thought that my suggestion had been inappropriate and that behaviour modification strategies would have been more effective in dealing with tantrums.

When, around two years later, I was asked back to the same pre-school to give another talk, I had forgotten about this incident. As soon as I arrived, to my horror, I saw the mother I had spoken to heading straight for me. She asked if I remembered her and the book by Thomas Gordon that I had recommended. I said yes and nervously asked how useful she had found it. She responded that it had been absolutely useless, no help at all in coping with her child's tantrums, but, had *'worked wonders on my husband!'*

This incident illustrates for me the value of learning active listening and the other interpersonal skills highlighted in this book. The skills are useful in a wide range of situations, personal and professional and across the age range from young children to old people. Teachers will find that active listening is useful in facilitating class discussions as well as counselling individual children. It is an essential skill for leading personal and social development activities such as 'Circle Time' which are discussed in Chapter 6. It is also useful in developing constructive relationships with parents and colleagues. Finally, it is a skill which is useful in all of one's relationships including those with family and friends.

In the next chapter, listening skills are seen as essential precursors to the implementation of a wide range of counselling skills, or intervention strategies, which can be used by teachers.

References

Bolton, R. (1979) *People Skills*. Englewood Cliffs, NJ: Prentice-Hall.
Brammer, L. M. (1988) *The Helping Relationship* (4th edn). Englewood Cliffs, NJ: Prentice-Hall.
Egan, G. (1982) *The Skilled Helper* (2nd edn). Monterey, CA: Brooks/Cole.
Ellin, J. (1994) *Listening Helpfully: How to Develop Your Counselling Skills*. London: Souvenir Press.
Gordon, T. (1970) *Parent Effectiveness Training*. New York: Wyden.
Hornby, G. (1994) *Counselling in Child Disability*. London: Chapman and Hall.
King, G. (1999) *Counselling Skills for Teachers*. Buckingham: Open University Press.
Rogers, C. R. (1980) *A Way of Being*. Boston: Houghton Mifflin.

4 Strategies for intervention

Garry Hornby, Eric Hall and Bob Manthei

> Just as a piano does not have a single best key or combination of keys, neither do you have one way that will always work best.
>
> (Hazler, 1998, p. 9)

This chapter presents various counselling skills or intervention strategies which teachers can use to deal with the concerns or difficulties which their students present. The chapter begins with strategies which build on the listening skills, which were discussed in the previous chapter. The emphasis is on the typical day-to-day interactions teachers have with students. Many of these are brief and take place in corridors, dining rooms, sports fields or as students make their way out of classrooms. These interactions provide possibilities for 'counselling on the run'.

The second half of the chapter focuses on strategies which teachers can use in more formal situations, typically one-to-one, in which teachers have more time and scope to provide help to students.

Counselling on the run

Mrs Collins turned the corner of the corridor to find Gerry from her Year Nine group trying to look invisible when he should have been out in the yard. 'What are you doing here?' she asked. 'Nothing Miss', came the reply. 'You're looking upset Gerry, is anything the matter?' 'Nothing Miss.' 'You say there's nothing the matter and yet you look as though you're about to burst into tears'. 'I just don't want to go out into the yard Miss.' 'Look Gerry, it's obvious that you're not all right. You can sit outside the office for the rest of break time and come and see me at the end of the last lesson and we will have a talk.'

Every sentence that Mrs Collins used could be seen as involving a counselling skill and yet the exchange lasted less than a minute. Counselling is an activity that is conventionally regarded as something that takes place between two people in private in which one of the participants is seen to need help or support for difficulties or problems in his or her life. Counselling skills, however, are important aspects of any skilful communication between people. The skills that have been described in the previous chapter are very effective in everyday interactions with students and colleagues alike. They can also be very helpful in what might be described as conflict or discipline situations. As well as teachers, all other staff in schools can benefit from an understanding of the use of counselling skills, including ancillary staff, secretaries, meals assistants and, in addition, students have also been shown to benefit from training in these skills.

Students are generally not inclined to seek out their teachers for counselling or a supportive conversation. The role of a teacher is complex involving information giving, controlling and disciplining. These activities can be seen to be at odds with supporting, listening and helping. Paradoxically Aspy and Roebuck (1977) demonstrated that training in counselling skills made teachers more effective in all aspects of their role. This would suggest that many aspects of the skills used in counselling could play an important part in daily interactions in the classroom as well as in situations where students are asking for help. This part of the chapter will consider how counselling skills can be used in many of the daily interactions that teachers engage in as well as in deal effectively with difficult and confrontational incidents with students. The skills can be used during events as they are happening in the classroom or on the corridors. They may be used for sorting out discipline problems at the end of a lesson or at the end of the day. The same skills are equally effective for relating to colleagues who are becoming emotional or behaving inappropriately. They are useful for sorting out a conflict between a teacher and a student if you have a pastoral role in which problems are referred to you. Under more normal circumstances the use of counselling skills in everyday interactions can be used to develop and reinforce relationships that are not problematic and may help to prevent the possibility of unfortunate interactions in the future.

Reframing the relationship

If your relationship with a student is consistently problematic, then it is worth considering changing your own behaviour in order to change a pattern that is becoming fixed and not working in the way that you would like. The first step to doing this is to change your perception of the situation.

Essentially, it is important to take a 'no-blame' approach to the relationship and to be able to stand outside of it and look at it objectively. This is advocated in the 'no-blame' approach to bullying (Maines and Robinson, 1992) in which all of the people involved in the bullying situation are seen as enmeshed in an unhelpful pattern of relationships, so it is the pattern that needs to change rather than any particular individual.

By stepping outside of the relationship it becomes possible to engage in what is described as second order change, which changes the system and thereby the relationship (Watzlawic *et al.*, 1967). This contrasts with first order change, which only produces superficial change. The more the teacher shouts, the more the student withdraws into an uncooperative shell. Behaviour is changing, but the pattern of the relationship, or the system, stays the same. Molnar and Lindquist (1989) discuss long-term solutions to problem behaviour where the teacher has the time to analyse the situation and plan for change. In this section we will consider situations where a response is needed on the spur of the moment and the responses recommended are in the form of counselling skills.

Changing interaction patterns

In the following section the use of counselling skills as means of changing difficult relationships in school will be explored. This will involve revisiting some of the skills described in Chapter 3 and applying them to situations in which they would not normally spring to mind. There is no guarantee that any particular intervention will work, but if your habitual responses are not working, then there is nothing to lose by trying out something new.

Using standard counselling skills in what might be a confrontational situation is a way of stepping outside of the relationship between you and the student. The 'problem' stays with the student. You do not have to become part of the problem by engaging in a moralistic or angry interaction, even though this form of response may be the first that comes to mind.

Reflecting content

Imagine that a student who has been sent to you arrives complaining: 'Mr Jones is always picking on me. As soon as I get into the class he starts telling me off.' An immediate response might be to reason with the student and explain how his or her behaviour is producing the telling off. An alternative response might be: 'So Mr Jones spends most of the lesson complaining about your behaviour.' All you have done here is to feed back to the student what they have said. This allows the student to let off some steam before you launch into finding out what the student has been doing. It is also a good indication that you have heard what the student has said, which may be an unusual experience for the student. A more difficult situation is one in which the student is responding to you in a threatening or offensive manner. You may feel that it is appropriate to respond in a controlling or disciplining manner. However, if you have tried this with the same student before with little effect, it may be time to try changing your response.

Student: Why should I do what you tell me? This is all a load of rubbish anyway.
Teacher: You think the lesson is a waste of time and you don't think it is worth doing the work?

The suggestion to respond in this way, at first sight, may seem a little unusual. However, it is important to test out this sort of response without rejecting it out of hand. Students are often not aware of what they are saying and to have it fed back to them can be a salutary experience. It is worth trying it out in a less demanding situation before using reflection of content when there is a more serious threat to your authority and self-esteem.

Reflecting content is a standard skill for effectively chairing a staff meeting. Regrettably, it is one that is not used very much and the chair will often respond to comments by providing what they regard as the right answer. There is a problem with using skills such as reflection of content in the staff room as you will get the reputation as a person who will listen. Teachers who have tried out using counselling skills with their colleagues have reported that colleagues want to spend much more time talking to them and it becomes difficult to find time for some peace and quiet. This requires a further counselling skill, which is drawing effective boundaries. The same is true for students. If you make it clear that you are willing to hear what students are saying, they will tend to come to you in the future when things are not going so well. This will, of course, enhance your reputation in the school community but it does take up more time.

Reflecting feelings

A large adolescent bursts into the classroom, bangs the door, knocks a book off one student's desk and then shouts an insult to another student across the room. A conventional response might be 'How dare you behave like that in my classroom?' Compare this with 'You seem angry today.' In the first example, the teacher is caught up in the situation and is reacting as if the student *is* a problem, while in the second example the teacher has stepped outside of the situation and is reacting as if the student *has* a problem. The unexpected response may stop students in their tracks and confuse them. This may sound manipulative, but it is a benign manipulation and is probably to the advantage of all concerned.

The same approach can be used with a colleague who approaches you in an aggressive manner. 'You sound very angry about it.' This form of response can often calm down the situation, whereas responding in kind is likely to set up a spiral of anger.

Feelings usually play an important part in the daily situations that arise in the school setting (Hall and Hall, 1988). The expression of disappointment, frustration, inadequacy, depression, loneliness, indecision, anxiety, anger, confusion, grief and apathy as well as a whole range of positive emotions is common and can occur in threatening situations. The response to a threat is often another outburst of emotion. Reflecting back the feelings that are being expressed can be a more useful response.

Expressing feelings

The suggestions made so far may sound passive in the face of threatening and emotionally charged behaviour. If you make a clear statement of your feelings about what has happened, then you are engaging in a skill that is used sparingly in counselling settings. It can be both challenging and confronting for the person on the receiving end.

There is evidence that indicates that helping professionals (which includes teachers) can help other people to deal with their feelings to the degree to which they are skilled at expressing their own feelings. The appropriate expression of feeling is considered to be an important counselling skill and one which our own research indicates that teachers experience difficulties with (Sirin *et al.*, 1995).

Unfortunately, the feelings expressed in challenging situations often emerge in distorted ways that are likely to be damaging to the student's self-esteem and be experienced as a put-down. This is often done in a way that writes off the student as a person, such as: 'You are really stupid.'

The recommended approach is to make a clear statement regarding your feelings about the student's behaviour, which can always be changed. For example, 'I get really angry when you disturb other people.' A statement of this nature does not invite a response, nor does it require obedience on the part of the student. It gives the responsibility for what to do next to students, rather than making them feel that they are being controlled.

Strategies for formal counselling situations

The need for teachers to widen their repertoire of intervention strategies is addressed in the remainder of the chapter. First to be considered are two approaches which can be used in a wide range of situations, requiring counselling skills, which teachers are likely to encounter. These are the problem-solving approach and the solution-focused approach. These are followed by brief outlines of a wide range of other counselling strategies intended to address more specific counselling needs.

Problem-solving approach

When teachers use listening skills in order to help students explore their concerns, as suggested earlier in this chapter and in Chapter 3, then students' need for help in solving their problems will often emerge. This is when teachers can adopt a problem-solving approach. The problem-solving approach to counselling presented here has been adapted from previous models by Egan (1982) and Allan and Nairne (1984) and is discussed in more detail elsewhere (Hornby, 1994, 2000). This is a practical approach, which is relatively easy for teachers to learn and use. It involves a three-stage approach to counselling with stages of *listening*, *understanding* and *action planning*.

The rationale for using this approach is based on the idea that any problem or concern which students bring to teachers can be dealt with by taking them through the three stages of the model in order to help them find the solution that best suits their needs. First of all, the teacher uses the skills of the *listening* stage to establish a working relationship with students, to help them open up and to explore any concerns they have. Then the teacher moves on to the second stage, using the skills of the *understanding* stage in order to help students get a clearer picture of their concerns, develop new perspectives on their situation, and suggest possible goals for change. Finally, the teacher moves on to the third stage, of *action planning*, in which possible options for solving students' problems are examined and plans for action are developed. Thus, different skills are needed at each stage of the model. It has been found that, once teachers have learned to use the listening skills (discussed in Chapter 3), needed for the first stage, then they are able to implement the problem-solving approach, since the skills of the other two stages are ones which teachers already have to some extent and which they can develop further with practice (Hornby, 1994).

In addition to being used for individual counselling, the problem-solving approach can also be used to facilitate class discussions (Allan and Nairne, 1984), taking whole class groups through the three stages in order to address a wide range of issues of concern to students. A brief warm-up stage is inserted at the start of the lesson, followed by the three main stages of exploration, understanding and action planning, before a brief termination stage at the end. This is illustrated below with extracts from a session on separation and divorce.

Warm-Up	Put your hand up if you know someone who is separated or divorced. Put your hand up if you have been through a separation or divorce.
Exploration	What is it like for children whose parents separate or divorce? What worries might they have?
Understanding	How do children behave at school when they are upset? Who can children go to for help when they are upset?
Action Planning	What can you do to help someone whose parents are separating? What can you do if this is happening to you?
Termination	What have you learned from today's discussion?

Used in this way the model can be a preventative strategy which, if used regularly, will result in students learning to apply the problem-solving approach in helping their fellow students as well as using it to work through any concerns which they may have.

Solution-focused approach

In solution-focused counselling the overall aim is to implement realistic, effective solutions to a student's problem rather than focus on analysing the problem itself. Usually, the focus of attention in interactions with students moves quickly to the goal setting and implementation stages and far less time is spent defining and clarifying the problem and what has caused it (Manthei, 1997). Because of this, the approach is regarded by teachers and school counsellors who use it as a practical, time-sensitive, effective tool for working with school-based problems (Murphy, 1996; Davis and Osborn, 2000).

Core beliefs of solution-focused counselling

Solution-focused counselling involves a clear set of beliefs about students and an identifiable set of questioning techniques. The central belief is that it is more productive and effective to focus on students' skills, abilities and resources rather than on their weaknesses or what is going wrong and why. Other important beliefs include the following (Gass and Gillis, 1995; Murphy, 1996; Manthei, 1997; Corcoran, 1998):

- Students and teachers already possess the abilities and skills to resolve problems that occur in the school.
- The seeds to these solutions can be found in those times when the problem is not present or is less of a problem; these times are called *exceptions* to the problem.
- It is easier for students to repeat successful behaviours than it is for them to stop negative behaviours.
- Problems can be thought of as non-productive patterns of interactions with others rather than individual weaknesses or deficits.
- Effective counselling builds on behaviours and thoughts that are already being used with success: 'If it is working, do more of it!' 'If things are not working, do something different!'
- By starting with small, simple changes to some aspect of a problem, larger changes become more likely.
- Students are not forced to accept help, nor are they given specific labels.

Accepting these beliefs is said to represent a paradigm shift in thinking about problems. The shift from a problem-dominated focus to one in which possibilities and hope predominate can be difficult for both teacher/counsellors and students to make. However, these beliefs are fully compatible with the humanistic model of counselling presented in Chapter 2.

The techniques of solution-focused counselling

The main skill in solution-focused counselling is the use of effective questioning. Presented below are several types of questions that are illustrative of how a positive focus on solutions, rather than problems, can be achieved with students and others who are 'stuck' (based on Manthei, 1997).

Pre-counselling improvement: It is not unusual for students to begin experiencing positive changes in their difficulties in between the problem being identified and the time when they talk to the teacher about it. These 'pre-counselling improvements' often signal ways in which the student has begun successfully dealing with the problem, even if unwittingly so. If such change has occurred, teachers should explore the reasons for those improvements and identify the helpful factors over which the student has control.

> Since the time you first thought about seeking help and now, have things improved at all? Even a little bit? If 'yes', ask: How did you manage that?

Compliments: As students talk, try to note all the things that they are doing successfully or well, and their skills and abilities. These are the things that can be used to construct successful solutions to their present problems or concerns. Complimenting students in an honest, sincere way helps to build an expectation of possibility, success and hope. Many things can be complimented, including: specific thoughts, ways of thinking, determination, fairness, motivation and patience. It is the teacher's job to be creative enough and astute enough to recognise student abilities and skills as they are presented.

> I admire your clear thinking on this problem. (direct compliment)
> How did you ever think of doing it that way! (indirect compliment)

Exception questions: As early in the interview as possible ask about times when the problem was absent, or when it was less serious. It is seldom the case that people's problems happen continuously, or at the same level of intensity. Therefore, it is important to know what triggers times of problem absence or abatement. Find out what was happening at those exceptional times: what the student was thinking, doing, feeling; what seemed to cause the exception? Answers to those questions will often contain clues to both achievable goals and possible solutions.

> Are there times when things are not so bad? What is going on then? Is it helpful? Could you do it again?

Coping questions: There will be times when it is clear that students have been managing great burdens, when they have had to handle multiple difficulties without much support or help. This huge effort may be worth complimenting; it may also be worth finding out more about how it has been accomplished. Coping questions convey a message of hope, competence and strength. Furthermore, the student's response usually indicates some small, positive things that can be complimented, built on and perhaps expanded.

> How do you cope with this situation day by day?

Scaling questions: Once the student's problem has been identified and explored (even if only briefly), it may be useful to find out how severe it is, for example. This can be done by constructing a scale that asks for an estimate of intensity, severity or enormity. For example, students can be asked to rate the seriousness of their problem at a point in time on a 1 to 10 scale where '1' is 'extremely serious' and '10' is 'no longer any problem'. The numbers on the scale have no objective meaning, nor does the number chosen by the student. It merely represents the student's subjective estimate of seriousness at that particular time. Once a scale is made teachers can refer back to it in the same or future interviews as a way of charting a student's progress or change. Scaling questions can also be used to gauge seriousness at different times, for example, now, two months ago or six months ago. Almost anything can be scaled: motivation, determination, success, a state of mind or physical traits. Scaling questions can be very useful in objectifying change. Students are quick to understand the concept and willing to engage in the exercise. Furthermore, they often report how helpful having things on a visual or concrete scale can be. Scaling questions can also be used to good effect in identifying possible solutions and establishing goals (Davis and Osborn, 2000).

> You say you are at 3 on the scale. What is making things better than if you were at a one or two? What would have to happen for you to get to four?

Miracle questions: There are times when students cannot think of exceptions to their problem, or they cannot identify a suitable goal or outcome. Therefore, it can be useful to ask a miracle, or a 'pretend that' question. This type of question helps students transcend the present, to break out of a cognitive straightjacket and do so in a playful, make-believe way. Their answers, of course, are often revealing of possible solutions, or goals that can be worked toward. As students begin to describe their miracle, help them to elaborate and expand their visions by asking: 'What else?' This simple device is useful at any stage of the interview.

> Suppose tonight a miracle happens to you and in the morning you notice that your problems have been solved, have disappeared! What is the first thing you would notice that would be different?

> Pretend for a moment that all your problems are solved. If that happened, what would be different?

Terminating: It is useful, even very early in an interview to talk about termination, or not needing counselling any more. This establishes the notion that counselling is brief, temporary, and will be successful.

> How will you know when you don't have to talk to me about this any more? What will be different?

Other intervention strategies

The three approaches presented so far, the problem-solving and solution-focused approaches and the application of listening skills in counselling on the run, are ones which teachers can use effectively to deal with the majority of situations in schools, which require counselling. They are also ones which teachers can learn relatively quickly, for example, after reading this book and attending a one-day workshop. However, there are a wide range of other counselling techniques or intervention strategies which can be very useful in the school setting, given the right circumstances. These strategies are more specialised ones, which require more extensive information than can be presented here and so require further reading. Teachers have successfully implemented many of these strategies with little or no additional training. However, ideally, they should obtain training on the strategies from qualified counsellors and then only use them in settings in which ongoing guidance from colleagues with experience of using the strategies are available. Brief outlines of a selection of such strategies, with suggestions for further reading, are presented below. More information on each of the strategies and a variety of other strategies which can be used in schools can be found in Thompson and Rudolph (2000) and Vernon (1993).

Cognitive therapy

This is an approach which is based on the view that the feelings and behaviour of students are influenced by their thoughts or beliefs (Hughes, 1988). Therefore, changing their beliefs will bring about behavioural and emotional change. The most widely used version is Rational Emotive Therapy (Ellis, 1994) which posits that dysfunctional feelings and behaviour are due to irrational, or non-productive, beliefs, such as, 'my unhappiness is caused by events or by other people' and 'I should be thoroughly competent in everything I do.' The focus of the therapy is to help students to identify these irrational beliefs and then, through 'disputing' the beliefs, to help students to change them to more rational and productive beliefs. There are three main phases to this approach (Cowie and Pecherek, 1994):

1   Help students to recognise that it is their beliefs about events, not the events them-
    selves that are causing their problems, and help them to identify the specific irrational
    beliefs, which are causing their problems.
2   Dispute these irrational beliefs to enable students to stop thinking on this basis and
    adopt new, more helpful beliefs.
3   Encourage students to act on the basis of their new beliefs even though it may feel
    awkward at first.

Gestalt therapy

The aim of gestalt therapy is to help children become aware of and express feelings and
integrate these into an awareness of themselves in the world (Passons, 1975). A wide variety of gestalt techniques have been used with children. Three major types involve: specific
language use; empty-chair techniques; and the use of drawing to facilitate expression of
feelings.

Specific language techniques are used to help students to maintain a focus on the present. Among these are: encouraging students to make 'I' statements to get them to take
responsibility for their feelings and behaviour; when students say 'can't' insisting they
change this to 'won't'; getting students to change any questions they ask into statements
(Thompson and Rudolph, 2000).

Empty-chair techniques are used to help resolve conflicts within and between people.
One empty chair is used when the child has 'unfinished business' with another person, for
example, someone close to them who has died. The child is told to imagine the other person is sitting in the empty chair, then go ahead and say to this person what it is they wish to
say. They can then transfer to the empty chair and reply as if they were the other person.
They can return to their own chair to continue the dialogue.

A two-chair technique is used to generate dialogue between conflicting thoughts and
feelings within one person. An example of this is to help resolve conflicts in which a part of
a young person wants to continue a relationship while another part wants to end it. Talking
from the opposing parts in separate chairs helps to clarify thoughts and feelings, and decide
what action to take (Vernon, 1993).

Drawing can be used to help children access and work through feelings. The simplest
example is the 'squiggle' where a random mark or wavy line is drawn on paper and the child
is asked to finish the picture. The child is then asked to tell a story about the picture. The
child projects feelings into the drawing which then stimulates the child to express these
feelings. Topics often used with children are their family, a house, a tree and a person, or
they can be asked directly to draw their feelings (Oaklander, 1978).

Focusing

Focusing techniques are used to help students, colleagues or parents to focus on troublesome feelings, bring them into awareness and make them dissipate or integrate them with
their thoughts. This enables them to link feelings and thoughts to action. It is a powerful
technique, which when learned, can be used alone when needed in the future (Gendlin,
1978). An example of the use of focusing with a teacher experiencing an intense stress
reaction is described in Chapter 14.

Play therapy

Since play is the child's natural medium for self-expression, play therapy provides opportunities for younger children to play out their feelings and problems in the same way that older children might talk them out (Axline, 1969). A variety of play media are employed but sand play is the most widely used as it is very attractive to children. Materials used consist of a tray full of sand and a variety of miniature toys and objects which children can choose from, such as people, animals and buildings (Allan, 1988). Children are allowed to play freely in the sand using their chosen objects. The therapist observes and reflects back the child's feelings and thoughts using the listening skills described in Chapter 3. A fascinating account of the use of play therapy with a very disturbed young child is provided in Axline (1964). Information on a wide range of other play therapy techniques can be found in West (1992), Oaklander (1978) and Geldard and Geldard (1997).

Art therapy

Since children often find it difficult to express their feelings or concerns directly, the medium of art provides them with the opportunity to explore these non-verbally in a safe situation (Case and Dalley, 1992). Art therapy is used to enable children to express feelings, anxieties and concerns through the use of such media as drawing, painting and sculpting. Once feelings and concerns are brought into awareness they can be worked through with the help of the therapist. For example, a widely used technique with children is to get them to imagine they are a rosebush and then to draw themselves as a rosebush. Allan (1988) has provided detailed instructions for this activity along with guidelines for interpretation of children's drawings. Allan (1988) also discusses several other art therapy strategies, based on a Jungian approach, which are very useful for children and adolescents. One of these is 'serial drawing' in which the child is asked to do a drawing or painting and then talk about it, in the presence of the therapist, once a week over a period of time. He believes that when children draw or paint regularly in this way it enables them to express and resolve conflicts and also enables the therapist to monitor progress.

Drama therapy

Drama therapy involves the spontaneous use of role play in which children can safely express strong feelings and learn from externalising the experience (Vernon, 1993). The roles which children play include themselves, others in their lives or symbolic characters. Dressing up in costumes and the use of puppets can be helpful in encouraging children to get fully involved in role plays and to facilitate the expression of feelings.

Another useful drama therapy technique is 'sculpting' (Satir, 1972) in which children are asked to make living sculptures of their relationships with important people in their lives by placing their bodies in relation to another person in such a way as to demonstrate how they experience that relationship. While part of the sculpt they are asked to describe how this makes them feel. Another example is a 'family sculpt' in which people in the room are arranged by the child to represent relationships with family members (Cowie and Pecherek, 1994).

Writing therapy

Since writing is a normal activity within schools it provides a non-threatening medium for counselling interventions. In their fascinating book, Allan and Bertoia (1992) demonstrate how children and adolescents can work through negative emotions and painful experiences by means of the writing process. Writing therapy can be used to help children improve their emotional well being and gain a better understanding of themselves and their world. This approach can be used with individual children, small groups of students or with whole class groups. Writing activities used range from completing sentence stems through writing journal entries, poems, letters and stories. The teacher's role is to provide a safe environment for students to express themselves and suggest appropriate topics and media. For example, 'Write a letter to, or a poem for, a friend who has died'.

Behaviour therapy

Teachers are already familiar with the use of behaviour modification techniques for managing behaviour, such as positive reinforcement, modelling and time out (Kazdin, 2001). There are many other applications of the behavioural approach which are used as intervention strategies for children experiencing emotional or behavioural difficulties. These include: contingency contracts; self-management techniques; systematic desensitization; social skills training, and assertiveness training (Liddell, 1987; Geldard and Geldard, 1999; Thompson and Rudolph, 2000).

Teacher as Key

Although all the above approaches and strategies are useful at various times and in a variety of situations, it must be emphasised that the teacher's personality and relationship with students represent the most important strategy (Rogers, 1979, 1980). The attitudes, knowledge and skills required for effective counselling, which were discussed in Chapter 2, when embodied by teachers, ensure that their interactions with students will be empathic, facilitative and empowering. The teacher's 'person' is therefore the key to effective counselling in schools, as highlighted by the following quotation.

> No printed word nor spoken plea
> Can teach young minds what men should be
> Not all the books on all the shelves
> But what the teachers are themselves.
>
> (Anonymous, cited in Purkey, 1970, p. 45)

References

Allan, J. (1988) *Inscapes of the Child's World: Jungian Counselling in Schools and Clinics*. Dallas, TX: Spring.

Allan, J. and Bertoia, J. (1992) *Written Paths to Healing: Education and Jungian Child Counselling*. Dallas, TX: Spring.

Allan, J. A. B. and Nairne, J. (1984) *Class Discussions for Teachers and Counsellors in the Elementary School*. Toronto: University of Toronto Press.

Aspy, D. N. and Roebuck, F. N. (1977) *Kids Don't Learn from People They Don't Like*. Amhurst, MA: Human Resource Development Press.

Axline, V. M. (1964) *Dibs: In Search of Self*. Harmondsworth: Penguin.

Axline, V. M. (1969) *Play Therapy* (Rev. edn). New York: Ballantine.

Case, C. and Dalley, T. (1992) *The Handbook of Art Therapy*. London: Routledge.

Corcoran, J. (1998) Solution-focused practice with middle and high school at-risk youths. *Social Work in Education*, 4: 232–44.

Cowie, H. and Pecherek, A. (1994) *Counselling: Approaches and Issues in Education*. London: David Fulton.

Davis, T. E. and Osborn, C. J. (2000) *The Solution-Focused School Counselor*. Philadelphia, PA: Accelerated Development.

Egan, G. (1982) *The Skilled Helper* (2nd edn). Monterey, CA: Brooks/Cole.

Ellis, A. (1994) *Reason and Emotion in Psychotherapy* (Rev. edn). New York: Birch Lane Press.

Gass, M. and Gillis, H. L. (1995) Focusing on the 'solution' rather than the 'problem': empowering client change in adventure experiences. *Journal of Experiential Education*, 18: 63–9.

Geldard, K. and Geldard, D. (1997) *Counselling Children*. London: Sage.

Geldard, K. and Geldard, D. (1999) *Counselling Adolescents*. London: Sage.

Gendlin, E. T. (1978) *Focusing*. Toronto: Bantam.

Hall, E. and Hall, C. (1988) *Human Relations in Education*. London: Routledge.

Hazler, R. J. (1998) *Helping in the Hallways*. Thousand Oaks, CA: Corwin Press.

Hornby, G. (1994) *Counselling in Child Disability*. London: Chapman and Hall.

Hornby, G. (2000) *Improving Parental Involvement*. London: Cassell.

Hughes, J. N. (1988) *Cognitive Behavior Therapy with Children in Schools*. New York: Pergamon.

Kazdin, A. E. (2001) *Behavior Modification in Applied Settings* (6th edn). Belmont, CA: Wadsworth.

Liddell, A. (1987) *Methods of Changing Behaviour*. Harlow: Longman.

Maines, B. and Robinson, G. (1992) *The No Blame Approach*. Bristol: Lame Duck Publishing.

Manthei, R. J. (1997) *Counselling: The Skills Of Finding Solutions To Problems*. Auckland, NZ: Longman.

Molnar, A. and Lindquist, B. (1989) *Changing Problem Behaviour in Schools*. San Fransisco: Jossey-Bass.

Murphy, J. J. (1996) Solution-focused brief therapy in the school. In S. D. Miller, M. A. Hubble and B. L. Duncan (eds) *Handbook of Solution-Focused Brief Therapy*. San Francisco: Jossey-Bass.

Oaklander, V. (1978) *Windows to Our Children: A Gestalt Approach to Children and Adolescents*. Moab, UT: Real People Press.

Passons, W. R. (1975) *Gestalt Approaches in Counselling*. New York: Harper and Row.

Purkey, W. W. (1970) *Self Concept and School Achievement*. Englewood Cliffs, NJ: Prentice-Hall.

Rogers, C. R. (1979) *Freedom to Learn*. London: Merrill.

Rogers, C. R. (1980) *A Way of Being*. Boston, MA: Houghton Mifflin.

Satir, V. (1972) *Peoplemaking*. Palo Alto, CA: Science and Behavior Books.

Sirin, A., Hall, E., Hall, C. and Restorick, J. (1995) Item analysis of the 'My Use of Interpersonal Skills Inventory'. *British Journal of Guidance and Counselling*, 23(3): 409–18.

Thompson, C. L. and Rudolph, L. B. (1988) *Counselling Children* (5th edn). Belmont, CA: Brooks/Cole.

Thompson, C. L. and Rudolph, L. B. (2000) *Counselling Children* (5th edn). Belmont, CA: Brooks/Cole.

Vernon, A. (1993) *Counselling Children and Adolescents*. Denver: Love.

Watzlawic, P., Beavin, J. H. and Jackson, D. D. (1967) *Pragmatics of Human Communication*. New York: Norton.

West, J. (1992) *Child-Centred Play Therapy*. London: Edward Arnold.

5 Empowering children and young people

Garry Hornby, Carol Hall and Eric Hall

We want to give people the process, not one experience. We don't want to give them a fish, we want to teach them how to fish.

(Gendlin, 1984, p. 298)

The goal of counselling in school needs to go beyond the initial focus of helping to solve students' immediate problems. Counselling should be seen as the first step along the path to facilitating the development of young people so that they become all that they can be. Counselling and supporting students with difficulties should be seen as a means of beginning the process of empowering young people to fully utilise their potential.

Empowering children and young people involves helping them to develop a sense of mastery and control over their lives. This includes helping them to identify their own resources, facilitating their problem-solving and decision-making abilities and helping them develop the behaviours required to deal effectively with other people. Empowering therefore goes beyond meeting current needs to focusing on essential life skill competencies and making students better able to mobilise their own resources. It requires that teachers identify and develop their students' capabilities and help students to develop the knowledge, attitudes and behaviours which will enhance these life skill competencies

The third stage of the three-stage counselling model, outlined in Chapter 2, focuses on taking students beyond coping with immediate difficulties and towards developing into young people who are functioning optimally. The first part of the chapter focuses on three main strategies for empowering students: supporting action programmes; consolidating changes; and promoting self-actualisation.

Teachers have a key role to play in empowering children and young people but various aspects of wider school functioning are also important, especially the implementation of personal and social education programmes. The teacher's role in empowering will be considered in the first part of this chapter followed by a discussion of the wider role of the school.

Supporting action programmes

Teachers need to provide on-going guidance to students to help them carry out any action programmes that have been developed to cope with the difficulties they have been experiencing. The guidance that teachers can provide ranges across a continuum of helping, and inevitably changes over time as students progress. The continuum of guidance ranges from *directing*, through *coaching*, and *supporting*, to *delegating* (Blanchard et al., 1986). This is illustrated by considering students who can benefit from learning to use assertiveness skills in order to accomplish their goals and maintain the changes these bring about. Initially, the guidance given will typically be in the form of *directing*, such as in teaching students specific assertiveness techniques in order to achieve their goals. The teacher provides specific instructions and closely supervises the learning and implementation of these techniques. As time goes on, the guidance provided will be more in the form of *coaching*, such as in using role play to help students refine the assertiveness techniques used. The teacher continues to direct and closely supervise the students but now seeks more of a contribution from them by asking for suggestions and helping them to reflect on progress. Later, the guidance will be in the form of *supporting*, possibly through the use of praise and encouragement to help students gain confidence in the use of the assertion techniques. The teacher's role becomes more of a facilitator and supporter and the responsibility for decision-making is now shared. Finally, the form of guidance given will be *delegating*, whereby the student is trusted to implement and adapt strategies with only occasional reference to the teacher. The teacher becomes more of a resource to be used when students need further guidance. Being flexible enough to deliver each of the four levels of guidance and being able to assess the levels which students need at each point in time enables teachers to provide help which supports students' action programmes while also promoting their independence.

Consolidating changes

An important aspect of the third stage of the model is helping students to maintain and consolidate the changes they have made. Kottler (2001) comments that much more attention has been given to bringing about therapeutic change than maintaining it. He suggests a variety of strategies for maintaining changes which are summarised and adapted for application with children and young people below:

- make sure students are committed to bringing about change in their lives;
- ensure their goals are realistic and achievable;
- reinforce positive expectations;
- prepare students for inevitable relapses and backsliding; .
- teach the use of self-monitoring to identify potential relapses at an early stage;
- teach students how to use coping skills for dealing with relapses;
- teach students cognitive strategies, such as positive self-talk, to prevent relapses;
- ensure students can tap multiple sources of support when they need it;
- encourage students to team up with peers with similar needs;
- encourage the use of rituals to ensure appropriate behaviour becomes habitual;
- promote the development of lifestyle changes which make relapses less likely;
- reinforce the value of learning from failures or relapses.

Teachers can help students to consolidate changes by using the above and other simple strategies, such as reminding students of the progress they have already made and by encouraging them to persevere in spite of the difficulties they are likely to encounter. Other useful strategies which can be implemented by teachers in order to help students consolidate changes include enhancing self-esteem (Lawrence, 1996); recognising and affirming students' strengths (Epstein *et al.*, 2000); and promoting learned optimism (Seligman, 1991).

Enabling self-actualisation

The main focus of stage three is to enable students' self-actualisation. Enabling involves facilitating the development of adaptive behaviours which will promote the growth of young people in order to help them to live their lives more effectively. The emphasis is on personal growth rather than simply addressing current problems. In practice, enabling involves a range of possible strategies, the first step of which is initiated when a student seeks help with a problem or concern. In this situation, the listening skills, described in Chapter 3, are used to help young people to explore their concerns and, typically, to help them work out a plan of action to deal with the situation. Counselling often ends at this point, but this is where enabling begins. The first step involves supporting young people in carrying out the action plans which they have chosen in order to cope with their problem situations. But enabling seeks to go beyond this in facilitating growth and fulfilment of potential to the fullest possible extent. So young people are helped to become aware of the life skill areas in which they have strengths that could be utilised and those in which they have weaknesses that need to be developed. Enabling may therefore involve the teaching of life skills that are unrelated to the problem situations that young people present with but which are related to aspects of their functioning that need to be developed if they are to progress toward self-actualisation (Gazda, 1984). Enabling also involves encouraging people to expand their range of options for how they will behave as well as increasing self-control and building self-esteem. Finally, young people are encouraged to develop their own self-help strategies such as reading books on personal effectiveness or study skills and by joining self-help groups.

A powerful technique for empowering young people, and enabling their self-actualisation, is mentoring. Mentoring basically involves providing a model of a highly effective person as well as using enabling skills to encourage, enthuse and support young people in aiming to develop their talents and fulfil their goals. Torrance (1984) suggests that the importance of mentors in facilitating success, has been recognised for centuries and argues that, for many people who achieve great success in their lives, someone has acted as their mentor. According to Torrance, mentors support and encourage mentees in expressing and testing their ideas. They also help them to develop their talents while ignoring the constraints which others attempt to impose on them.

Torrance (1984) reports the results of a study in which he surveyed a group of 212 young adults who he had interviewed twenty-two years earlier when they were in primary school. He found that forty males and fifty-seven females had had mentors. He also found that having a mentor was correlated with several indices of adult achievement and was a better predictor of the level of achievement of these young adults than their IQs! In addition, he found that those young adults who had mentors completed a greater number of years of education than their peers who did not have mentors. This research emphasises the potential power of mentoring in facilitating personal development and suggests that it is a relatively frequent, but by no means universal, experience.

Developing personal mastery

At any age, growing up is a tough process. It can be tough emotionally, socially and intellectually, as well as physically. During the school years, the process becomes even tougher. When we enter nursery or infant school what was previously a relatively private, family affair, is suddenly and rudely made public. Without the supportive guidance of a classroom teacher bridging the gap between home and school, it can be a lonely and psychologically isolating experience for the child. If a child feels swamped by distress and no attention is paid by the teacher to building active coping and self-management strategies, there will follow an inevitable loss of self-confidence and belief in self-efficacy (Bandura, 1997).

Schools which provide students with programmes of personal and social education (PSE), giving them time to attend to their feelings, understand where they come from, what they mean and learn to express them appropriately, will reap the rewards in better student social and academic adjustment during this turbulent transition to school life. In their study, Hall and Delaney (1992) describe a personal and social education intervention programme for students of infant school age, designed to enhance patterns of friendship in a classroom characterised by poor interpersonal relationships. They found that as a result of the programme students perceived an improvement in friendliness in the class and the class teacher reported that despite the imminent move to junior school, the class remained friendly and calmer than the other classes of similar age who were unsettled by the prospect of the transition. The personal and social learning gains reported in the study are interesting in that very little intervention work of this nature has been reported with children of this age group but the outcomes demonstrate similarities with intervention programmes for students of older junior to secondary age (Thacker, 1985).

Promoting the emotional and social development of all students in our schools remains one of the greatest challenges still facing us in education today (Senge, 1997). As a society we will continue to pay a high price for failure to take responsibility for equipping our young people with the personal skills to live decent, productive and worthwhile lives if educationists do not face up to this challenge.

The notion of emotional or intrapersonal intelligence have been popularised recently by Gardner (1993) and Goleman (1996) who provide evidence that emotional maturity is a better predictor of success in life than conventional intelligence. In spite of this, academic development remains the central focus of schools and emotional development is receiving even less attention than it did twenty years ago when programmes of personal and social education were much more common (Watkins, 1999). The professional competencies required to develop students' emotional maturity rarely form part of initial teacher training programmes. Indeed, in a recent research project to promote emotional development in a family of schools, two of the authors interviewed all the teachers involved about their experience of training for work in this area. The staff of the seven project schools reported little more than the occasional half-day course. Only one teacher out of twenty-eight reported a significant training input in college. Research however suggests that 'emotional intelligence' (Goleman, 1998) can be developed just as any other competence and that EQ can be mapped just as IQ (Cooper and Sawaf, 1997).

Emotionally healthy schools

In order for schools to be able to develop the emotional health of the students they serve, they need to be emotionally healthy places in which to work and learn. Experience tells us that this is not always the case and that many schools are actually emotionally dysfunctional places. The following can be used as a check list against which to gauge a school's emotional health. If there is evidence of the following features then emotional dysfunction rather than emotional health will be present.

- Strong feelings of anxiety and insecurity in staff and students due to the emphasis on 'academic excellence' without reference to the emotional health of the school.
- The fracturing of relationships and breakdown in social cohesion due to a survival culture which emphasises short-termism and individualism over vision, co-operative problem-solving and support.

- Signs of student disaffection, high truancy rate, complaints about boredom and staff not seeing themselves as part of a community.
- Evidence of staff and students feeling incompetent, helpless and with a reluctance to take risks, change attitudes or behaviours for fear of losing face in front of peers.
- A denial or reluctance to take responsibility evidenced by a blame culture and an inability to talk frankly and openly about problems being experienced.
- A tendency to predict negative outcomes to events with a low expectation of success.
- Form tutors seeing their role as monitorial rather than developmental.
- Little teacher training in emotional development, experiential learning and counselling skills.

Using group work to develop social and emotional competence

The emotional health of the school as a community can be nurtured and sustained in classrooms through using group work approaches to personal and social education. The focus of PSE in schools is to direct students' attention to the ways in which they relate to themselves, each other, authority figures like teachers and the wider patterns of familial and community relationships. Citizenship education must begin with the phenomenal world of the student, not end with it, if they are to become responsible community members, rather than merely mouthing idealistic platitudes or taking extreme positions which they know will annoy the teacher and fellow classmates. The teacher's focus in leading or facilitating group work activities designed to foster social and emotional intelligence must be firstly on creating a safe psychological space for students to explore their own issues and secondly to structure lessons in ways in which learning emerges naturally by the students themselves.

In this way, teachers model *a way of being* (Rogers, 1980) with students which consistently and unobtrusively directs their attention to emotional and social *health* rather than *difficulties*. Negative emotional states, such as hopelessness, despair, anger or cynicism, when powerfully expressed, verbally or non-verbally, can quickly take hold of a group and reality can become distorted. The teacher must remain alert to this possibility and hang on to the role of reality checker for the group. However, the teacher's own self-awareness needs to be acute if he or she is to fulfil this function well. While a teacher must always accept the students' rights to have such feelings and express them appropriately, their primary task is to create a learning environment where such feelings can be explored safely and ways of moving on, letting go or growth out of reflection and understanding can occur. Pointing out alternatives, choices, possibilities, giving, affirming, encouraging feedback and visioning exercises (Day, 1994) all help to give a more balanced, optimistic view of reality.

One of the functions of counselling in schools is to help students to understand, talk about and manage their feelings. This is also an important part of group work, which has the added advantage that no child is 'problematised'. Through group work, students learn that relationship difficulties or entanglements are an inevitable consequence of social relations. The challenge is to face up to them in an assertive, pro-social way, which leaves the protagonists with a sense of personal dignity.

In order to effectively carry out group work in schools teachers need to learn about group dynamics and group leadership skills. These are considered next.

Group leadership skills

The key skills needed to lead group work with young people are the listening skills which were discussed in Chapter 3. However, the skills required in order to lead such groups are more comprehensive than those needed for individual counselling. Dinkmeyer and Muro (1979) agree that, first and foremost, group leaders need to be skilled listeners. However, they suggest that leaders also need to be able to develop trust within the group and to maintain a focus on the goals of both the group as a whole and of the individuals within it. Further, that leaders need to be spontaneous and to be responsive to what is happening within the group at any point in time. They need to be able to combine the ability to stand firm with a good sense of humour. Finally, to be effective, they need to be perceived by group members as being with them as a group and for them as individuals.

Another perspective on leadership skills which is particularly useful is that provided by Trotzer (1977) who considers that group leaders need the skills of *reaction, interaction* and *action*. These are briefly outlined below.

The *reaction skills* which group leaders need are:

- *listening:* in order to communicate respect, acceptance, empathy and caring;
- *restating:* to convey to group members that they are being heard;
- *reflecting:* in order to convey understanding and help members to express themselves;
- *clarifying:* in order to better understand confusing aspects of what is said;
- *summarising:* to provide an overview, stimulate reactions and move on to new ground.

The *interaction skills* which group leaders need are:

- *moderating:* to ensure that all group members have the opportunity to talk;
- *interpreting:* to help members gain insight into what is happening within the group;
- *linking:* to tie together common elements within the group and promote cohesiveness;
- *blocking:* to prevent undesirable comments or actions by one or more group members;
- *supporting:* to encourage members to share of themselves safely within the group;
- *limiting:* to prevent actions which would infringe the rights of group members;
- *protecting:* to prevent group members from being unduly criticised or hurt;
- *consensus taking:* to help members see where they stand in relation to others.

The *action skills* which group leaders need are:

- *questioning:* to help members consider aspects they had not thought of;
- *probing:* to help members look more deeply into their concerns;
- *tone setting:* to establish an atmosphere and qualitative standard to be adhered to;
- *confronting:* to help members face things about themselves which they are avoiding;
- *personal sharing:* to show that the group leader is human and is prepared to open up;
- *modelling:* to teach members interpersonal skills such as active listening.

Group dynamics

In addition to leadership skills, group leaders also need to have a good understanding of group dynamics, that is, the processes which occur within groups. There are several models of the process of group development and each suggests that all groups need to pass through several stages or phases if they are to function well and achieve their goals. A useful one for understanding what happens in groups is that proposed by Williamson (1982), which has four stages: *inclusion; work; action;* and, *termination*. These are outlined below.

Inclusion. The first stage of any group is one of developing a group cohesiveness so that all members feel a part of the group. Participants need to feel comfortable about belonging to the group. They need to be willing to share aspects of themselves and to explore concerns and issues within the group. As this process develops, group norms or implicit group rules will begin to be established.

Work. The second stage is one in which the members begin to work on resolving the concerns or issues related to the purpose of the group. This is usually the longest stage in the group's life. It involves members in activities such as discussing ideas, expressing feelings and listening to others in order to gain insight into their own situation. It is in this stage that group members will experience the greatest benefit. However, some members will resist change and there will be conflict and tension within the group. At the same time relationships between other group members will deepen and become more meaningful.

Action. In the third stage, the understanding and growth which occurs in the work stage needs to be translated into some form of action, otherwise the group will not fulfil its purpose. Individual members, or the group as a whole, need to decide what action to take to address the concerns which brought them into the group. Since change is difficult for members to cope with, the group leader needs to provide them with considerable support during this stage.

Termination. The final stage is one in which the group comes to a close with members experiencing a sense of completion, accomplishment and gratitude for what the group has helped them achieve.

When groups progress through these four stages then the experience can be a very powerful one in promoting learning and personal growth in the members. Unfortunately, however, because groups can be so powerful, when they are badly led they can result in members having their self-confidence threatened. So it is essential to ensure that qualified and experienced leaders are employed for any group work carried out in schools.

Background to group work: experiential learning and humanistic education

The use of group work activities encourages students to use their own experience as the content of a lesson, rather than a discussion of issues in the abstract, or an information giving session, for example, on drugs education. This type of learning is often described as experiential learning. We define this as learning which takes place in a structured workshop, classroom or laboratory setting when students are encouraged to be active in exploring their personal repertoire of feelings, attitudes, values and behaviours. The experiential learning cycle can be neatly summarised as DO – REVIEW – LEARN – APPLY (Hall and Hall, 1988). With skilful facilitation, exploring the self and relations with others can be highly rewarding and result in lasting changes which generalise to other life situations. A plethora of experiential activities were developed in the US, strongly influenced by humanistic psychologists such as Carl Rogers, who applied his research about personal empowerment to education (Rogers, 1979). Experiential exercises in workshops are now commonplace in the practical training of helping professionals and also management training, where businesses recognise clearly the link between development of a manager's interpersonal skills and their managerial effectiveness. Similar exercises have been designed for working with students in schools to provide a curriculum in which the content is the personal experience of the students themselves (Hall and Hall, 1988).

There are four main characteristics typical of a humanistic approach to education:

1   Emphasis is on personal meanings.
2   Development of personal authority and autonomy.

3   Learning focussed on process rather than content.
4   Awareness of feelings considered to be of equal importance to intellectual understanding.

The use of experiential learning considered here is only one of many approaches to social learning. There are other related and overlapping models used in schools which, in varying degrees, take a more cognitive approach to social relations. For example, values clarification (Simon and O'Rourke, 1975; Haydon, 1997) involves the discussion of beliefs, attitudes and values related to all aspects of living and can be applied by teachers to ongoing issues in the classroom. Alternatively, Pring (1984) discusses the use of hypothetical moral dilemmas, based on the work of Kohlberg (1971) to stimulate discussion for moral development as part of a programme of personal and social education. This approach can result in heated discussions which may touch on important ethical issues, for example, abortion or crime and punishment, but may still remain distanced from immediate classroom issues and will not necessarily lead to important self-disclosure or personal reflection by the students. A recent development in secondary schools in the UK is to replace personal and social education with a form of citizenship education (Lynch, 1992) which again moves to a discussion of issues rather than an examination of what is happening in the immediate classroom situation.

There is an abundance of resources which provide materials for working in a humanistic mode which help to foster social relations in groups of students. These include Canfield and Wells's (1976) influential book *100 Ways to Enhance Self Concept in the Classroom*. The 1970s and 1980s produced many useful resources for schools such as those by Castillo (1974) and Fugitt (1983). The exercises suggested in these books were developed into whole schemes of work for schools, such as *Group Tutoring* (Button, 1982), *Life Skills* (Hopson and Scally, 1981), *Building Self-Esteem in the Secondary School* (Reasoner and Dusa, 1991) and *Teaching Social Behaviour* (Warden and Christie, 1997). Many schools devised their own schemes of work using these resources. Other more recent and useful resources outlining good practice include those by Galloway (1990), Thacker *et al.* (1992), McNamara and Moreton (1995) and MacGrath (1988). These sources provide a wide range of practical activities which offer students of all ages an opportunity to develop their emotional and social competence in a classroom setting. Recently, Weare (2000) has provided a thorough review of the theoretical and research background which supports the use of these activities.

What characterises many schemes of work is their concentration on 'topics'. There is a clear need to have a coherent organisation of lessons, which demonstrates a planned, developmental process. Unfortunately, schemes which front-load topics into the curriculum can mean that the teacher once again falls into the trap of 'needing to get through the material in the lesson'. What is really needed is the interpersonal astuteness to strike a delicate balance between the 'here and now' learning priorities of the group and the dictates of the topic itself. Some teachers need the safety net of the topic if they do not possess the self-confidence or experience to take a lighter, less content-driven approach. Our own work with teachers and students over a period of twenty-five years has led us to encourage the use of broad structures that the teachers can use with content appropriate to the specific group of students involved. These structures are considered in the following chapter with some examples of possible content.

References

Bandura, A. (1997) *Self-Efficacy: The Exercise of Control*. New York: W.H. Freeman.

Blanchard, K., Zigarmi, P. and Zigarmi, D. (1986) *Leadership and the One Minute Manager*. London: Willow.

Button, L. (1982) *Group Tutoring for the Form Teacher*. London: Hodder and Stoughton.

Canfield, J. and Wells, H. C. (1976) *100 Ways to Enhance Self-Concept in the Classroom*. London: Allyn and Bacon.

Castillo, G. (1974) *Left-Handed Teaching*. New York: Praeger.

Cooper, R. and Sawaf, A. (1997) *Executive EQ*. London: Orion Business Books.

Day, J. (1994) *Creative Visualization with Children*. Shaftesbury: Element.

Dinkmeyer, D. C. and Muro, J. J. (1979) *Group Counselling: Theory and Practice* (2nd edn). Itasca, Ill: Peacock.

Epstein, M. H., Rudolph, S. and Epstein, A. A. (2000) Using strength based assessment in transition planning. *Teaching Exceptional Children*, 32(6): 50–4.

Fugitt, E. D. (1983) *He Hit Me Back First*. Rolling Hills Estates, California: Jalmar Press.

Galloway, D. (1990) *Pupil Welfare and Counselling: An Approach to Personal and Social Education*. London: Longman.

Gardner, H. (1993) *Frames of Mind: The Theory of Multiple Intelligences*. London: Fontana Press.

Gazda, G. M. (1984) Multiple impact training: a life skills approach. In D. Larson (ed.) *Teaching Psychological Skills: Models for Giving Psychology Away*. Monterey, CA: Brooks/Cole, pp. 87–103.

Gendlin, E. T. (1984) The politics of giving therapy away: listening and focusing. In D. Larson (ed.) *Teaching Psychological Skills: Models for Giving Psychology Away*. Monterey, CA: Brooks/Cole, pp. 287–305.

Goleman, D. (1996) *Emotional Intelligence*. London: Bloomsbury.

Goleman, D. (1998) *Working with Emotional Intelligence*. London: Bloomsbury.

Hall, E. and Hall, C. (1988) *Human Relations in Education*. London: Routledge.

Hall, C. and Delaney, J. (1992) How a personal and social education programme can promote friendship in the infant class. *Research in Education*, 47: 29–39.

Haydon, G. (1997) *Teaching About Values*. London: Cassell.

Hopson, B. and Scally, M. (1981) *Lifeskills Teaching*. London: McGraw-Hill.

Kohlberg, L. (1971) Stages of moral development as a basis of moral education. In C. Beck, B. Crittendon and E. Sullivan (eds) *Moral Education Interdisciplinary Approaches*. Toronto: University of Toronto Press.

Kottler, J. A. (2001) *Making Changes Last*. Philadelphia, PA: Brunner-Routledge.

Lawrence, D. (1996) *Enhancing Self-Esteem in the Classroom* (2nd edn). London: Paul Chapman.

Lynch, J. (1992) *Education for Citizenship in a Multicultural Society*. London: Cassell.

MacGrath, M. (1998) *The Art of Teaching Peacefully*. London: David Fulton.

McNamara, S. and Moreton, G. (1995) *Changing Behaviour*. London: David Fulton.

Pring, R. (1984) *Personal and Social Education in the Curriculum*. London: Hodder and Stoughton.

Reasoner, R. and Dusa, G. (1991) *Building Self-Esteem in the Secondary School*. Palo Alto, CA: Consulting Psychologists Press.

Rogers, C. R. (1979) *Freedom to Learn*. Columbus, OH: Merrill.

Rogers, C. R. (1980) *A Way of Being*. Boston: Houghton Mifflin.

Seligman, M. E. P. (1991) *Learned Optimism*. New York: Knopf.

Senge, P. M. (1997) *The Fifth Discipline*. London: Century Business.

Simon, S. B. and O'Rourke, R. D. (1975) *Developing Values With Exceptional Children*. Englewood Cliffs, NJ: Prentice Hall.

Thacker, J. (1985) Extending developmental groupwork to junior/middle schools. *Pastoral Care in Education*, 3: 4–12.

Thacker, J., Stoate, P. and Feast, G. (1992) *Groupwork Skills: Using Groupwork in the Primary School.* Devon: Southgate Publishers.

Torrance, E. P. (1984) *Mentor Relationships.* Buffalo, NY: Bearly.

Trotzer, J. P. (1977) *The Counselor and the Group.* Monterey, CA: Brooks/Cole.

Warden, D. and Christie, D. (1997) *Teaching Social Behaviour.* London: David Fulton.

Watkins, C. (1999) Personal and social education: beyond the National Curriculum. *British Journal of Guidance and Counselling,* 27(1): 71–84.

Weare, K. (2000) *Promoting Mental, Emotional and Social Health: A Whole School Approach.* London: Routledge.

Williamson, D. L. (1982) *Group Power: How to Develop, Lead and Help Groups Achieve Goals.* Englewood Cliffs, NJ: Prentice-Hall.

6   The emotional development curriculum

Carol Hall

> The rules for work are changing, we're being judged by a new yardstick: not just how smart we
> are, or our expertise, but also how we handle ourselves and each other.
>
> (Goleman, 1998, p. 3)

The previous chapter outlined the theoretical issues related to working with groups of students on personal and interpersonal issues. This chapter goes on to outline the practical classroom strategies which can be used to support the delivery of a curriculum specifically designed to focus on the emotional development of students and their teachers. This curriculum was developed by the Centre for the Study of Human Relations at the University of Nottingham and has been trialled extensively with clusters of inner city schools, both primary and secondary.

The curriculum cuts across age and culture because it speaks to our experience of what it means to be human. It is an emotional development curriculum designed for teachers as well as students and can be used as the basis for the in-service training of teachers who wish to develop their own emotional intelligence. It expands Goleman's (1998) elements of emotional intelligence; self-awareness, motivation, self-regulation, empathy and adeptness in relationships into a curriculum which can be developed systematically through an experiential programme.

The emotional development curriculum

Learning to relax: developing awareness and the ability to stay in control
Learning to listen: to myself and others
Learning to talk: so others can hear
Learning to feel: so that I can understand myself
Learning to express feelings: so that others can understand me
Learning to love, care and support: myself and others
Learning to lose: changing, grieving and letting go
Learning to live: being fully alive to experience
Learning to think: reflecting on behaviour and developing skills and strategies to change
Learning to handle challenging moments: being skilful in crisis.

This chapter sets out to outline the broad principles, strategies and practices for teachers who wish to implement this curriculum through group work in their own schools.

The role of the teacher – attitudes, behaviours and interventions in group work

An experiential group work approach to the 'formal' delivery of an emotional development curriculum requires not only a different set of classroom strategies but also that the teacher consciously attempts to model the Rogerian core conditions for healthy interpersonal relationships of authenticity, positive regard and empathy (Rogers, 1962). Thorne (1985) added a further interpersonal quality to this list, that of tenderness and we would add a fifth, the ability to communicate hope. Teachers, who have a tendency to pessimism, depression, self-deprecation rather than a healthy optimism, belief in themselves and the future will need to guard against this tendency when working with students. When facilitating group work teachers should:

- consciously and consistently work to create a trusting, supportive relationship with the group;
- use students' first names often and avoid using them in a punitive or punishing way;
- greet each student individually and be generous in giving positive feedback;
- talk about feelings in an assertive, authentic way and encourage students to talk about theirs;
- model accepting and respectful behaviours when students disclose personal feelings;
- never prompt, probe or exert psychological force to get students to talk;
- discuss clear guidelines for group confidentiality and behaviour and discuss strategies for managing transgressions;
- discuss appropriate ways to respond and support strategies if an individual's feelings become unmanageable within the group;
- emphasise group cooperation and be extravagant in praise of cooperative behaviours;
- keep the group focussed on surfacing creative win/win problem-solving strategies;
- model emotional self-regulation by staying calm and disclosing personal survival methods when under pressure;
- demonstrate relaxation techniques for keeping or regaining composure;
- help students to identify their emotional growing edge and plan ways to extend their competence.

The traditional modes of communication for instructional or didactic teaching need to change in order to encourage relevant self-disclosure in the group. The teacher needs to develop the skills of a facilitator, using the core conditions mentioned above. The skills borrowed from training counsellors can be used by teachers in their daily interactions with students, whether it is in the teaching of academic subjects or for working with the contributions from students during group work. It is particularly important in facilitating a group discussion to avoid the talk being dominated by the teacher or for closed questions to be asked which bring the discussion to an abrupt end. The use of listening skills, reflecting back what the student has said and expressing and reflecting feelings all play an important part in group discussion. Here are a few examples of facilitative modes of enquiry. The following suggestions offer forms of open questions and self-expression, which can be helpful to encourage students say more about their experience.

Use questions beginning with: 'What?' 'How?' and 'When?'

Avoid using questions beginning with 'Why?' Why questions ask for motives and reasons for behaviour which are not always accessible immediately to us. If the student is unclear about their motives, 'Why?' questions can create confusion and defensiveness as a reaction to feeling interrogated or probed.

A useful pair of linked questions to 'What? 'How?' and 'When?' are,

'What is good about …?' and 'What is bad about … ?'

There are 'good' and 'bad' sides to most aspects of our life experience and it is often helpful to ask the student to discuss both elements. To ask, 'What's good about coming home late?' and 'What's bad about coming home late?' in a neutral, non-judgemental tone can permit the student to explore his/her experience more fully. To prompt further exploration of feeling, use the simple but very potent question: 'How do you feel about …?'

Inviting students to use the first person singular, with sentences beginning with 'I' to own and take responsibility for their thoughts, feelings, behaviours and attitudes is also a potent method for developing self-awareness.

'I feel anxious', rather than, 'This is a worrying situation.'

'I don't like what's going on.' rather than, 'We don't approve of what's happening.'

These suggestions may appear to be simple and are certainly easy to understand. Applying them in the classroom is much more difficult and may involve changing years of habitual teacher behaviour. Oaklander (1978) provides a moving account of the impact of using these simple forms of language with disturbed adolescents. In an earlier book (Hall and Hall, 1988), we explain how the same sets of language skills can be used to calm aggressive behaviours or hostile professional interactions with 'difficult' colleagues.

The issue of personal choice is an important ethical consideration in group work. When a teacher is working with a group of students on emotional, personal and social issues it is important that students are given the choice as to whether to join in a structure or not. This option is not normally offered in academic subjects, it is expected that the students participate without question. One of the main aims of experiential learning is to extend the behavioural choice repertoire of individuals. To make wise decisions about what are healthy and unhealthy attitudes and behaviours. Unless students are given the responsibility to make real choices about what they feel able or emotionally ready to work on, they will participate only grudgingly and resist learning.

Students can be told that they can sit out if they wish but that it is important not to disturb others who are taking part. In the examples of centring and using imagery given, the students are invited to close their eyes. A useful suggestion to add is, 'You can peep if you want to.' If the students are given choices in this way, then they are cooperating whether they join in or not. It is not possible to disobey the teacher's instruction. Effectively they are being put into a positive or benign double-bind.

Confidentiality is also a vexed question and should be addressed by the staff team as a whole, not left to individual teachers to make their own rules up as they go along. We would recommend that there should be no blanket rule of confidentiality in the classroom. It is neither a confessional nor a counselling room. Students are in the process of learning and their learning in the main will be uncontroversial. If a student working in a pair or small group requires that self-disclosure remain confidential then they might articulate that need and hope that it be respected, although this can never be guaranteed. This issue is certainly one which should be discussed within the group and the teacher's own professional limitations on confidentiality should be frankly aired.

If feelings run high

Recently a colleague was working with a group of Year 9 students on the emotional development curriculum and had reached the section 'Learning to lose'. Students were reflecting on losses in their own lives. At the end of the lesson, three students were in tears. Together with his head of department, he spent the lunch break talking to them. The students had all experienced personal bereavements in their immediate families and found that the adults at home were reluctant to talk about their own feelings or encourage their youngsters to talk about theirs. At school there never seemed the time, space or opportunity to discuss with a supportive listener the depth of their feeling. The lesson had been the first real opportunity where they had been given permission to talk about their grief. The colleague reported after this experience his relationship with one of the girls in the group, who was looked on by staff as being particularly difficult, subsequently changed dramatically. He had seen a different side. Vulnerable and tender, she had disclosed profound feelings of loss and abandonment. In his turn, he had been an empathic listener who did not shy away from either her vulnerability or her tears.

It must be recognised that the outward expression of emotion will sometimes result in behaviours that make others feel uncomfortable. Teachers need to remain calm and alert to the needs of the individual and the rest of the group. Usually, peers are the appropriate people to provide support. Teachers do not need to rush in with the emotional band-aid to make everything all right. What is necessary is to ensure that the student who is overcome by strong feeling feels that they can cope or can decide what conditions they themselves need to work through their feelings. This might mean sitting with a friend outside the room having a good cry or taking time out to calm their own anger. This is all part of the experience of learning to love, care and support others. Not denying, avoiding or demonising feelings but seeing them as natural forms of authentic self-expression which can aid self-understanding and personal growth. Teachers need to be a role model for the class in how to handle these situations with calmness, dignity and caring.

Although strong feelings of grief and anger are common in schools, there is often no forum in the school for these feelings to be expressed legitimately or appropriately. Consequently, they may be acted out in distorted and destructive ways. If the teacher is uncomfortable with authentically expressed feelings it may be an indication that they have not yet reached the emotional maturity to be of real help to students in need and will need further opportunities to work on their own emotional development. In our view, the curriculum of affect should play an important part in the initial training of all teachers.

Getting started: preparing a group work session

There are very basic ways in which teachers can prepare themselves and the classroom for group work. It helps to think of the session as if preparing to tell a story which is to capture the imagination of the group. The physical setting of the room needs to promote an atmosphere of safety and intimacy. A circle of chairs enables each member of the group to have eye contact and students can speak directly to each other. A carpeted room will be less noisy when chairs are moved for paired or small group work and contributes to a comfortable atmosphere. The most appropriate arrangement of the room will vary, but as a rule of thumb the starting point is to begin with a circle of chairs while the teacher introduces the theme of the session. Younger students may be used to sitting on a carpeted floor or even in a large hall. It would be absurd to expect a Physical Education (PE) teacher to hold a gym lesson in a classroom. In the same way it is essential that a teacher using group work uses the appropriate physical space.

Beginning a session with a short relaxation exercise helps to centre both students and teacher, bringing awareness to what is happening inside themselves and focussing on physical and emotional sensations, as well as watching a train of thought. This forms a useful buffer between the turbulence of the class and the session to come, as well as training students in basic relaxation and breathing techniques. Students can literally be encouraged to leave any emotional 'baggage' outside the door using imagery. A primary teacher and her students decorated the outside of the classroom door to make it resemble a magical doorway. Inside, only good things happened and as students entered the room they were encouraged to make a wish or think a positive thought. The teacher noted that other classes eyed the door enviously and asked their teachers to help make their rooms magical places too. A teacher in a Californian school we visited, used a gym bench turned upside down and as students entered the room they were challenged to walk along the narrow edge of the balance. It took the young students all their concentration to walk along the bench without toppling off and they began the session in a much calmer frame of mind. After a period the bench was removed and the students used their own personal relaxation technique to begin the day.

Sessions can be paced so that after the initial relaxation, a slightly more stimulating or emotionally taxing piece of work can be introduced. This should still be well within the emotional competence range of the group. However, during the middle section of the session, students should be given increasing levels of challenge, either by introducing material or ideas which push their limits further so that they experience what Joyce (1984) terms 'dynamic disequilibrium', when preconceptions may need to be revised or overturned as new learning takes its place. After an emotionally taxing period, the level of arousal needs to be diminished. It is useful to form a circle at the end of a session, so students can share individual experiences. Not everyone will want to join in this whole group discussion and they should never be forced to do so. However, students who do not normally join in classroom discussions will do so when they have been personally involved in the issues and the fear of failure is eliminated. Hearing others talk about their experience deepens empathic understanding within the group, as well as being an emotional relief to hear others articulate feelings, especially as it can serve to *normalise* your own.

Structured group work for the emotional development curriculum

The following list of experiential structures is by no means exhaustive but gives a brief flavour of the variety of techniques which can be productively employed, from individual reflection exercises such as the learning journal to a large group carousel. Use them imaginatively to pace and structure the session.

Learning to relax

Learning to relax. A colleague was once asked to teach a yoga class in a local school. This was a daunting proposition as he had wrongly assumed that adolescents would be very supple and relaxed. Nothing could have been further from the truth. As a group they appeared to be tense, physically stiff and had lost much of their youthful flexibility. They also reported being amazed by the effects of a short period of relaxation. It was as if they had never before experienced being deeply relaxed. This suggests that the 'laid back' pose adopted by many adolescents is merely a pose and belies the underlying reality of tension or rigidity. In fact many students are in a hyper-aroused stressed or anxious state. The accompanying physiological states, tension in the muscles, increased heart rates and blood pressure, higher levels of hydrochloric acid in the stomach and an increased production of adrenaline, will be contributing to their overall levels of stress. Learning to relax and moving to what is called a parasympathetic state is an important skill for students to learn and will likely have a knock on effect on behaviour as well as academic achievement. It is helpful if the class is relaxed when any of the following experiential structures are introduced and learning to relax on its own provides a powerful tool for emotional as well as physical self-regulation. What follows are general guidelines and scripts for enabling a group to relax.

At the beginning of a relaxation exercise, invite students to pay attention to sense data in their immediate environment.

> Take your attention to the noises outside the classroom ... people walking along the corridor ... the sound of the wind/birds outside the window ... . At the moment you can hear people shuffling in their seats ... some people are coughing ... . Notice the feel of your clothes against your body and the feel of your back against the chair ... . Does it feel cold or warm in the room? What does the air feel like on your hands and face? ... Be aware of the taste in your mouth ... . You might still be able to taste the last thing you ate or drank ... . Take a deep breath ... . What can you smell? ... Notice how you are breathing ... the breath coming in and out.

Build into the relaxation anything that happens unexpectedly in the immediate environment, such as loud conversations on the corridor, a chiming clock, coughing or even giggling and offer the suggestion that such sounds will only be an aid to deeper relaxation.

> There may be noises outside the room but you will still be able to relax and let go. If you feel the need to cough or sneeze just go ahead and do it; this won't interfere with the sense of being relaxed.

Embed suggestions or commands in sentences by emphasising key words and dropping the pitch of the voice for a particular phrase.

> 'If there are noises outside, you will still be able to *become relaxed*. In a moment you might feel that you want to *close your eyes*.'

It can also be useful to embed such suggestions in your everyday language. Conventionally teachers phrase commands in the negative. 'Don't make a noise', 'Don't move out of your seats', or 'You must not hit other people in the class', but they have the unfortunate effect of unintentionally embedding suggestions to make a noise, wander about and hit other students!

Embedding suggestions of pro-social behaviours in your verbal messages, such as, 'Keep as quiet as possible', 'Stay in your places' and 'Please respect the other students', will over time mean that student behaviour will shift to match them. Unfortunately the opposite is more common and the behaviour of students shifts toward the negative. Changing language use requires careful attention to speech habits. Feedback from a supportive colleague can provide data for learning about unconscious speech patterns. Also notice the speech patterns of students and work to alter them if they veer towards the negative. These ideas can also form the basis for a session on the power of positive self-talk.

Young children and adolescents rarely have legitimate opportunities to relax purposefully during the school day. Here are two simple scripts for encouraging relaxation and learning to use the techniques in other situations. Students can relax sitting in chairs or if possible, lying down on the floor. If a student does not want to take part, then it is best to let him or her opt out with the proviso that they do not disturb the rest of the class. Do not be put off by restlessness, noises or even people coming into the room. Be clear with students about the purpose of the exercise and bring them back to the room gently. Do not hurry them back into activity and do not be surprised if the students just want to sit quietly for a moment. Like any new activity, students improve at relaxation over time. In fact, at first they may notice just how tense they feel and this might be unsettling. The teacher will need to explain that this is a natural phenomenon and goes away with practice.

Watching the breath. Make yourself as comfortable as you can and try to keep your eyes closed, but it doesn't matter if you open them … now be aware of your breathing … breathing in … and breathing out. If you watch carefully you might notice your chest and stomach rising and falling … over and over again … just like the waves of the sea lapping on to the beach. Just watch your breathing for a while and be aware of what happens … . Now turn your attention to the end of your nose and feel the air brushing against your nose. If you watch carefully, you might notice that cold air is coming in and warm air is going out. Now try to be aware of the breath changing from going in to going out. Notice what happens as the breath changes. Keep on watching the breath for a while, as you take this time for yourself to relax.

Breathing in the light. Make yourself as comfortable as possible and try to keep your eyes closed, but it doesn't matter if you open them … Now be aware of your breathing. As you breathe, imagine that you are breathing in a bright white light. Soon the body begins to fill up with this shining bright light. As your body fills up with the light, you become very calm, quiet, and relaxed. The white light starts to melt all your worries, fears, anger and sadness … . They all just melt and float away, leaving your body totally relaxed and full of the light. Keep breathing and as you breathe, you will find that you become more and more relaxed and the whole of your body will begin to glow with the relaxing light … .

It is important to bring students out of the relaxation gently. Some may even have fallen asleep and others will take some time to return to normal alertness. Use this form of words at the end of each script.

Gently, and in your own time, begin to bring your attention *back* to the room. If your eyes are still closed, you may wish to open them. You might want to breathe a little deeper and move your fingers and toes. Take your time. (Let a few moments elapse.) Is everybody ready to move on?

Students can also be taught to meditate (Fontana and Slack, 1997; McLean, 2001), which does enable them to relax. An increasing number of primary and secondary schools are adopting this activity as mental preparation to combat the strain of exam pressure.

Use of imagery and scripted fantasy

A powerful way of enabling students to develop self-awareness and to share their feelings with other people is through the use of forms of imagery; in particular, the use of scripted fantasy; a form of a guided imagery, (Hall *et al.*, 1991). This book details both theory and practice of scripted fantasy and also provides a large number of fantasy scripts. A further useful resource for developing imagery work with students is de Mille's (1976) *Put Your*

Mother on the Ceiling. Hall *et al.* (1991) list the benefits that accrue for the use of imagery as a tool for learning as

- the acquisition of basic relaxation skills for self-awareness and stress control;
- the development of listening skills;
- valuing and respecting the contributions of others;
- creating a cooperative, friendly, accepting classroom environment;
- improving the use of genre in writing;
- improving vocabulary to express subtle feeling states and enhancing self-expression;
- the ability to articulate aspects of personal experience clearly and concisely and to make personally meaningful interpretations of that experience;
- increasing levels of creativity and imaginal capacity;
- increasing self-awareness and self-understanding.

To lead students through a scripted fantasy, invite them to relax, close their eyes and simply follow the script of the imagery journey read aloud by the teacher. Here is a script which can be used to build up students' sense of personal control in a stressful or pressured environment.

A Safe Place

Take two deep breaths and allow your body to relax ... . Just let the tension go ... . As you breathe in I want you to imagine you are breathing in feelings of relaxation and as you breathe out, you are breathing out any tension you feel in your body ... . As you begin to relax a little more deeply, I want you to take your attention to some of the things that are making you anxious at this time in your life ... . I am not going to ask you to talk about them to anyone else unless you want to ... . You don't need to go into them in any detail, but just be aware that there may be some things in your life at the moment that you may not be too happy about.

Now have the sense that there is a safe place you can go where you don't need to worry about any of these things ... . Allow a picture to build up in your mind of the sort of place you could go to where you would feel safe ... . What is the place like? ... Take a good look around ... . Really explore it ... . What sort of things do you have in your safe place? ... What are the colours like? ... What does it smell like? ... Feel some of the things around you ... . Now have the sense that you are actually in your safe place ... . What are you doing right now in this safe place? ... How are you feeling? ... How does your body feel? ... In a moment I am going to ask you to let the image fade but I want you to remember that you can go back to this safe place in your imagination any time you want ... . Try to hold on to this feeling of warmth, safety and relaxation as you gently come back to the room and on into the rest of the day.

The precise language used for a script of this nature will vary with the age and background of the group involved but can be used with students as young as five to adults. Asking the group to draw their image of the safe place or even of a feeling from the fantasy and discuss it in pairs or trios can further develop the exercise. Training in 'turn taking' will help this process so that all participants have equal airtime in conversation. Later, the teacher might ask if anyone wants to share their experience with the whole class group. There will almost certainly be responses from the more vocal students and even individuals who seldom contribute may feel encouraged to do so.

Students are often eager to share their descriptions of the safe place, but they should not be pressed into sharing their anxieties. Teachers may need to decide for themselves strategies for dealing with any sensitive material which may emerge. Problems with relationships, family breakdown, physical, abuse, bullying, loneliness, ill health or death in families and employment, are all issues which might be present in a cross-section of students regardless of age. Certainly the discussion of such topics would fall within the remit of an emotional development curriculum designed to meet students' needs and concerns so that the safe place script offers them one way of developing personal coping strategies.

The suggestion is sometimes made that personal material of deep psychological significance is being raised through the use of imagery and that it requires the help of a skilled therapist to handle them. Certainly the images that emerge may be important to the students but usually they are very happy to have taken part in the experience and are able to draw their own conclusions from it. We have had feedback from several hundred teachers on the outcomes of using imagery in this way with their classes. Out of the thousands of students involved, there have been no reports suggesting psychological damage and no complaints from parents regarding the activity. However, we would add the caveat that, as with all experiential work, the teachers should have been through these experiences for themselves in a training situation first, before using them as a learning tool in the classroom.

Paired work

Work in pairs is the basic training technique in teaching students to listen attentively and respectfully to others. The following exercise is an example.

Learning to listen. Invite the students to form pairs and sit facing each other. They will have five minutes each to talk. Provide an appropriate topic, geared according to the age of the student and fitted to the theme of the session.

Examples might include:

> What do you remember about your first days at school?
> What are your favourite and least favourite lessons?
> How did you feel when you came to this school?
> Recall a dream you had recently.
> What makes you mad (or sad or glad)?
> When the first student begins talking, the role of the partner is to listen and try not to interrupt or say anything about him or herself. Their task is to encourage their partner to say more about their feelings and experience. Swap after five minutes and the partner now takes a turn.

Variations on this focussed listening exercise can involve more subtle forms of demonstrating attentive listening:

- invite students to make appropriate eye contact;
- ask them to lean forward slightly while they are listening;
- invite listeners to reflect back and summarise what their partner has said during the conversation.

Finally it is important to ask students to reflect on the *process* of the exercise, to share what it felt like to listen in that way. How might they have listened more attentively?

Ask the partners to give each other feedback about the way they felt when they were listened to. Some may choose to share in the whole group. Draw the session together by inviting pairs to comment on their learning to the whole group.

Small group work

Small group work can be geared to provide opportunities for students to express feelings.
  Here is an example:

Expressing feelings. Invite the group to divide up into groups of only children, eldest children, youngest children and middle children. The teacher may choose to join one of the groups. Then ask them to share the advantages and disadvantages of having this place in the family; how it feels to be this position in the family. A spokesperson reports a summary of the discussion to the larger group.

  The potential gains of an exercise like this are that the usual social groupings of the class are mixed up and personal material is being shared in these new groups. Appropriate self-disclosure by the teacher can help this process, as long as the teacher does not dominate the discussion. Teachers may feel anxious that students may not stick to the task. However, if students are off task, this could be an indication that the material is too threatening or sensitive in some way. However, as adults know, the best conversations often develop a powerful momentum of their own, which is exciting precisely because we do not know where they will end up. Teachers should allow for and tolerate such creative digressions.

Fishbowl

Learning to listen and learning to talk. Invite the group to form pairs. Ask them to decide who is A and who is B. The As then make a circle of chairs looking inwards and the Bs sit out-side the circle in a place where they can get a good view of their partner. The inner circle is given a topic to discuss within a time limit, say 10 minutes, such as 'What is a reasonable time to be home at night?' Observers take notes of their partner's behaviour according to a schedule provided. This might include helpful and unhelpful group behaviours such as:

- listens to other people's ideas;
- interrupts others;
- asks for other peoples' views;
- dominates the discussion;
- sits attentively and makes good eye contact;
- summarises the discussion;
- sabotages the discussion.

  After 10 minutes the teacher calls time and the original pairs re-form and the observers give feedback to their partners. The exercise is then repeated with roles reversed. In con-clusion, the pairs should be invited to discuss how it felt to give and receive feedback as well as how their behaviour in the group could be improved upon.

  The fishbowl is a particularly potent variation of work in smaller groups and since it involves giving personal feedback between students there may need to be some preliminary training in the skills of giving and receiving feedback.

Carousel

Learning to think. Invite the group to form pairs and decide who is A and who is B. Present the topic for the pairs to discuss, fitted to the session's theme. Then ask the As to form a circle, with chairs facing outwards. The Bs then sit in an outer circle facing their partners. The Bs are then invited to move two seats in a clockwise direction, to further mix up the pairs. A then begins and B just listens or prompts A to say more. The topic might be for example, 'One important thing I have learned about me in group work this term'. Then As are asked to move two places anti-clockwise and talk to a new partner. This process could then be continued with, 'One thing about group work that I don't enjoy', giving a total of four paired listening sessions.

The carousel is an effective way of setting up discussions in which the participants find themselves paired with someone they might not naturally choose and so offer the potential to deepen relationships through sharing personal feelings.

Circle Time

Learning to live. One particular group structure, which has been found to be particularly effective for promoting emotional development and heightening awareness of the self and others in a group, is known as Circle Time. This structure has been used for many decades, both in the US (Ballard, 1982) and in the UK (White, 1991; Lang, 1998; Moss and Wilson, 2000; Tew, 1998). The term is used for activities which range from simply inviting students to sit round in a circle to discuss an issue, to the comprehensive and potent model developed by Mosley (1996) using the title, 'Quality Circle Time'. All these activities aim to enable students to focus their attention on the 'here and now' interpersonal relations in the group.

The circle should be as close to being round as is possible in the space available and the teacher should be an equal member sitting on the same level as the students. There are usually guidelines or rules for operating Circle Time, which are clearly articulated and discussed within the group. We would suggest that the group begin by creating a set of guiding principles for working which will help to create a stronger sense of self-determination. Here are some useful pointers:

- there should be no put-downs by any members of the group;
- contributions from group members should be accepted and not criticised;
- group members are only allowed to speak if they are holding an agreed object, for example a book;
- everyone has the chance to speak if they want to;
- there will be no pressure for anyone to speak;
- the rules apply to the teacher as well as students.

This is an opportunity for community or individual issues to be aired in a safe, supportive environment. It needs to be acknowledged that feelings can run high and that teachers should be prepared emotionally to handle whatever emerges in the group. The issue of confidentiality will need to be discussed and for the teacher to be clear that some forms of personal disclosure cannot remain confidential to the group, for instance disclosure of sexual abuse.

Goal-setting/personal action planning

If the learning from the classroom sessions are not being applied in other situations and the transferability of the learning is limited, then it is clearly not being effective. Setting personal goals which encourage both the application, self-monitoring and evaluation of outcomes is the most important challenge of emotional and interpersonal learning. It may be very enjoyable to sit in a lesson and talk about yourself and aspects of your behaviour that you need to work on, but the real test is out in the hurly-burly of the playground or in a lesson with a teacher you do not like. Students can negotiate in pairs or small groups, behaviour they can try out in other contexts, such as at home or in their social lives. Outcomes can then be reported back to a partner in the group or in the whole group. The possibilities for areas to experiment with change are legion. The process of identifying an area for change provides an opportunity for an important issue to be focussed on constructively. An example of a simple goal-setting sheet is presented in Figure 6.1. The language used on the sheet will need to be adapted to the group involved and for younger students, these sheets can be illustrated and they can draw pictures to denote their personal goals.

My Goal

My goal for the next four weeks is to:
....

My evidence for the need to work on this goal is:
....
....

The advantages of achieving this goal are:
1. ....
2. ....
3. ....

The disadvantages of achieving this goal are:
1. ....
2. ....
3. ....

Who can help me?
....
....

Who might hinder me?
....
....

Having thought about it, I will change my goal to:
....
....

Figure 6.1 Example of a goal-setting sheet.

Personal learning journal

Keeping a personal learning journal can be an extremely valuable tool for helping students reflect deeply on their experience in and outside group work sessions, particularly in relation to their goal-setting activities. It is important for the teacher not to apply the same injunctions and restrictions that would normally be applied to working in exercise books.

Feelings, thoughts, intuitions and ideas can be expressed in drawings as well as words in the journals. It is important that the journal remains confidential to the student unless they wish the material to be shared. However, if teachers are permitted by the student to share the journal, or even write in it, they are often surprised at the quality and sensitivity of the writing as well as the sophistication of the emotional expression.

It is very useful to offer students simple prompts for journal writing to enable personal reflection:

- What did we do during the session?
- How did I feel during the session (critical moments)?
- What personal goals do I need to set?

Progoff (1980) claims that diaries and journals can stimulate a therapeutic, healing process for the individual. Journals should not be merely streams of consciousness. They are intended to build a bridge between the learner's subjective experience and a more detached, self-aware perspective. The journal becomes a reflective commentary on personal learning.

Conclusion

The desire to be socially and emotionally literate is a basic need in all of us, so that we might lead rich and fulfilling lives. There appears to be some positive indications that the promotion of emotional development of our young people is once more taking centre stage on the educational agenda. There is a genuine concern that schools could be doing more to promote the social and emotional development of young people in order to decrease school exclusion, juvenile crime, teenage pregnancy, substance abuse and other expressions of anti-social behaviour. Educators have a professional and a moral duty to provide the learning opportunities in which students can explore their own emotional lives (Day, 1993). Teachers can find inspiration for this moral imperative in the emotional development curriculum presented in this chapter when planning for the social and emotional development of young people in schools today.

References

Ballard, J. (1982) *Circlebook: A Leader Handbook for Conducting Circle Time*. New York: Rivington.

Day, C. (1993) Research and the continuing professional development of teachers. Inaugural Lecture, delivered at the University of Nottingham, School of Education.

de Mille, R. (1976) *Put Your Mother on the Ceiling*. Harmondsworth: Penguin Books.

Fontana, D. and Slack, I. (1997) *Teaching Children to Meditate*. Shaftsbury, Dorset: Element.

Goleman, D. (1998) *Working with Emotional Intelligence*. London: Bloomsbury.

Hall, E. and Hall, C. (1988) *Human Relations in Education*. London: Routledge.

Hall, E., Hall, C. and Leech, A. (1991) *Scripted Fantasy in the Classroom*. London: Routledge.

Joyce, B. (1984) Dynamic disequilibrium: the intelligence of growth. *Theory into Practice*, 23(1): 26–34.

Lang, P. (1998) Getting round to clarity: what do we mean by circle time? *Pastoral Care in Education*, 16(3): 3–10.

McLean, P. (2001) Perceptions of the impact of meditation on learning. *Pastoral Care in Education*, 19(1): 31–5.

Mosley, J. (1996) *Quality Circle Time*. Cambridge: LDA.

Moss, H. and Wilson, V. (1998) Circle time: improving social interaction in a year 6 classroom. *Pastoral Care in Education*, 19(1): 11–17.

Oaklander, V. (1978) *Windows to Our Children*. Moab, Utah: Real People Press.

Progoff, I. (1980) *The Practice of Process Meditation: The Intensive Journal Way to Spiritual Experience*. New York: Dialogue House Library.

Rogers, C. (1961) *On Becoming a Person*. Boston: Houghton Mifflin.

Rogers, C. (1962) The interpersonal relationship: the core of guidance. *Harvard Educational Review*, 32(4): 416–29.

Tew, M. (1998) Circle time: a much neglected resource in secondary schools. *Pastoral Care in Education*, 16(3): 18–27.

Thorne, B. (1985) *The Quality of Tenderness*. Norwich: Norwich Centre Publications.

White, M. (1991) *Self-esteem: Promoting Positive Practices for Responsible Behaviour – Circle-time Strategies for Schools, Set A*. Cambridge: Daniels Publishing.

7 Peer counselling and support

Hans Everts

> ... in adolescence, young people in distress often turn first to a peer for help. A growing body of evidence suggests that, with the right sort of training and support, it is possible to create systems which facilitate this natural process ... .
>
> (Cowie and Sharp, 1996, p. 12)

Introduction

The purpose of this chapter is to highlight the potential which exists within student peer groups for active participation in counselling-related activities. Troubled students often find it easier to talk with peers as a first point of contact in the process of seeking help. In addition, an effective network of students, trained in peer counselling and peer support, significantly extends the scope of the guidance network provided by teachers and counsellors. Constructive collaboration between these student and adult networks is of mutual benefit to both parties, and teachers can play a very significant role in such a partnership. This kind of collaboration also provides an alternative, more positive perspective on the role of the student peer group.

This chapter does not focus on specific problem issues faced by students and teachers, as is done elsewhere in this book. Rather, it sets out to define and describe a range of peer counselling and peer support systems, to analyse those elements which are essential to their success, and to highlight the implications of these findings for the role and contribution of teachers. The demands that peer counselling and peer support place on young people in terms of personal maturity and skill level tend to make these activities more fitting to the secondary school. However, many elements in such networks are highly relevant to primary schools, and can be developed there with caution.

Examples of successful peer counselling and peer support systems

Buddy system

A buddy may be defined as a peer who provides friendship and support, at a level of counselling skills that is relatively unsophisticated. The aim of a buddy system is to break down the sense of isolation or alienation experienced by many students, often newcomers or members of minority groups. A buddy can help the transition process into an unfamiliar school system or peer group. While the friendship and support provided may be limited in the level of sophistication of counselling skill used, the quality of relationship is vital to the buddy system's success. Buddies are usually chosen on the basis of their personal experience, maturity and sociability. The training normally undertaken is augmented by ongoing support and supervision from staff members involved in a buddy system set up to address a particular situation.

McWhirter *et al.* (1993) refer to the usefulness of buddies for second-language learning students; they provide personal encouragement, opportunities to practice the language, and make up a valuable source of suggestions on how to adjust to the school. Herring (1997) discusses a related situation in which international students are allocated a local buddy who, apart from providing personal friendship and support, helps research that international culture in order to carry out a joint presentation of it to the wider school community. It should be noted that in many instances the buddies benefit from the entire experience in terms of self-worth, empathic understanding of others, and relationship skills (Taylor, 1996).

Peer support

At a more formal and comprehensive level, peer support is a term commonly used to describe a secondary school-based programme in which senior students are trained as group leaders in a personal development programme for younger students, like new entrants to the school. Peer support typically requires full backing from senior administration, and links closely into the school's wider curriculum in such subjects as health, physical well being and social sciences. Much of the original conception came from Hopson and Scally's Life-Skills programme developed in the UK in the 1980's (Hopson and Scally, 1981), and a range of more specific action-orientated personal development activities (Brandes, 1984; Bond, 1986; Johnston *et al.*, 1993). Peer support as a specially designated programme has been comprehensively developed in a number of countries like Australia, since 1971 (Campbell, 1993a,b), and New Zealand, since 1985 (Peer Support New Zealand, 1995). The peer support training programme for senior students comprises up to twenty sessions focusing on communication, self-awareness, confidence building, trust, personal relationships, valuing and goal setting. It also includes training in leadership skills, facilitation and specific techniques like 'fish-bowls' (see Chapter 6). After initial training, leaders receive ongoing supervision and support over several years. This leader or leaders will then be:

> a supportive friend to a small family of new entrant students. (You) are not expected to solve problems or counsel, but (you) can help members by providing an environment where they can sort out their own ideas and values and learn to make sound decisions about their lives.
>
> (Campbell, 1993b)

Where needed, referrals for more sophisticated help may be made to the training teacher, counsellor or other appropriate person.

Another example of a powerful peer support system in action is found in a local high school known to the author. Students Against Driving Drunk (SADD) is a derivative from the well-established organisation known as Mothers Against Driving Drunk. SADD is a student-initiated peer support network with many branches in a loosely organised national body, which very actively promotes non-drinking for young people when they drive. The local group meets regularly; signs up members who contract to not drink when they drive; runs promotions in the form of plays, mock crashes and special weeks ('Alive at 25'); and raises funds for its promotions and its participation in the national body.

SADD branches are actively supported by schools, the Road Safety Council, the police and parent bodies. The existence of a strong peer support system in the school means many young people in this local SADD branch are already trained in peer support and basic counselling skills. Teachers and other adults are involved to a limited and variable degree in liaising with school and community organisations, in consulting with the local branch, and in facilitating certain events. Much emphasis remains on SADD being a student-initiated and student-run organisation.

Peer tutoring

At a more academic level, peers may be involved as tutors in specific subjects, extending the work of the teacher in a manner which is well-recognised in many educational traditions (Herring, 1997; McWhirter et al., 1993; Hornby et al., 1997). While some peer tutoring programmes are relatively limited in structure, most are based on a more highly organised system of lessons, closely related to the class curriculum, taken in brief daily sessions, and with specific outcomes (Jenkins and Jenkins, 1985). Many peer tutoring programmes focus on the reading area. Tutors are trained to give clear directions, to encourage, to confirm correct responses, to correct errors in a non-punitive manner, and to avoid over-prompting (Herring, 1993). While tutors are often recruited from senior classes, a tutor may come from the same class as the peers. In a variation on the theme, it is possible to set up a cooperative learning group in which both tutor and peers have a stake in its success; this can be greatly beneficial for all involved (Johnson and Johnson, 1989). Peer tutoring has been demonstrated to have a cost-effective and positive impact on the academic performance, attitudes and social relationships of those tutored (Cohen et al., 1982). It has also been found that peer tutoring can have significant benefits for the tutor, whose sense of self-esteem and confidence are enhanced and who in many cases make more academic progress than their tutees (Goodlad and Hirst, 1990; Hornby et al., 1997).

Peer counselling

Peer counselling, or peer facilitation as it is sometimes called, differs from peer support and peer tutoring in that the person involved provides actual counselling. Peer facilitation is a process in which trained and supervised students perform interpersonal helping tasks; listening, offering support, suggesting alternatives and engaging in other verbal and non-verbal interactions, that qualify as counselling functions with similar-aged clients who either have referred themselves or have been referred by others (McWhirter et al., 1993).

Such peer counselling is designed to address the personal and relationship problems of young people. These problems are many, and include personal crises like accidents, depression or suicide; the presence of personal disability or handicap; tensions arising out of cultural difference; discrimination, bullying or harassment; substance abuse; and stressful family relationships. All these problems affect the wider group of peers and, as demonstrated in the case of bullying in the UK, may create a cyclical pattern that has serious effects on the personal and academic functioning of pupils (Smith and Sharp, 1993).

Many schools have developed policies to address issues that affect the personal well-being of pupils, particularly problems like bullying, harassment or drug taking. They may also have taken an appropriate initiative in setting up programmes and structures that translate such policy into action. For example, Cartwright (1996) describes a whole-school anti-bullying policy, developed in a secondary school in Stafford, in the UK, comprising well-recognised principles, procedural guidelines, a system of rewards and punishments, a contract signed by all pupils, a student helper scheme and a comprehensive curriculum theme.

The successful development of such a network typically starts with the selection of a core group of perhaps 8–12 students, based on their seniority in the system, their demonstrated personal and social maturity, their commitment to this kind of programme, and their representation of different gender, ethnic and other groups in the school (Sue and Sue, 1990; Corey and Corey, 1997; Jacobs et al., 1998). Both written submissions and personal interviews help in selecting a suitable group.

Training this group takes considerable time and skill from staff experienced in counselling. Initially such training should take the form of facilitating the development of a strong mutual support group, followed by the training of its members in the skills and resources needed to perform their peer facilitation role. Developing a strong mutual support group requires members to develop: self-awareness; understanding and caring towards others, both group members and clients; openness and honesty; the ability to comfort as well as challenge others; and being at ease in a multicultural group. As a result of such initial development, the support group provides a safe environment, characterised by trust, commitment, cohesion, genuine caring and sharing (Capuzzi and Gross, 1998; Jacobs et al., 1998).

Alongside this more affective facilitation agenda lies the need for group members to learn specific skills of empathic listening and understanding, problem identification and problem solving, mediation and referral (Vernon, 1993; Sexton et al., 1997). At an organisational level, group members must also learn the discipline of running a smooth rostered team, of functioning within the boundaries of their competence, of avoiding personal entanglement in the lives of their clients, of referring on rather than becoming involved in psychotherapeutic activities and of guarding against burnout (Barak, 1994; Corey and Corey, 1997).

With such training and support from adult staff, there is clear research evidence that peer counselling programmes are effective, both at primary and secondary school levels (Sexton et al., 1997). For example, Paterson et al. (1996) outline the success of a student-managed Anti-Bullying Campaign in a secondary school in Camden, London. An active peer counselling programme provides an essential first point of contact for students who are harassed or bullied. They feel at ease talking to another young person; they appreciate the immediate support provided by a peer group which openly opposes harassment. When more formal action by the school authorities is required, the peer counsellor can provide appropriate referral; and he or she may continue to act as a support person in formal meetings or hearings.

The additional role of the peer counselling network as an advocate for certain principles is a very powerful one in the student body, as highlighted in the case of harassment or the use of alcohol and drugs. This is also true for matters of human rights, as discussed in the next section. All of this requires that the adults involved must have considerable time over a long period, and be able to function as counsellor and facilitator, as skill trainer and as organiser. Genuine liking and respect for young people, honesty, an active leadership style and much positive feedback are important (George and Dustin, 1988; Capuzzi and Gross, 1998). While some of such leadership is best supplied by specialists in guidance and counselling, it is both appropriate and valuable for teachers with a pastoral role to be closely involved with aspects of the training and programme-maintenance phases of such a project. For example, Gillard (1996) describes the establishment of a staff working party on bullying in a middle school near Oxford, which undertook a survey on the extent of bullying in the school. They then developed a personal and social education programme, created a bully-box for complaints and established a bully court based on a no-blame approach. While this chapter provides a broad outline of various peer counselling activities, a more detailed account of several projects and programmes in the UK, like Gillard's, are described in Cowie and Sharp's *Peer Counselling in Schools* (1996).

Peer advocacy

At times it happens that members of a particular peer group in the school, normally a minority group, take the initiative in advocating for the rights of that group. While this has features similar to the activities and programmes described above, peer advocacy is distinctive in that the initiative comes from students, with or without any backing from the system. The decision to support such initiatives, and the manner in which this is carried out, requires consideration in its own right. Even when it involves the actions of only one person, it poses a challenge to the teaching staff.

In one striking case known to the author, a 16-year-old young man, Gary, approached his year tutor in a single-sex school. He started off by telling the year tutor that he wanted help with a project. Gary then explained that he was gay, that he himself felt all right about this, but that he wanted the tutor's help in countering the many forms of direct and indirect prejudice against homosexuality that existed in the school. He noted that there was not a single statement anywhere in school policy which made it clear that differences in gender identity were acceptable, in spite of the school's professed affirmation of student rights. Such a statement of policy would help other students who were gay to feel more comfortable in coming out. It would also help to counter the informal slights and put-downs that he was getting a lot of the time from other students. One further way in which this lack of policy came out was in the fact that the library contained no books which discussed or portrayed homosexuality openly, let alone from a positive point of view. Gary did not want the tutor to do any of these things for him, just to give him advice and support. After reflection, the tutor agreed, and Gary proceeded to consult with him over a long period of time. The tutor used his own network to help Gary with making personal contacts, provided advice and informal support, and accompanied Gary in some meetings. Gary, however, insisted on taking personal responsibility wherever he could and the tutor was very careful to respect his initiative to the full. After considerable time and effort, the school's executive agreed to make an explicit and positive policy statement about the right of students to make decisions about their own gender preference, and the right of students to not be discriminated against as a result of such a decision. Gary was invited to write an article about the experience of being a gay in the school magazine, and the library was authorised to buy several books about homosexuality.

Peer empowerment and mediation in cultural and ethnic groups

High schools have increasingly developed into multicultural communities, representing students with widely different ethnic, national or religious beliefs and customs. Some such groups are well established, some are newly arrived; some come from stable and comfortable backgrounds, others have fled from traumatic situations like war or persecution. Some have intact families and communities; others are alone or with the tattered remains of their families. Sometimes the differences between pupils and teachers are vast, not only in terms of age but also in terms of cultural heritage. These circumstances in the school as a community constitute as much an opportunity for enrichment as one for separation, stress, misunderstanding and conflict. The latter is increasingly common and is a challenge for staff and students to work together in fostering goodwill and collaboration between diverse cultural groups.

One approach to the resolution of such inter-group tensions is through the development of a collaborative network of students and staff based on the principles of empowerment and mediation. Empowerment through providing all groups with a sense of recognition and identity. Mediation through helping them find mutually acceptable solutions to the tensions of living together within the same community. Once again, elements of this approach are similar to what has been outlined above, but the overall thrust of this kind of activity is unique in nature and intent. An example of such a programme is provided by Frayling, who is establishing a three-phase development project to address inter-cultural relationships (Frayling, 1998). The three phases are: first, the establishment of a group of cultural leaders, who develop their own inter-cultural sensitivity and relationship skills through a systematic training programme. Second, provision by them of positive support and empowerment for the various cultural groups they identify with through, for example, welcoming new entrants, providing information about subject choices and non-academic activities, sharing the frustrations of using a foreign language, and personally supporting students in difficulty at school, especially when parental support is lacking. Third, the development of skills to help them provide safety for students being bullied or harassed, and to contribute to mediation processes in handling inter-group tensions.

A group of cultural leaders, representing ethnic and other cultural minority student groups in the school, constitutes a powerful resource network. It consists of young people who have personal experience of being in that cultural group, often complicated by facing the stresses of adapting to the process of migration and its attendant inter-generational tensions (Sue and Sue, 1990). Such stresses are often discussed more readily within the peer group rather than with teachers or counsellors, partly because it involves less loss of face (Soong and Au, 1990), partly because professional resource people are often less highly regarded as a source of psychological help in many non-European cultures. At the same time, a well-resourced peer support network, associated with the school's guidance network, allows that school to meet its obligation to client groups under stress (Ibrahim, 1991; Highlen, 1996). As such, cultural leaders may develop roles of advocate, adviser, facilitator of indigenous support systems and change agent (Sue et al., 1996).

To succeed in these tasks, cultural leaders must be carefully selected for their tolerance of diversity, willingness and capacity for full participation and personal commitment (Reynolds and Pope, 1991; Corey and Corey, 1997). Their group must also reflect a balance of age, gender, ethnicity and stage of migration. Once selected, they are put through a training programme, culturally foreign to many of them (Yu and Gregg, 1993), designed to develop their self-concept and cultural esteem (Sue and Sue, 1990), as well train them in the facilitation or counselling skills. This learning process is a very active one, with constant cross-cultural sharing and comparison, and the development of mutual understanding and respect. The uniqueness of this multicultural group is respected through the use of somewhat more formal procedures, less urge to reach depth in personal sharing (Corey and Corey, 1997), and avoidance of early confrontations between members and cultural identities (Kinzie et al., 1988; Yu and Gregg, 1993). With time, the group's formation phase flows into the active outreach phase of the programme – in the form of fostering positive support and empowerment for various cultural groups in the school.

Not surprisingly, ongoing support, supervision and training of members of the cultural leader group is vitally important. The multiple challenges of the programme require the selection of competent adult trainers who can create a strong atmosphere of trust and safety, who themselves represent cultural diversity, who model the mutual understanding and respect which the programme fosters, and who can draw on a range of teaching and counselling backgrounds (Capuzzi and Gross, 1998). Ultimately, this area can be seen to represent a distinctive and powerful way in which peer facilitation and teacher collaboration combine to contribute to the psychological well-being of the school as a multicultural community.

Components of successful peer counselling and peer support groups

While the above examples indicate that there are important differences between types of peer counselling and peer support systems, there is equally significant evidence that there are common elements in all which are crucially important for the success of their operation. To highlight these elements or components is valuable for all those involved in establishing a peer helping system, responsible for its effective running, or contributing to its evaluation. The foregoing section indicates that an effective peer helping system requires it to take in mature individuals, to run a group which is personally satisfying, to train its members in essential skills and to be seen to be successful in its external responsibilities. Put that way, the successful peer counselling and support network may be described as resilient or hardy.

Resilience has become an increasingly useful and popular concept to describe individuals or groups. At the individual level, researchers like Rutter (1993) in the UK and Grotberg (1995) in the USA have highlighted the characteristics of resilient children. At an interpersonal level, resilience has been defined as the ability of a group of people, or a couple in an intimate relationship, to be able to cope successfully with its external tasks at the same time as maintain, if not enhance, the quality of its own relationships (Everts, 1999). In the author's study designed to ascertain the components of couple resilience, four clusters of components were found: individual resources; relationship attitudes; relationship skills; and the relationship between couple and wider community (Everts, 1999). These clusters appear highly relevant to the task of defining the essential qualities of a successful peer helping system, and will be used as a tentative template for summing up points made in the preceding section.

Personal qualities

In terms of personal resources or qualities, the preceding findings indicate the importance of selecting peer helpers who are optimistic, and have a positive attitude towards other people, challenging situations, and the future. Such an attitude, translated into a counselling strategy called reframing (Bandler and Grinder, 1982), has been found to be very powerful in helping clients change their own negative perceptions into more positive and adaptive ones. In addition it is important to select people who have a personal resilience or hardiness, a capacity to hold up under stress, and ones who understand themselves, and who are aware of others at a psychological level. Nothing in the literature cited notes whether a religious or spiritual faith is important, but it would seem fitting that peer helpers have a sense of the meaning and purpose of life.

Relationship qualities

Both the peer group and any student clients obviously need the peer counsellor or support person to have a clear attitude of caring and empathy towards them. This is a quality which must be there at the time of selection, is strongly fostered during training, and is central to the integrity and cohesion of the support group. In addition to this quality of caring, and somewhat different from it, is the notion that peer helpers must have a sense of commitment towards others and towards the helping process, for better or worse. They are involved for some time, and expected to remain so even if it is emotionally demanding. It would be impossible to imagine an effective peer helper who is not tolerant and accepting of differences in the needs and characteristics of peers and clients. Yet, at the same time it is important that members of the peer helper group share basic values like an interest in others and a tolerance of differences.

Relationship skills

Personal and relationship qualities are closely intertwined with more cognitive and behavioural skills or resources. Once an atmosphere of trust and caring is established in the training group, much time is devoted to the development of interpersonal skills, with emphasis on the communication skills and strategies noted in earlier chapters. Closely associated with these are collaboration skills, or the ability to work together in a practical sense of tackling the group's internal cohesion tasks as well as its external working brief. As soon as this can be achieved, the group and its members hope to accumulate a track record of learning experiences which can be drawn on to help in dealing with subsequent challenges. In addition to all the hard work, groups normally emphasise the need for some recreation to give a sense of break and build up the optimistic sparkle noted above. It is interesting to recognise that the conflict situations which peer counsellors and supporters get to address, and the skills they are taught to use in dealing with them, are strongly supported by recent work in so-called Reaction Pattern Reset (Rink and Ott, 1997). In this research it was found that the majority of young people know about and choose to use solutions which are regarded as partially satisfactory: accommodation to the needs of the other party; favouring self at the expense of the other; or avoidance of conflict. Relatively few know how to negotiate their way through a conflict and achieve a win–win solution. Yet, these are the very skills which peer helpers learn to use in their own group work and to apply in counselling or support activities with clients.

Community relationships

In terms of their relationships with the wider community, the thrust of findings above emphasises the peer helper group's strong need for external social support from significant others like teaching staff, the wider student population, the school's administration and parents. Such support, as well as the availability of past and present role models, helps the peer counselling or support group to maintain its collective strength, and protect itself against inevitable external pressures and detractors.

The teacher's role: rising to the challenge

While the forgoing section indicates the crucial involvement of students in making peer support and counselling successful in the school, it is evident that the teacher's active contribution to such activities is equally necessary. This contribution varies enormously in depth and extent. At a relatively modest level, teachers, regardless of role or skill level, can provide much needed informal support. At a more sophisticated and time-consuming level, teachers may be involved in a training capacity. Such training can be of two kinds. In some situations, illustrated above, the trainer is one who facilitates the expression and development of personal functioning in students. Here the trainer must demonstrate counselling-related personal qualities of caring, respect and genuineness as he or she uses invitational strategies to encourage students to express themselves, experience themselves fully, reflect on this experience, relate openly to others, learn to understand and respect others in their uniqueness and difference, and be affirmed for such experiences. By contrast the teacher, displaying the same personal qualities, may act in a much more structured and directive role by training students in communication, problem solving, assertiveness, mediation or collaboration skills. In and of itself, such a training role is challenging as well as potentially very satisfying.

Even if this training role is limited in scope, it is normally part of a wider programme and thus raises issues about the nature and sophistication of the teamwork, which exists to underpin such programmes. Some programmes, like a limited buddy network to welcome students, need not involve many staff or require much training. Others, described above, require a much more sophisticated guidance network, with skilled counsellors and a defined budget of time and resources. Such a network is able to develop more sophisticated programmes, and use a wide range of staff in creative and satisfying ways to provide training, ongoing support, supervision and programme monitoring. A well-functioning guidance network is also able to take its contributing teaching staff much further in the quality of service delivery that any one of them could develop on their own.

In all, this chapter highlights the great pastoral care potential which resides in the student population, and the innovative and effective ways in which the peer group may be encouraged to meet the school's personal and social needs, as noted in other chapters. Active collaboration between all staff and students interested in such needs can result in many programmes and activities at different levels of sophistication, which enhance the resilience of the student peer group. Such a partnership greatly extends the scope of the guidance network's activities, and does so in ways that only the student peer group can do. All teachers are in a position to contribute to peer support and counselling, and may well find their own job satisfaction and effectiveness enhanced in the process.

References

Bandler, R. and Grinder, J. (1982) *Reframing: Neuro-Linguistic Programming and the Transformation of Meaning*. Moab: Real People Press.

Barak, A. (1994) A cognitive–behavioral education workshop to combat sexual harassment in the workplace. *Journal of Counseling and Development*, 72: 595–602.

Bond, T. (1986) *Games for Social and Life Skills*. London: Hutchinson.

Brandes, D. (1984) *Gamester's Handbook Two: Another Collection of Games for Teachers and Group Workers*. London: Hutchinson.

Campbell, E. (1993a) *The Teacher's Manual for the Peer Support Program*. Sydney: Campbell.

Campbell, E. (1993b) *The Student Leader's Manual for the Peer Support Program*. Sydney: Campbell.

Capuzzi, D. and Gross, D. R. (1998) *Introduction to Group Counseling* (2nd edn). Denver, CO: Love.

Cartwright, N. (1996) Combatting bullying in school: the role of peer helpers. In H. Cowie and S. Sharp (eds) *Peer Counselling in Schools*. London: Fulton, pp. 97–105.

Cohen, P. A., Kulik, J. A. and Kulik, C. L. C. (1982) Educational outcomes of tutoring: a meta-analysis of findings. *American Educational Research Journal*, 19: 237–48.

Corey, M. S. and Corey, G. (1997) *Group Process and Practice* (5th edn). Belmont, CA: Brooks/Cole.

Cowie, H. and Sharp, S. (eds) (1996) *Peer Counselling in Schools*. London: Fulton.

Everts, J. F. (1999) Couple resilience: an empirical exploration of the concept. *New Zealand Journal of Counselling*, 20: 47–65.

Frayling, I. (1998) Personal communication. Auckland: University of Auckland.

George, R. L. and Dustin, D. (1988) *Group Counseling*. Englewood Cliffs, N.J.: Prentice-Hall.

Gillard, D. (1996) Peers facing the problem of bullying in school. In H. Cowie and S. Sharp (eds) *Peer Counselling in Schools*. London: Fulton, pp. 106–13.

Goodlad, S. and Hirst, B. (1990) *Explorations in Peer Tutoring*. Oxford: Blockwell.

Grotberg, E. (1995) *Resilience in Children*. The Hague: Bernard van Leer.

Herring, R. D. (1997) *Counseling Diverse Ethnic Youth*. New York: Harcourt Brace.

Highlen, P. (1996) MCT theory and implications for organizations and systems. In D. W. Sue, A. E. Ivey and P. B. Pedersen (eds) *A Theory of Multicultural Counseling and Therapy*. Pacific Grove, CA: Brooks/Cole.

Hopson, B. and Scally, M. (1981) *Lifeskills Teaching*. London: McGraw-Hill.

Hornby, G., Atkinson, M. and Howard, J. (1997) *Controversial Issues in Special Education*. London: Fulton.

Ibrahim, F. A. (1991) Contribution of cultural world-view to generic counseling. *Journal of Counseling and Development*, 70: 13–19.

Jacobs, E., Masson, R. L. and Harvill, R. L. (1998) *Group Counseling Strategies and Skills* (3rd edn). Belmont, CA: Brooks/Cole.

Jenkins, J. and Jenkins, L. (1985) Peer tutoring in elementary and secondary programs. *Focus on Exceptional Children*, 17: 1–12.

Johnson, D. W. and Johnson, R. T. (1989) Towards a cooperative effort: a response to Slavin. *Educational Leadership*, 45: 58–64.

Johnston, M. *et al.* (1993) *Action Against Bullying: A Support Pack for Schools*. Edinburgh: The Scottish Council for Research in Education.

Kinzie, J. D., Leung, P., Ben, R., Bui, A., Keopraseuth, K. O., Riley, C., Fleck, J. and Ades, M. (1988) Group therapy with Southeast Asian refugees. *Community Mental Health Journal*, 24: 157–66.

McWhirter, J. J., McWhirter, B. T., McWhirter, A. M. and McWhirter, E. H. (1993) *At-Risk Youth: A Comprehensive Response*. Pacific Grove, CA: Brooks/Cole.

Paterson, H., Bentley, M., Singer, F. and O'Hear, P. (1996) The Anti-Bullying Campaign (ABC) at Acland Burghley. In H. Cowie and S. Sharp (eds) *Peer Counselling in Schools*. London: Fulton, pp. 114–23.

Peer Support New Zealand (1995) *Peer Support Programme for Secondary Schools*. Christchurch, N.Z.: Rotary Peer Support Trust.

Reynolds, A. L. and Pope, R. L. (1991) The complexities of diversity: exploring multiple oppression. *Journal of Counseling and Development*, 70: 174–80.

Rink, J. E. and Ott, W. (eds) (1997) *Youngsters Between Freedom and Social Limits*. Leuven/Appeldoorn: Garant.

Rutter, M. (1993) Resilience: some conceptual considerations. *Journal of Adolescent Health*, 14: 626–31.

Sexton, T. L., Whiston, S. C., Bleuer, J. C. and Waltz, G. R. (1997) *Integrating Outcome Research into Counseling Practice and Training*. Alexandria, VA: American Counseling Association.

Smith, P. and Sharp, S. (eds) (1993) *School Bullying: Insights and Perspectives*. London: Routledge.

Soong, C. and Au, S. (1990) Towards an indigenized approach to counselling. *New Zealand Journal of Counselling*, 15: 13–17.

Sue, D. and Sue, D. (1990) *Counseling the Culturally Different* (2nd edn). New York: Wiley.

Sue, D. W., Ivey, A. E. and Pedersen, P. B. (1996) A *Theory of Multicultural Counseling and Therapy*. Pacific Grove, CA: Brooks/Cole.

Taylor, G. (1996) Creating a Circle of Friends. In H. Cowie and S. Sharp (eds) *Peer Counselling in Schools*. London: Fulton, pp. 73–86.

Vernon, A. (ed.) (1993) *Counseling Children and Adolescents*. Denver, CO: Love.

Yu, A. and Gregg, C. H. (1993) Asians in groups: more a matter of cultural awareness. *Journal for Specialists in Group Work*, 18: 86–93.

8   Empowering parents and families

Mariana Chadwick

> The goals of families and schools can be met most effectively by these two institutions working together. This can be accomplished by recognising the family as a resource and working to empower parents through counselling.
>
> (Kraus, 1998, p. 14)

The model of family counselling that underpins the workshop outlined in this chapter is based on Minuchin's (1984) structural model that emphasises the development of clear, direct and specific communication between parents and children. This approach has been developed by the author and a colleague (Fuhrmann and Chadwick, 1995) on the basis of their professional experience as family therapists at the Centro de Terapia Sistemica, Santiago, Chile. We call this the 'Empowering Families' model and the aim of this chapter is to prepare teachers to conduct parent workshops using a preventative perspective based on this model.

Parenting is so much more than behaviour management and discipline. It is the joy of watching children grow, not just in the physical sense but also to mature, become independent, develop self-worth and adopt healthy behaviours that help them function in society. Parenting also involves helping children develop social skills, personal interests, respect for others and themselves, and ways of handling and expressing their emotions. Parents need to feel confident about what they have to offer in terms of their own wisdom and intuition.

This chapter outlines a workshop approach to working with families which encourages parents to reflect on and explore their attitudes and those of their extended family members, to family life. This is complementary to the individual and group counselling approaches already used in schools (Kraus, 1998). It is considered that an individualised search for alternative behaviour patterns for the family is more valid than the imposition of external recommendations. Each family needs to discover its own style, according to its own beliefs and values.

In training teachers as facilitators for the parenting workshop, the development of flexibility, leadership and respect for diversity is emphasised. Teachers should first have the opportunity to learn these skills in a workshop experience where the leader will model a friendly, non-judgmental attitude toward all participants. Teachers should also go through the eight sessions of the parent workshop with their own families before they conduct a parent group.

It is potentially even more enriching if parents work through each section of the workshop at home by themselves and then meet with a group of other parents who are following the same programme. In these meetings, the teacher's responsibility is to provide parents with a setting where they will learn from each other, share their experiences and ideas and provide an emotional climate in which participants can express their sufferings and difficulties, joys and successes.

How families function

Every human being is part of a family which forms part of an extended family, a cultural community, a country. A family as a unit is more than a conglomerate of individuals. It forms an open, constantly interacting, hierarchical system in which any variation in one of the sub-systems will affect the family's functioning (Hoffman, 1981). Also, the family affects the behaviour and development of each of its members. Families can provide love, affection and the opportunity for both physical and psychological development. Families can also provide identity through the sense of belonging and maintaining family bonds. The identity of each family member will be shaped by the continuous interaction of personal and familial characteristics.

The social context of the family

It is imperative to understand the family in the social context in which it occurs. Bronfenbrenner (1979) provides an ecological model of family functioning which highlights four different levels of influence on the family. These are:

- *The Microsystem* which is the nuclear family of parents and children.
- *The Mesosystem* which includes the extended family and the community in which the family lives.
- *The Exosystem* which consists of wider social factors, such as the quality of health, education and social welfare resources.
- *The Macrosystem* which includes the attitudes, beliefs and values inherent in a particular society, all of which influence the way that families develop.

Family functioning is influenced not only by the interactions within the family's microsystem but also by its interactions with other levels of the entire social system. For example, a strong marriage, supportive extended family, a strong spiritual network and gainful employment are factors that predict whether a family can maintain its objectives in a team approach, whereas, very young, immature, single parents are likely to have fewer resources at their disposal.

Family communication

A smile, a word or silence are all forms of communication that enable family relations to take place. Family communication is a process of reciprocal influence, a continuous process in which family members simultaneously affect and are affected by others. Communication can occur through any behaviour in the presence of another person, including a lack of response. Thus, it is impossible for family members not to communicate. It is possible to determine the social organisation of a family by analysing family communication patterns among the different sub-systems. Good communication is essential to healthy, happy relationships between family members. It is a complex area of learning that many parents have difficulty mastering (Snell-White, 1993). How can parents be sure that they are sending the message they want? First, they need to be aware that their body language, tone of voice and actions must reflect the message. They also need to choose their words carefully. They can use 'I messages' to express their feelings, which otherwise might be difficult. For example, 'I feel angry when you don't listen to me', rather than, 'you are a bad boy for not listening to me'. Parents need to pay attention to their children's behaviour in order to obtain feedback on the impact of their messages.

How can parents get children to talk to them? Children and teenagers find it easier to talk to someone who really listens. To be good listeners, parents should stop what they are doing and give children their full attention while they speak. They should let children know that their point of view is understood and encourage them to speak openly about their opinions, feelings and ideas. Another component of good family communication is being assertive and having self-confidence in expressing opinions. Some parents are aggressive, others are passive or manipulative. After listening to the children, parents can be assertive and make a decision without hurting other members of the family. Generally, this involves saying what they want or feel and why, and then clearly stating the decision or action they have chosen.

Family members need to communicate to solve problems. People have a natural tendency to close down communication during periods of stress. In some families, closed communication is the rule, not the exception. This closed system is maintained by yelling, blaming or, more ominously, by silence (Golden, 1993). An educational approach can help otherwise competent parents who simply need to improve their communication skills. However, severely disturbed communication patterns indicate a need for family therapy. The workshop described here is not intended as therapy but as an educational experience for parents to reflect on and empower their own families.

When parents hold an 'executive' position in the family organisation, children are granted freedoms based on their demonstrated responsibility. However, some parents surrender authority too soon, often in the hope of avoiding conflict with the child, or because they have neither the patience nor the sensitivity to deal with setting limits. Most children from these families do not develop inner control and, as they grow, become more difficult to guide.

Teachers can help parents establish appropriate authority in several ways:

- by asking them to reflect and set family goals;
- by supporting and expressing confidence in the parents' decision-making;
- by pointing out the many different paths parents can take.

Quick assessment of family functioning

Experience has shown that well-trained teachers can empower families and thus help prevent their students from developing serious social and emotional problems. Many families can benefit from preventative interventions but some will require long-term intensive therapy to solve their child's problems. Golden (1993) proposes a quick assessment of family functioning to help teachers choose the families to work with. This assessment includes the following variables:

- *Time frame of the child's problem.* Is it of short duration?
- *Communication.* Is communication between family members clear and open?
- *Hierarchy of authority.* Are parents effective in asserting authority?
- *Parental resources.* Can parents provide for the child's basic needs and still have time and energy for a behavioural plan?

- *Relationship between helping adults.* Does a working relationship exist between teacher and parents? Do parents return phone calls, attend meetings?

Golden suggests teachers respond to the above questions on a scale of 1 to 5: [5] definitely yes; [4] yes; [3] moderately; [2] no; [1] definitely no. An average score of '3' or higher suggests that behaviour change can be achieved by a brief approach. Thus, this quick assessment could be used to decide which parents can benefit from the workshop described in this chapter.

Basic skills for facilitating parent workshops

Understanding your own family is a first step in learning how to facilitate parent workshops. This can be done effectively using the family circle method (family mapping), which provides a simplified picture of your own family dynamics in order to enhance openness and discussion (Thrower *et al.*, 1982). This is used in the first and last sessions of the workshop described later in this chapter. Having gained an understanding of their own family dynamics, and indeed worked through the other sessions, the teacher then needs to develop the listening skills described in Chapter 3 and possess the following broad communication skills for facilitating a workshop.

The basic skill in facilitation is to permit the workshop participants to generate their own solutions to problems and not have solutions imposed on them. So you might phrase a task in this way,

> Remember a situation in which you were made to change when you didn't want to. Look back in your personal history to a point when you were forced to act against your will. Choose a situation that was really uncomfortable. What did the other person do to force you to change? Assess how this imposed change affected you in both short and long term ways.

Or

> Think about the positive changes in your life. List the persons who influenced positive changes. Remember what these people did to make you feel the need for change. How did these persons manage to help you make a decision?

It is important to relate to all the workshop participants as equally as you can. Usually we like to get close to people with whom we sympathise and to distance ourselves from those whom we dislike. When conducting a workshop teachers need to be equally friendly to all participants. In order to create a context for change, the teacher as facilitator should be perceived as a democratic authority who knows the objectives of each activity and focuses on the abilities of the parents to grasp the concepts and principles of each session. In other words, teachers should be well-prepared, take responsibility for organising and timing the different activities but not feel responsible for changing parents' attitudes or behaviour.

A good place to hold a workshop could be the teacher's classroom or the staff-room which probably will assure more comfort and privacy. From the very beginning, participants should agree on the basic rule that confidentiality should be respected. The time limit encourages a focus on the objectives of each session and how to incorporate the new ideas into family functioning. The parent group should meet regularly or every fortnight after school hours or on Saturdays according to the teachers' and parents' schedules. The length of each session should be between an hour and a half and two hours. Teachers will find it much easier to work with a co-leader. As a team they can prepare for each session and better assess parents' progress. When, during the session, the large group breaks into two smaller groups, the co-leader leads one of the groups. When the time comes to record parents' comments, it is also useful to have one leader structuring time and the co-leader writing comments on the flip chart.

It is useful to invite parents to the workshop with an attractive letter, setting out the objectives of each session. It is also useful to include a space for parents to answer when it is possible for them to attend. Workshops can function with five to eight couples of parents or ten to sixteen parents. It is best to have solo parents working together. They have specific needs and are more comfortable working with other parents in the same situation. Each parent should be provided with a notebook to write the new ideas emerging from each activity, the principles and basic concepts of each session and a summary of their family meetings.

Counselling or communication skills are the basis for communication in the workshop, which will enable parents to experience being heard and respected by others. In order to achieve empathy with the workshop participants, the teacher will need to be flexible and put aside his or her own beliefs in order to look for another understanding of the same reality. When teachers lead parent groups, they must accept all descriptions and interpretations of a problem even when those statements disagree with their own personal views. Some ways by which teachers can show acceptance without judgement include:

- Expressing your approval with comments like, 'How interesting, your opinion appears to differ from that of other parents';
- Exploring the reasons why some parents have an opinion that you don't share by asking, 'Could you please explain this in more detail?' or 'Tell me more about why you think that is so'.

No learning experience is complete without evaluation. In the parent workshop, evaluation is expected both from the teachers, as facilitators and from the parents. Honest feedback and evaluation helps each of us to learn, to modify and change our own approach and to devise methods which can improve effectiveness. After each session, the teacher and co-leader need to self-assess their facilitating skills. This evaluation will help them reflect on their interactions with parents in a way which will empower their leadership style.

The parent training workshop: step by step

The following parent education programme is based on a systemic approach to working with families (Hoffman, 1981) and involves a participatory methodology which enables the training of facilitators from different professional backgrounds.

Structure of each session

Each session focusses on specific objectives and is structured into four activities:

- The first activity, 'What have we done to empower our family?' is an opportunity for parents to share how they have worked through at home their chosen objectives for improving their family's functioning. They also discuss difficulties they have encountered and what has made it easier to fulfil the goals set in each session.

- The second activity focuses on some of the specific objectives of each session. Tasks are usually completed individually by the parents and then shared in small groups.
- The third activity focuses on the rest of the objectives of the session. The activities completed individually by parents, or in small groups, are shared with all the parents.
- The fourth activity, 'New ideas to take home' is a moment of reflection and summary of the session. Parents write down and then share with the whole group the principles and concepts they have learned that will help them empower their family.

Session 1: Family mapping

OBJECTIVES

- To obtain a simple representation of each participant's family system;
- To make parents conscious of family structure: emotional closeness, hierarchy, decision-making, communication patterns and personal boundaries;
- To increase parents' awareness of possibilities for identifying and setting specific goals for changes in their families;
- To identify and understand different family structures.

ACTIVITY 1: THE CIRCLE OF MY FAMILY

The family circle is a metaphor for each family system. After distributing a form entitled, 'The circle of my family', on which there is a large circle occupying most of the page, the teacher explains:

> We are interested in you and your family. Let this circle stand for your family as it is now. Draw in some smaller circles to represent yourself and your family members. These circles can be touching each other or far apart; they can be large or small depending on their significance or influence.

ACTIVITY 2: THE QUESTIONS

When they have finished, ask participants to describe their family circles according to the following questions:

- How would you describe your family circle?
- Why are the circles this size? Why are some smaller than others?
- Why are some closer to or farther apart from others?
- Who does your family circle suggest is most important in your family?
- How do you feel about the size and location of the circle that's you?
- How do you think the other members of your family would feel about their circles?

ACTIVITY 3: THE CIRCLE OF MY IDEAL FAMILY

Give the parents a form entitled, 'The circle of my ideal family', on which there is a drawing identical to that of 'The circle of my family' and the following questions:

- Would you like to make some changes to your family circle? If yes, which ones? Draw the ideal representation of your family on this page. Show how you would like your family to be.
- What personal changes and goals will help to create your ideal family?

ACTIVITY 4: NEW IDEAS TO TAKE HOME

- Ask parents to reflect on their family circles and write down what new principles and suggestions will help them empower their own families.
- Suggest that parents have a family meeting during which each member of the family will draw and then describe his/her family circle.
- Have parents share different possibilities for having a successful family meeting.
- Have parents share their final conclusions, perhaps by using a 'round' where each parent in turn makes a comment. Write them on a flip chart or a blackboard.
- Suggest that parents write the ideas that fit their family lifestyle into their notebook.

Session 2: The stubborn problems

OBJECTIVES

- To show parents that in every family children have problems;
- To empathise with parents when they recognise they have done the wrong thing;
- To offer parents a method for problem solving;
- To give parents confidence that they can cope with family problems.

ACTIVITY 1: WHAT HAVE WE DONE TO EMPOWER OUR FAMILY?

Ask the parents to discuss whether increasing awareness of their family structure has had any effect since the previous session:

- Are they giving more time to their family?
- Are they enjoying family life in the same way?
- What new thoughts can they share about their family circles?
- Did they organise a family meeting? How successful was it?
- What did they learn from their children's family circles?

ACTIVITY 2: ONE PROBLEM UNDER THE LENS

Invite parents to discuss which of their children's difficulties concern them. Then ask them to split into two groups and:

- List the problems of each child in their family.
- Choose one of the children's problems.
- Describe the problem in a clear and concise way.
- Explain the circumstances during which the problem appears.

ACTIVITY 3: WHY THE PROBLEM PERSISTS

- Brainstorm the possible reasons why the problem persists.
- List all the persons affected by the child's problem.
- Write what you think each person will say about the problem and why it persists.

ACTIVITY 4: NEW IDEAS TO TAKE HOME

- Ask parents to reflect on the session.
- Suggest that parents have a family meeting during which each member of the family will state what he/she thinks about the problem and why it persists.

- Have all the parents share their final conclusions, write them on a flip chart and suggest that parents copy the ones that fit with their family lifestyle.

Session 3: *The voice of our children*

OBJECTIVES

- To increase parents' ability to listen to their children, so they will listen to them;
- To explore children's criticism with love and respect;
- To learn, from other parents' experiences, different ways of making children feel that they are respected as unique individuals.

ACTIVITY 1: WHAT HAVE WE DONE TO EMPOWER OUR FAMILY?

Invite parents to discuss how the problem-solving process suggested in the last session has helped them to handle a family problem:

- What difficulties have they encountered in applying it?
- When or how it has been especially useful?
- What new information have they gathered from the family meeting?
- Can they suggest new explanations for the problem?
- Ask parents to make a new plan to solve the problem.

ACTIVITY 2: GOOD GUESSES

- Ask parents to think what criticisms their children may have about family rules.
- Ask them to write down the possible criticisms from each child.
- Have the parents share their intuitions about their children's criticisms.

ACTIVITY 3: LET'S HAVE A FAMILY TALK

- Ask parents to set up a 'mailbox' at home into which their children can drop complaints and suggestions.
- After a set time, get parents to collect the complaints and compare them with their guesses.
- Have parents plan a family meeting during which they will listen carefully to their children's complaints.
- Then ask the children to suggest solutions for their complaints, including suggestions for parents' changes as well as their own personal changes.
- Have parents share different ideas for holding a successful family meeting dealing with complaints.

ACTIVITY 4: NEW IDEAS TO TAKE HOME

- Ask parents to reflect on the session;
- Remind parents to have the family meeting;
- Have parents share their final conclusions and write them on a flip chart.

Session 4: *The value of diversity*

OBJECTIVES

- To increase respect for different points of view;
- To use a disagreement between parents to reach a deeper understanding of how the family functions;
- To arrive at compromises that will provide energy to strengthen parenting roles.

ACTIVITY 1: WHAT HAVE WE DONE TO EMPOWER OUR FAMILY?

Invite parents to discuss how they have used the communication skills they worked on during the last session:

- How accurate were their predictions about their children's criticisms?
- What ways did children suggest to solve their complaints?
- How did they integrate children's ideas into planning how to solve their complaints?
- How useful was it to explore the children's complaints?
- What did they learn by having the family meeting and listening to their children?

ACTIVITY 2: CHOOSING A DISAGREEMENT

- Ask parents to discuss parenting issues on which they disagree.
- Make a list of the disagreements and underline one that really concerns both parents.
- Ask parents to think about the reasons for their point of view and write down the benefits that the family receives from this position.

ACTIVITY 3: THE OTHER SIDE OF THE COIN

Ask parents to pretend they are their partner and have them answer the following questions on a separate page and then discuss the answers:

- What are the reasons for my point of view on this issue?
- How do our children benefit from my position?
- What would be my parents' opinion about this disagreement?

ACTIVITY 4: NEW IDEAS TO TAKE HOME

- Ask parents to reflect on the session.
- Suggest that parents hold a family meeting during which each member of the family will say what they think of a family disagreement – the advantages and disadvantages of each point of view.
- Have all parents share their final conclusions and write them on a board.

Session 5: My family shield

OBJECTIVES

- To draw a symbolic representation of family values;
- To determine why parents enjoy parenting;
- To find out what makes parenting difficult for them;
- To set goals for better parenting.

ACTIVITY 1: WHAT HAVE WE DONE TO EMPOWER OUR FAMILY?

Ask parents to share their experiences of compromising to respect diversity:

- Do they have greater respect for their partner's point of view?
- Have they identified the reasons for each partner's position?
- Have they looked for the disadvantages of their own personal arguments?

- What did they learn from the family meeting which sought their children's opinions?
- Have parents arrived at a flexible compromise that reflects each other's values?
- What is the outcome of the compromise?

ACTIVITY 2: ANSWERING THE QUESTIONNAIRE

Give the parents the following questionnaire to reflect on their family values:

- What I like best about my family is ... .
- What worries me about my family is ... .
- As a parent, I find it easy to ... .
- As a parent, I find it difficult to ... .
- My ultimate goal as a parent is ... .
- My motto as a parent is ... .

ACTIVITY 3: DRAWING A METAPHOR OF FAMILY VALUES

After parents have completed the above statements, ask them to go back to each one, close their eyes, and create an image that represents it. Ask parents to draw these images on a page that has a big shield divided into five sections with the space for the motto at the bottom.

ACTIVITY 4: NEW IDEAS TO TAKE HOME

- Ask parents to reflect on the session.
- Ask them to write what new ideas will empower their own parenting roles.
- Suggest that parents hold a family meeting during which each member of the family will draw his/her family shield.
- Have parents share their final conclusions.

Session 6: *The origin of our identity*

OBJECTIVES

- To remember what each parent knows about his/her partner's ancestors;
- To draw the maternal and paternal branches of the family tree;
- To share family stories and anecdotes with their children;
- To reflect about how these two family histories have influenced the family.

ACTIVITY 1: WHAT HAVE WE DONE TO EMPOWER OUR FAMILY?

Ask parents what effect making their family shield has had on them:

- What new ideas do they have about enjoying parenting?
- What options can they use to overcome parenting difficulties?
- What did they learn from the family meeting and their children's family shields?
- Have they set new parenting goals?

ACTIVITY 2: OUR ANCESTORS

Ask parents to remember what each of them knows about his/her partner's family:

- Look for ways in which families are different.
- Determine how these differences have affected interactions with their children.
- Share conclusions in small groups.

ACTIVITY 3: THE FAMILY TREE

Show the parents how to draw a genealogical tree for three generations

- Show them how they can use the following symbols: a circle to denote a woman; a square for a man; a horizontal line for a couple; a vertical line for a child of the couple.
- Ask them to gather information about their family's values, interests, activities, personal characteristics, physical traits, stories and anecdotes by talking to individual family members.
- Suggest they have a family meeting to enlist their children's help in this research.

ACTIVITY 4: NEW IDEAS TO TAKE HOME

- Ask parents to reflect on this session.
- Remind parents to have a family meeting to share anecdotes of their ancestors.
- Have parents share their conclusions.

Session 7: *The power of our exploration*

OBJECTIVES

- To remember how love and affection were expressed in each parent's family of origin;
- To explore how each family of origin reacted to anger, frustration and pain;
- To think about authority in each family of origin;
- To list all of the 'I would have liked to …' statements in relationship to each family of origin's ways of expressing emotions.

ACTIVITY 1: WHAT HAVE WE DONE TO EMPOWER OUR FAMILY?

- How they have progressed in making their genealogical tree;
- How their family stories have influenced their nuclear family;
- What they have learned from their children's collaboration.

ACTIVITY 2: WAYS TO EXPRESS AFFECTION

Ask parents to recall a scene from their childhood where they felt loved by their family:

- Have them describe how this love was expressed in their family.
- Have them imagine how they would have liked their family to show affection.

Then ask parents to bring to mind a scene where there was anger, frustration or pain.

- Have them describe how such feelings were expressed in their family.
- Have them imagine how they would have liked their family to react.
- Ask parents to share in small groups the ways their family expressed affection.

ACTIVITY 3: AUTHORITY IN MY FAMILY

Ask parents to think about authority in the family in which they grew up:

- Could they tell what behaviour was allowed and what wasn't?
- How were rules for children's behaviour established?
- Who gave permissions and determined punishments?
- What happened when they disobeyed?

- How and when were they punished or rewarded?
- Was it possible to anticipate the consequences of their behaviour?
- How would they have liked the authority in their family to have been different?

ACTIVITY 4: NEW IDEAS TO TAKE HOME

- Ask parents to reflect on the session.
- Remind parents to have a family meeting to discuss ways of expressing affection and the way authority is used at home.
- Have parents share their conclusions and write them down on a flip chart.

Session 8: Second family mapping

OBJECTIVES

- To have a new representation of each participant's family system;
- To make the parents conscious of their family's structural development: emotional closeness, power hierarchy, decision-making, communication patterns and personal boundaries;
- To increase parents' awareness of setting specific goals for change;
- To accept and understand different rhythms or changes in family structures;
- To evaluate how the family has changed since beginning this programme.

ACTIVITY 1: WHAT HAVE WE DONE TO EMPOWER OUR FAMILY?

Ask the parents to reflect on how the uniqueness of their ancestors has been integrated into their family organisation:

- What was the benefit of spending time exploring their family of origin?
- What was their most important discovery?
- What did they learn from their family meeting about the way they express affection, react to anger, pain or frustration and handle family authority?
- What other issues would they like to work through as a family?

ACTIVITY 2: THE SECOND FAMILY MAPPING

Have parents draw their current family circle, answer the questions and then draw their ideal family circle, repeating the methodology of the first session:

- What can they say about this new family representation?
- Share in small groups their new representations and thoughts about their ideal family structure.

ACTIVITY 3: PROJECTING TOWARD THE FUTURE

Ask parents to compare their present family circles with their first representations of their family:

- What changes appear?
- Are there differences in size and distribution of space?

- What interpretation can they give to their new ideal family?
- What would they like to do with the new information?

ACTIVITY 4: NEW IDEAS TO TAKE HOME

- Ask parents to reflect on the session.
- Have all participants share their final conclusions and write them on a flip chart.

Conclusion

In the last decade, schools have opened their doors for family collaboration and have begun to train their staff members to interact with parents more effectively (Hornby, 2000). Teachers are able to help parents to develop the awareness and skills to support their families more effectively and thus help to prevent social and emotional problems from developing in students. Training teachers as facilitators to empower families should focus on the principle that teachers with high self-esteem are more likely to appreciate and support the potential of others. In other words, people who feel capable of thinking, feeling and problem solving will better promote the development of confidence within and among family members, not by directing from the front, but rather by working alongside parents in a climate of empathy, respect and co-operation. Teachers tend to establish rapport more easily with parents who are verbally skilled and psychologically sophisticated. Some parents who seem to be unresponsive may feel intimidated by professionals or may lack fluency in English. Teachers must make a particular effort to reach out to these parents and will find that most of them will make good workshop participants.

This chapter offers teachers the opportunity to develop the knowledge and skills to enable them to help students by working more closely with their parents, thus empowering them to be more effective within the family environment. Teachers may also wish to consider inviting those parents who have completed the workshop and have the necessary leadership skills to co-lead future workshops. This constructive, humanistic and democratic orientation will thus bring the benefits of parent education to a larger community. My final hope is that this chapter will help teachers and parents empower themselves by looking at the image and the reality of their own family life, tracing the footprints into their past, and more confidently and assertively directing them into the future. This experience will enable teachers and parents to appreciate their hidden treasures, discover a potential of resources for building their children's future, and grasp the beauty within their own lives right now.

References

Bronfenbrenner, U. (1979) *The Ecology of Human Development*. Cambridge, MA: Harvard University Press.

Chadwick, M. and Fuhrmann, I. (1998) *Pensar nuestra familia: Dialogos entre padres e hijos [Thinking About Our Family: Dialogues between Parents and Children]*. Santiago, Chile: Andres Bello.

Fuhrmann, I. and Chadwick, M. (1995) *Fortalecer la familia. Manual para trabajar con padres [Empowering our Family: Manual for Facilitators to Work with Parents]*. Santiago, Chile: Andres Bello.

Golden, L. (1993) Counselling with families. In A. Vernon (ed.) *Counselling Children and Adolescents*. Denver: Love, pp. 272–90.

Hoffman, L. (1981) *Foundations of Family Therapy*. New York: Basic Books.

Hornby, G. (2000) *Improving Parental Involvement*. London: Cassell.

Kraus, I. (1998) A fresh look at family counselling: a family systems approach. *Professional School Counselling*, 1(4): 12–17.

Minuchin, S. (1984) *Tecnicas de Terapia Familiar. [Family Therapy Techniques]*. Buenos Aires: Paidos.

Thrower, S., Bruce, W. and Walton, R. (1982) The family circle method for integrating family system concepts in family medicine. *Journal of Family Practice*, 15(3): 451–7.

Snell-White, P. (1993) *Pathways to Parenting: A Caribbean Approach (Volume II: A Facilitator's Manual for Parenting Groups)*. Kingston, Jamaica: Parenting Partners.

9   Cultural issues in counselling

Belinda Harris

If you want to be my friend
Forget I'm black
If you want to be my friend
Never forget I'm black
       (Source unknown)

Despite the continual development of multicultural and pluralistic societies across Europe and North America, cultural differences are still viewed as barriers to effective communication rather than as opportunities to deepen our understanding of and compassion for diverse human experiences. It is widely accepted that attitudes and behaviours are learned in cultural contexts and that people develop multiple identities to help them manage a complex and changing world (Pederson, 1996). However, the politics of minority versus majority cultures represents a key additional dimension within the cross-cultural counselling or helping relationship. This chapter discusses this phenomenon within a British context and focuses on the relationship between majority teachers and minority students. In particular, it focuses on the challenges and opportunities involved in counselling and supporting students whose lives have been affected by the additional experience of racial discrimination. Children of African and Asian descent will be discussed because of the degree of psychological harm resulting from being stereotyped, racially abused and excluded from dominant white British cultures (Henley and Schott, 1999). Throughout this chapter, such children will be referred to as 'black'. In this way the centrality of colour in relationships between black students and white teachers is highlighted and developing pride in black identity is presented as an aide to self-esteem and an antidote to racism.

Throughout the 1980s, as a teacher and counsellor, I found myself working with diversity issues in inner city areas, without the advantage of any professional training or support in the cultural dimensions of my role. After concerted efforts to understand the values, traditions and inheritance of Bengali, South Asian, Chinese and Afro-Caribbean students, I was no more effective as a helper! Sometime later I asked a newly appointed senior member of staff of African descent, what I should do to improve my ability to work well with all students and told her of my efforts to date. Having listened patiently and attentively, she responded by asking me why I had wanted to work in a multi-racial community and how I perceived myself as different as a result of both my experiences and the cultural knowledge I had acquired.

Initially confused, I recognised the necessity for awareness and understanding of my own cultural roots and motivating forces. The life stories, patience, support and challenges of numerous black 'teachers' of all ages have enriched my understanding of the psychological destructiveness and pain caused by living in an intolerant and oppressive society. I have learned to appreciate the centrality of my own cultural identity and preferences to the development of healthy, empowering relationships with students and adults whose attitudes and behaviours sometimes strike me as strange and puzzling.

As a white woman I am writing primarily to encourage other white teachers and counsellors to examine their cultural roots, to reflect on their experience and to renew and extend their commitment to working with diversity. To this end, the chapter has been written interactively and a series of structured questions have been included to encourage reflection on personal and professional issues. It is not necessary to show or discuss your responses with anyone else, but you might want to pay attention to your felt sense as you read and write, particularly in those instances where you find it difficult to respond. Taking time to reflect on what lies behind this difficulty may help to deepen cultural understanding.

Explore your cultural roots

How would you describe your family culture when you were growing up? What were important family sayings?

Who were your cultural 'heroes' – the people who influenced you and who you looked up to most? What did they teach you about yourself and your place in the world?

Do you remember the first time you became aware of skin colour? What happened and what was that like for you? How do you account for that within your family culture?

How were people of different skin colour referred to in your family of origin? What effect did these messages have on you?

What, if anything, has happened in your life to reinforce or challenge these messages about differences?

The challenge of helping: the teacher

Teachers are experiencing unprecedented levels of stress (Travers and Cooper, 1996), and living in a 'climate of fear' (Watkins, 1999), in which their self-esteem is under threat and little attention or care is given to their pastoral needs. Equally, issues of race and culture have slipped from the agenda and the pastoral needs of students have been overlooked in favour of performance measures. Within this context, some teachers are anxious about and resistant to any new demands on them and may tend to deny or conceal their personal vulnerability and anxiety behind a mask of professionalism. Such teachers not only protect themselves from their own pain and distress, but also withdraw from emotionally demanding situations in school, so that they may become immune to the suffering of young people around them.

Additionally, the distance between adult and student created by the professional mask can give the teacher permission to objectify and label students. Falling back on stereotyped views of black youth, for example, may simplify the teacher's world and reduce their openness to learning about difference. The statistics on the exclusion of male students of African and Asian descent bear testimony to the failure of many schools to provide appropriate conditions, in which young black people may thrive and develop their personal, social and intellectual talents (CRE, 2000). Relationships between teachers and black students are often perceived as 'difficult' and there is an implicit assumption that the problem resides in the student, either by virtue of their ability, their attitude or their circumstances.

Examining cultural resources

What motivated you to want to become a teacher?

What do you see as your core purposes as a teacher/counsellor?

How do you respond to emotionally challenging situations in school?

What effect does this have on achieving your core purpose and your enjoyment at work?

One of the most challenging aspects of working with diversity is recognising that culture is in fact complicated, fluid and in a constant state of change. Every interaction involves a cultural negotiation of values, behaviours and expectations. A successful negotiation is one in which both parties are changed and enriched by their contact, neither of them an object in the eyes of the other. From this perspective culture does not lend itself to crude categorisations of people, neither does it demand the fragmentation of self. By contrast it supports a deeper and more expansive view of the self and the other as whole people and energises our curiosity and sense of wonder about humankind (Pederson, 1998). Culturally sensitive and effective teachers will therefore feel comfortable owning their naivety as they seek to understand the student's behaviour within its cultural context. Naivety is a stance that many teachers may find challenging in the current climate, but one that is important if we are to deepen our understanding of the way students experience their world and be open to learning from them. Young black boys, for example, may be berated in school for their loudness, which can be experienced as threatening unless understood within the context of extended families, where being loud is viewed as normal, healthy behaviour for a growing boy.

Teachers need to recognise the power of their position and to understand that their consciously and unconsciously expressed values, beliefs and attitudes towards the black student may cause potential difficulties in their relationship. The effective teacher therefore might be presumed to be one who integrates self-awareness with a unique cultural identity and who is sensitive, open and supportive of each student's need to develop a unique cultural identity. In other words, both teacher and student are engaged in a voyage of cultural self-discovery, which leaves each one richer as a result of their contact. For example, a teacher may encourage students to consider how particular concepts or ideas would be received within their home environment. If teachers disclose their own viewpoint, communicate that it is culturally formed and positively welcome different perspectives, then students may be encouraged to engage in honest discussions about the role of cultural influences in their lives and help them to identify their cultural preferences.

The following key attributes and skills may be seen as crucial in creating a climate where issues of culture can be discussed openly:

- Motivation to offer culturally sensitive support.
- An attitude of naivety and desire to understand.
- Self-monitoring to acknowledge preconceived ideas about what constitutes 'normal' behaviour and to recognise this as culturally specific.
- Self-disclosing culturally formed values and beliefs.
- Active listening to enable exploration and understanding of the student's experience and cultural context.
- Taking account of and where appropriate, harnessing the student's support systems (peers, family, community) in the helping process.

The challenge of helping: the student

Young black people are painfully aware that they are not fully accepted within British society. They know this because over their short lifetime they have experienced the hurt and distress of feeling 'invisible', of being actively ignored, avoided and snubbed, and of being absent in the history books and literature of scholarly accomplishments that form core aspects of the curriculum. Simultaneously, they feel highly 'visible' and suffer a range of abusive responses from white people because of their blackness, including name-calling, taunting, non-verbal intimidation and physical violence. They have learned to anticipate rejection from white people and to bear the shame of false accusation because of an implicit assumption that they are untrustworthy, inferior and inherently bad. They know that their chances of professional advancement are negatively affected by the colour of their skin and fear that despite the rhetoric of a pluralist society, race relations in Britain are getting worse. This perception is at odds with an optimistic view of the situation by white people (Anwar, 1998) and the disparity may account for some of the frustrations that young people bring into school and some of the difficulties white teachers may have in taking their concerns seriously.

Young black people report that white teachers do not understand the daily experience of living with racism. Worse, they sense that teachers do not want to understand. James, a twelve-year-old boy of African descent tells of his experience:

> I was coming to school feeling wound up like a spring … they tripped me up, called me 'black this' and 'black that' and when was I going to go back to the jungle … . I got into trouble as soon as I got into class because X made a comment and I exploded. I tried to explain to my form tutor but her eyes glazed over and I knew she wasn't listening. She just told me whatever had happened was no excuse.

Developing cultural empathy

Are you able to imagine what it's like:

- To walk past racist slogans and symbols on your way to school?
- To be the only black face in a sea of white?
- To wish your skin colour away?

Internalised racism

The psychological damage of racism is greatest where messages of black inferiority and lack of worth have been swallowed whole. This 'internalised racism' has a significant impact on self-esteem and on peer relationships. One example of this at work is a preoccupation with skin tone, where paler black skins are considered more attractive than dark and straightened hair is prized more than a natural black look. Leroy, for example, the only black student in his Year 10 class at a suburban independent school, vaselines his hair to straighten it and therefore be more acceptable to his classmates.

Students who feel ashamed of their blackness need little by way of reinforcement. They believe core messages about themselves, including, 'I don't belong'. 'I am unlovable' and 'I should not exist'. Such hopelessness may predispose the student to act in ways that will reinforce these beliefs by attracting negative attention from teachers (Vernon, 1993). It is therefore important that teachers seek to resolve inappropriate behaviours and difficult situations with a view to constructive change and reinforce a culture of hope. Healing shame messages is a complex and protracted task and more within the remit of a professional counsellor. White teachers cannot 'cure' internalised racism, but they have an important role to play in offering a reparative relationship with a white adult in which they feel valued, respected and in which the teacher demonstrates belief in their competence and joy in their difference. A school which is committed to raising the self-esteem of all its students, is more likely to create systematic opportunities to 'drip-feed' messages of pride, care and respect for differences and hence reinforce the one-to-one relationship work of the pastoral tutors. An expectation of and belief in students' ability to self-monitor and self-discipline is more likely to create a culture of positive behaviour.

Key skills for helping students overcome internalised racism

- Appreciation of the student's personal and cultural history as significant in determining current behaviour – we are not all the same!
- Commitment to engage in conflict resolution work with the student, which recognises cultural influences and seeks to develop goals and strategies which are acceptable in the student's cultural context.
- A whole school approach to developing self-esteem, self-reflection and self-discipline through relationships and reward systems.

Bi-culturalism

Migration and dislocation are recognised as taking a toll on the mental health of migrants (Furnham and Bochner, 1986) and consequently having a negative effect on black identity formation over several generations. Second and third generation Asian young people, for example, speak of feeling separated from their parents' history, culture and language the moment they step out of the security of their home. They feel the need to 'split off' part of themselves as if it were an item of clothing only suited to one context. Equally, they can feel under pressure from their family to leave their British self outside the door of the home. It is difficult for all adolescents to establish an independent identity, but for the Asian student this may be a more demanding task. Guernina (1992) found that the threat to identity is greater because of the sense of belonging to two cultures whilst simultaneously being lost in both. The task of resolving the mismatch between the values, expectations and behaviours of family and a dominant white culture requires opportunities for students to work through the differences openly and honestly. Over time, this process can help heal inner fragmentation and create a self-identity that enables them to proudly take their place in society as a British Asian. I set up a lunchtime discussion group for Year 11 girls to help them manage the stress of examinations and leaving school. The predominantly Muslim group members however, identified the tension they experienced between their cultural traditions on the one hand and being British on the other as a major source of stress. Many conversations centred on their relationships with boys, their sexual curiosity and emerging sensuality, the pressure from boys to be sexually active and their fears about dishonouring their family and being rejected by their community. The intimacy and support achieved through engaging honestly and openly with the issues meant that group members learned to value themselves and each other in new ways. By exploring the relationship between self, family and community in this way they were able to identify culturally relevant strategies for managing conformity and non-conformity with integrity and the group continued to meet for many months after the girls had left school.

Students of African descent may suffer the loss of African spirituality, history, scholarship and traditions. In their case, the loss is more difficult to mourn as it is embedded in the physical destruction of generations of black people. One of the legacies of slavery is an identity founded on the white colonial myth of savage slave. The school curriculum may unwittingly reinforce this by focussing on the slave trade as the main reference to black history and students may suffer from a pervasive sense of hopelessness and a lack of meaning, which affects their motivation to learn and contribute to a learning community. Although many teachers may recognise such symptoms they cannot be expected to offer the professional counselling such students might need. However, McLaughlin (2000) found that students particularly appreciate teachers who listen to them and recognise that such teachers are able to foster closer working relationships and positively enhance students' capacity and will to learn. Moreover, her research suggests that students are hungry for the kind of dialogue with teachers in which both people are emotionally involved, self-reflective and open to learning through the experience. In other words, through dialogue teachers can enhance emotional development, learning and a positive self-identity.

For mixed race students the situation is particularly complex and is illustrated by Jolene's story, as reported by a black education project worker:

> Several teachers complained about Jolene, a mixed race teenager, because she appeared withdrawn in class and any attempts to engage her met with a cheeky response. When approached by her form tutor, Jolene reacted angrily and stormed out of school. Distressed and concerned by this unusual response, the tutor phoned Jolene's mother, who recognised that this behaviour might be connected to weekend visits to her father's black family. Jolene identified herself as 'white' and was uncomfortable in her grandparents' home. Together, the tutor and mother enlisted support from a local black education project. As a result, the black worker invited Jolene to a cultural identity workshop, where, with other black and mixed race teenagers she started to appreciate her black identity. Longer-term support involved developing a relationship with a black mentor who helped Jolene understand and integrate her feelings. Eventually, she recognised that

her fear and denial of being black stemmed from her unresolved grief about her father leaving the family when she was eight and empowered her to disclose her feelings.

Jolene's education and her reputation in school were at risk, because of a split in her sense of self, which was causing her distress. It is particularly difficult for mixed race students who live with a single parent to equally embrace their black and white heritage. Understanding and valuing both aspects of herself enabled Jolene to integrate her bicultural identities, to understand her emotions more fully and to own the anger underlying her 'difficult' behaviour.

Cultural identity workshops run by black educators for black, Asian and mixed race young people can help to build a sense of social pride and belonging. Teachers can support identity development by enabling black students to see and find themselves in the curriculum (Gaine, 1995). Both Leroy and Jolene would have been helped in school if they had learned about famous black scientists, writers, artists, scholars and freedom fighters. Learning about people who epitomise pride and achievement in black culture can inspire and bring sparkle and energy to a troubled student.

Key skills for supporting identity development

- Willingness to understand the impact of living in two overlapping cultural contexts (home and school).
- Proactivity in establishing links with local/regional black education projects and community resources.
- Commitment to embed cultural diversity into the curriculum.
- Curiosity – encourage students to talk about their experiences of values, expectations and behaviours at home and at school – promote appreciation of diversity.
- Management of process issues – the here and now interactions between class members.

Many black students will come from loving homes and live in vibrant communities, in which their cultural heritage and traditions are honoured and celebrated. Saturday schools, for example, may help to develop awareness and knowledge of black culture and a sense of cultural pride. For black students living outside of black communities, they may additionally provide access to a support network. In these environments students may develop a healthy 'counter identity' which meets their needs for safety, self-esteem, validation and belonging (Maslow, 1968). Such students know they are special and are able to make a constructive impact on their environment. They are likely to develop self-esteem and self-efficacy to help them manage experiences of racism outside the safety of their home and community.

A minority of black students grow up in homes where racism, dislocation and poverty have taken their toll on the self-esteem and identity of parents or carers and there is little love or energy to spare for their children. Black education workers report this to be most evident where adults have lost touch with their cultural roots and traditions and have themselves been unsupported to develop a positive sense of their black identity. Such children may grow up starved of self-esteem, self-love and validation, and full of fear, grief and confusion come to school alienated from mainstream white culture, their pain and distress manifesting itself as aggressive behaviour.

Aggressive behaviour may also be an exasperated expression of black students' loss of faith in the education system and in teachers' ability to make person-to-person contact with them. A black teacher complained,

> White colleagues regularly enlist my help in getting black students to listen to them. They will for example, seek me out five minutes into a lesson and ask me to go to their class and enforce some school rule, such as the removal of sports caps.

The behaviour of such teachers suggests that they had either given up on black students or that they were fearful of them. Enlisting the support of a black colleague is an option in a crisis and can have a calming effect. However, as a longer-term strategy, it is not to be recommended because it reinforces divisions between black and white people, fails to acknowledge the inter-dependence of adults and students within a learning community and minimises the possibility of improving the relationship.

In this instance, the black colleague can be seen to play the role of 'toxic handler' a term used to describe those who mediate between senior managers and harassed employees in organisations (Frost and Robinson, 1999). These people play an important role in soaking up some of the distress caused by the ego needs and poor interpersonal skills of those in positions of power, for example, where the attitudes and behaviour of colleagues could cause harm and distress to black students. Paradoxically, it is the teachers' frustrations and sense of powerlessness that can drive them to act in unhelpful ways towards students. It is therefore imperative that the school offers tutors and Heads of Year structured opportunities to talk through difficult situations, express their frustrations, reflect on the impact of their behaviours and discuss alternative strategies for dealing with challenging behaviour. Developing relationships with other black and white professionals who are committed to being culturally effective can help to maintain commitment, a sense of proportion and humour.

The concept of black teacher as 'toxic handler' is premised on a view of the aggressive black student as a misunderstood, vulnerable, desperate young person displaying difficult behaviour. Such behaviour signifies an attempt by the student to protect themselves from further pain. Secondary teachers will be familiar with an adolescent's veneer of indifference or 'front', designed to test their commitment and patience and ultimately to challenge their authority. Black students may develop further survival strategies to additionally protect themselves from racism. Thomas (1999) suggests that from the age of three, they develop a particular gift for distinguishing between friend and foe. These cultural 'antennae' tell a student when it is necessary to adapt their behaviours in the presence of significant others in order to minimise the risk of harm. In short, the young person will present a 'false self', seeking to keep the dangerous 'other' as distanced from her inner reality as possible. The resulting behavioural manifestation might be passivity, withdrawal or confrontation, which are subsequently used to categorise the student as 'difficult'.

Key skills for managing difficult situations

- Establish effective support and supervision systems for teachers.
- Commitment to intervene in situations where a colleague's communication with students is disrespectful and potentially damaging.
- Commitment to challenge students assertively and constructively where their behaviour is inhibiting their own and others' learning.
- Demonstrate respect for the students' defences by giving space and non-verbal affirmation.

Creating an enabling school environment

Is this school willing and committed:

- To use every opportunity to raise the self-esteem of black students?
- To provide opportunities for young people to learn about black cultural heroes?
- To offer a 'difficult' black student a safe, secure and supportive relationship?
- To create a safe and supportive learning environment for teachers?
- To develop constructive relationships with black and white professionals who are committed to black students' welfare?

Moving forward

The 'false self' represents perhaps the greatest challenge to the white teacher's capacity to create a safe and supportive relationship with the student. It may only be possible to build successful relationships in such circumstance, if teachers are prepared to accept uncomfortable facts about themselves. The culturally aware teacher will understand that in the eyes of the student his/her colour automatically represents a symbol of white dominance, with the capacity to affect negatively the young person's sense of self. Coming to terms with the self as representative of every white person that has ever wounded, terrified or abused a black student is uncomfortable and disconcerting. The path to successful contact with the student is through a rigorous and honest confrontation with the privileges enjoyed by virtue of skin colour and professional status.

Creating conditions for effective helping relationships

Are you willing and committed:

- To appreciate the extent to which being white may be a prop to your self-esteem?
- To recognise what your white skin might signify to a black student and what the student's black skin signifies to you?

As we have seen, the culturally attuned teacher will view the young person's behaviour as a creative or defensive adjustment to hostile circumstances and recognise that an equally creative but non-defensive adjustment to the role of teacher is required if real contact is to be made. The central issue here is one of safety:

> In the choice between giving up safety or giving up growth, safety will ordinarily win out. Only a student who feels safe dares to grow forward.
>
> (Maslow, 1968, p. 49)

The teacher is a key player in forging a new relationship between the young person and an oppressive society. Armed with self-awareness and knowledge they will seek to build an interpersonal bridge with the young person. Within the Citizenship curriculum, for example, the teacher may actively initiate an exploration of underlying issues of prejudice and power in relationships. The teacher might offer students a case study of equally qualified black and white school leavers applying for the same jobs with differential success rates. Discussing the impact of these stories on black/white relationships, the teacher could demonstrate empathy and understanding for the black student's experience, by saying, for example, 'If I were in your shoes, I would find it difficult to know whether you can trust me or any other white professionals'. Such observations however, need to be offered tentatively (Khan, 1999) as it is not normal to disclose personal information outside the family in some communities and students need to know that such cultural preferences will be respected by the helper.

Similarly, it is important to affirm the young person's need for a 'false self', to let them know that the teacher will not abandon them whether they choose to retain or remove the mask. In this way the teacher actively demonstrates his/her commitment to the student and communicates unconditional acceptance. Patience and persistence are needed to allow the students to make sense of their own responses to the teacher's efforts. They may feel angry or confused by the difference between the predicted and presenting response of the teacher and need time to acknowledge this as genuine. If and when they choose to engage it may be necessary for the culturally committed teacher to help articulate differences in cultural values and behaviours and thereby honour the cultural complexities within and between each of them. If successful, young persons may remove their mask and be willing to discuss issues that cause them concern.

Within a 'safe zone' the young persons may then express any pain or hurt without needing to fear or protect the teacher who will seek to accept their pain and distress. If teachers value and respect their personal power they will find healthy ways of using this to benefit the young person's self-esteem. They will seek to enable the student to exercise their power within the safety of the relationship. Offering students opportunities to make real choices about the issues they wish to discuss, to set their own goals, to ask key individuals for support and to decide how they will celebrate achieving their goals are all ways of helping them experiment with power. Sukhi, a thirteen-year-old girl in my tutor group, revealed that she often dreamed about her twin sister who had died within days of their birth. Discussion of this event was taboo at home, leaving her feeling dissatisfied although respectful of her mother's feelings. As we discussed her feelings and I shared with her the recent loss of a close friend, Sukhi decided she would like to hold a ceremony of remembrance. With the help of the tutor group, she created a simple and moving service to honour her sister's memory and symbolise her loss. She reported that her dreams continued but were no longer disturbing.

Key skills for moving forward

- Commitment to initiate contact and explore differences.
- Persistence in the face of resistance.
- Self-disclosure to build bridges across experiences.
- Creativity in power sharing.

Have you got what it takes?

Are you able and willing to:

- Hear and respond to the pain and distress caused by racism?
- Learn and grow through your relationships with young black people?
- Allow the student's needs to dictate the pace and intensity of contact?
- Accept mistrust, rejection and rage as a healthy part of the process?

Many teachers reading this will be concerned about the amount of time, energy and commitment involved in culturally sensitive helping. The following story illustrates a culturally attuned teacher at work in a comprehensive school, and demonstrates the core competences in action:

> A number of small thefts coincided with the arrival of Ali, a Somali refugee, a bright boy with some language problems. As the academic year proceeded and he left the unit where he had received language support to spend more time in mainstream classes, he found it difficult to concentrate. He often got up and walked around and did not respond well to the admonishments of teachers. He became known as 'awkward', a 'nuisance' and untrustworthy. One day he was so distressed that he locked himself in the toilet and refused to come out until the arrival of Toni, the teacher in charge of special needs, who was called on because of her reputation with 'difficult' students. Having calmed Ali down, Toni took him with her to her classes where she paid him lots of non-verbal attention and later took him home to his mother, who was grief stricken by the murder of her husband, and suffering from depression. Toni realised that Ali was adrift without an anchor in a hostile environment. She made a deal with Ali that he could come to her classes whenever he wanted to as long as he brought his work and didn't disturb other students. Her colleagues, who already thought she was a 'soft touch', were angry with her and let her know that in their eyes she was acting unprofessionally and undermining the 'assertive discipline' culture of the school. Despite this, Toni kept her promise to Ali. Slowly she began to give him some responsibilities and trusted him to do little jobs for her. As a reward she allowed him to take home his favourite classroom resources and games to play with his mother. On one occasion he lost part of a game and she expressed her concern but not judgement. By lunchtime Ali had found the missing item and returned it. Given his reputation as untrustworthy, she was visibly touched by his display of honesty. She encouraged him to draw and write about Somalia and to share his experiences with other refugee students. She spent a few minutes with him whenever she could and gave him her full attention at these times. Gradually, Ali spent more and more time with his year group and one term later he had started to make friends in class and achieve according to his abilities. He now spends one or two lunch-times a week with other newly-arrived refugees and helps them to feel at home. Staff acknowledge that Ali's behaviour and achievement has improved.

Toni and Ali entered into a committed healing relationship that was never confined to a counselling room or specific time, but which was proactive and responsive to Ali's needs.

It was her very ordinariness, her willingness to be proactive and to enter into a partnership which gave Ali an emotional anchor. This affirmed his cultural identity and his independence. Toni acted from and was affirmed in her core values, which included the right of each student to experience care, trust and support through difficult situations.

Reflections

- What is your professional response to Ali and Toni's story?
- What do you admire, envy, question?
- What do you struggle to understand? What does that mean to you?
- How would Ali have fared in your school?
- What aspect of Toni's approach could you learn from?

This chapter set out to demonstrate that where there are difficult students, there are difficulties with interpersonal relationships and difficult environments within which to help those struggling against the odds to develop a healthy sense of self. The way forward is in acknowledging and embracing the white self and the black other as unique culturally complex individuals. Acknowledging and transcending the differences 'between' them can help heal the student's pain, enhance self-esteem and develop an identity founded on a real experience of personal choice and power in relationship with a white person.

Teachers who willingly embark on the road to becoming a culturally attuned helper and create meaningful, principled relationships with black students will inevitably experience difficulties along the way and find themselves working at the limits of their competence. There is however, very little that is more professionally rewarding than the experience of being fully alive and engaged in helping young people to grow to love their difference and hence to love themselves.

References

Anwar, M. (1998) *Ethnic Minorities and the British Electoral System*. Coventry: University of Warwick.

Commission for Racial Equality. (2000) *Learning for All: Standards for Racial Equality in Schools*. London: CRE.

Frost, P. and Robinson, S. (1999) The toxic handler: organisational hero and casualty. *Harvard Business Review*, July–August, 97–106.

Furnham, A. and Bochner, S. (1986) *Culture Shock: Psychological Reaction to Unfamiliar Environments*. London: Methuen.

Gaine, C. (1995) *Still No Problem Here*. Stoke-on-Trent: Trentham Books.

Guernina, Z. (1992) Counselling adolescents of immigrant parents: a transcultural approach. *Counselling Psychology Quarterly*, 5(3): 251–5.

Henley, A. and Schott, J. (1999) *Culture, Religion and Patient Care in a Multi-Ethnic Society*. London: Age Concern.

Khan, E. (1999) A critique of nondirectivity in the person-centred approach. *Journal of Humanistic Psychology*, 39(4): 94–109.

Maslow, A. (1968) *Towards a Psychology of Being*. London: Nostrand Reinhold Company.

McLaughlin, C. (2000) The emotional challenge of listening and dialogue. *Pastoral Care*, 18(3): 16–20.

Pederson, P. B. (1996) *Culture-Centred Counseling Interventions*. Thousand Oaks: Sage.

Thomas, L. K. (1999) Towards a positive self-identity for Black children. *Race and Cultural Education* (Journal Division of the British Association for Counselling) No. 19, 22–26.

Travers, C. J. and Cooper, C. L. (1996) *Teachers Under Pressure: Stress in the Teaching Profession*. London: Routledge.

Vernon, A. (ed.) (1993) *Counselling Children and Adolescents*. Denver: Love.

Watkins, C. (1999) Personal-social education: Beyond the National Curriculum. *British Journal of Guidance and Counselling*, 27(1): 71–83.

10 Coping with loss and trauma

Garry Hornby

I have two younger children, and their schools, with the best of intentions, told the other pupils not to mention the death of my seventeen-year-old son in order not to upset them. Fortunately for my daughter, who was ten, a teacher at her school who had recently lost her husband realised that this was a mistake and countermanded these instructions. She told the other children that they should certainly talk to my daughter about her brother when she returned to school, at least to say how sorry they were. So my daughter was surrounded by loving, concerned friends, who talked to her quite openly about her brother .... My fourteen-year-old son was not so fortunate. His school mates obeyed the instructions ... he was deeply hurt by this apparent lack of concern: it seemed to him that the death was not important enough to mention. He was deprived of the support and care which his sister had enjoyed.

(Mulder, 1994, p. 5)

Children's experiences of loss

A survey of 836 adolescents in their first year of secondary school in the North of England highlighted the high proportion of young people who have experienced significant losses (Branwhite, 1994). Students were asked to indicate which of a variety of different life events they had personally experienced. The results indicated that the majority of students had experienced at least one major loss in their lives, as outlined below.

- *Loss of a pet*: 69 per cent of the sample reported having a family pet die sometime in the first twelve years of their life.
- *Loss of a relative*: 61 per cent of the sample reported having gone through the loss of a relative. That is, grandparent, sibling or parent.
- *Moving house*: 55 per cent of the sample reported moving house in the first twelve years of their life and would have experienced the losses often associated with changing homes, including changes of school, as well as the loss of friends and family.
- *Hospital treatment*: 42 per cent of the sample reported receiving hospital treatment. It was not recorded how many of these would have been for outpatient treatment only, but it is likely that a proportion of these children had undergone the trauma of hospitalisation.
- *Parental separation*: 26 per cent of the sample reported having gone through the separation or divorce of their parents. Therefore, a quarter of the young people had experienced the loss of an intact family and many of these would be experiencing increasing loss of contact with one of their parents.

Adaptation to loss or trauma

It is clear that by the time they reach secondary schools, the majority of children will have experienced a significant loss or trauma in their lives. Therefore, teachers need to understand the process of adaptation which children and adults go through in gradually coming to terms with loss or the effects of traumatic events. The most useful way to conceptualise the process of adaptation is by means of a stage model like that presented below. The model is based on the work of several authors (Kubler-Ross, 1969; Worden, 1991; Hornby, 1994). It suggests that the adaptation process can be viewed as a continuum of reactions through which children must pass in order to come to terms with their loss. These are:

- *Shock*: The initial reaction of children when they first find out about the death or other traumatic event is typically one of shock and confusion which usually lasts from a few hours to a few days.
- *Denial*: Denial or disbelief of the reality of the situation typically follows shock. Children find it difficult to believe or take in that the traumatic event has occurred. As a temporary coping strategy denial is useful in providing time to adjust to the situation; it is only when denial is prolonged and intense that it is problematic.
- *Anger*: Following denial, when children are beginning to accept the reality of the situation, they tend to experience anger associated with the loss. They may search for a reason for the loss having occurred, for someone to blame. Alternatively, underlying the anger may be feelings of guilt about somehow being responsible for the situation.
- *Sadness*: Sadness may follow anger and is a reaction which, more than any other, is reported to pervade the whole adaptation process. Some children spend a lot of time crying while others cut themselves off from contact with friends. It is important for teachers to realise that sadness and even temporary depression are a normal part of the adaptation process.
- *Detachment*: Following sadness children tend to experience a feeling of detachment, when they feel empty and nothing seems to matter. Life goes on from day to day but it has lost its meaning. This reaction often indicates that the child has accepted the reality of the loss and is therefore thought to be a turning point in the adaptation process.
- *Reorganisation*: Reorganisation follows detachment and is characterised by realism about the situation and hope for the future. Children begin to focus less on the negative aspects of the loss and can find something positive about the situation.
- *Adaptation*: Finally children reach a point when they have come to terms with the situation and exhibit an emotional acceptance of the loss. They are fully aware of the significance of the loss but are determined to get on with life as best they can.

However, in reality, the adaptation process is not as clear-cut as simply moving from stage to stage would suggest. Although one reaction may be uppermost at a particular time, the other reactions will also be present to some extent. For example, children who seem to be mainly reacting with aggression and anger will also be feeling sad as well. In contrast, children who appear to be withdrawn and detached will also be experiencing anger and sadness. The adaptation process is considered to be a normal healthy reaction to the experience of loss. In some cases it is possible to work through the process in a few days, whereas for others it can take years to reach a reasonable level of adaptation. It is considered that most adults will take at least two years to come to terms with any major traumatic event and this is probably a reasonable guideline for children too. The fact that people move through the adaptation process at different rates has consequences for families. At any point in time family members may be at different places along the continuum. So while a mother is feeling sad about the loss, the father may be experiencing anger and the children may still be in denial. This often leads to conflict within families who are all grieving but are at different points on the continuum of response.

It is also important to realise that passage through the adaptation process can be accelerated or retarded by what people do and say. Children who refuse to face up to the loss and do not allow themselves to experience the feelings triggered by the adaptation process will take longer to come to terms with the situation. It is important to do the 'grief work' associated with a loss in order to adjust to it (Webb, 1993). In cases where the loss has been anticipated, for example, a death through terminal illness, children and their parents may have partially worked through the adaptation process in anticipation of the loss. The reality of the loss is then often accompanied by some feelings of relief.

Many losses are associated with developmental transitions which children will need to negotiate. These include: starting school; changing classes at the end of every school year; changing schools to move from primary to secondary school; leaving school to attend college.

As well as developmental transitions there are also other traumatic events or losses which are very common although not experienced by all children, as noted from Branwhite's (1994) survey reported at the start of this chapter. For example, 42 per cent of the sample reported receiving hospital treatment. Studies have shown that hospitalisation can have a profound effect on young children suggesting that this can be a traumatic event for them. I know that this was the case for me when I broke my arm at age five and spent a night in the hospital alone. It was the first time I had been separated from my parents overnight, I was in pain and very frightened. Cowie and Pecherek (1994) suggest that children typically go through three stages in response to hospitalisation. First of all, *protest* in which they call out for their parents. Second, *withdrawal* in which they show little interest in staff or their peers. Third, *detachment* when they become more active but relate to children and adults in superficial ways. When they are re-united with their parent's children may often exhibit angry outburts, cold rejection or excessive clinging.

Two traumatic events experienced by many children are the death of a relative and separation or divorce of parents. Branwhite (1994) reported that 61 per cent of the young people had experienced the loss of a relative and 26 per cent had gone through the separation or divorce of their parents. These are major losses, which are likely to be extremely traumatic for children to endure. It is, therefore, vital for teachers to understand what will be happening to children and know what they can do to help.

Other children will have to cope with the loss of a close friend or someone they know less well, but is nevertheless significant to them, such as a classmate or teacher. Since parents and teachers often know very little about children's reactions to death or how to help them cope with bereavement, they may avoid the issue. The result of this is that many children have problems coming to terms with their losses.

Rutter (1975) was the first to systematically study the emotional and behavioural difficulties that are often experienced by children in coping with bereavement. He found that twice as many children who had lost a parent by death attended the Maudsley Hospital psychiatric clinic than would be expected from death rates in the general population and 14 per cent had been bereaved of a close relative in the recent past.

Children's difficulties in coping with bereavement

Most teachers and parents are not sure what to do when a child has suffered a bereavement, so they typically do nothing. When the death of a parent or child occurs it affects all members of the family. Parents may be struggling to cope themselves and therefore may not be able to give grieving children the emotional support they need. Parents also may not be aware of the extent of children's understanding of death or of the likely effects of bereavement on children. To make matters worse children are often aware that their parents are upset following the death and tend to put on a brave face to avoid burdening parents further. So, because of these factors children's needs can be overlooked, or underestimated.

Death of a parent

The death of a parent is generally thought to be the most traumatic event that can happen to a child. Morgan (1985) suggests that, when a parent dies, a child is faced with three major tasks. First, the child must come to terms with the reality of the death itself. Second, the child must adapt to the changes in the family, which will result from the loss of a parent. Third, the child must learn to cope with the permanent absence of one parent. Young children may believe that bad things happen because they have been naughty, and consequently they may blame themselves for their parent's death. Children may react by regressing to an earlier stage of development or may attempt to deny the reality of the death by carrying on as normal and apparently being unaffected by it. Alternatively, children may experience physical symptoms such as loss of appetite, sleep problems or bed-wetting (Morgan, 1985).

Children sometimes exhibit hostile reactions to the dead parent or others because they feel they have been unjustly abandoned or deserted. Alternatively they may idealise the deceased as a means of avoiding the negative feelings they may have. Identifying with parents who have died by perhaps taking on some of their interests is seen as a constructive reaction. Whereas trying to take their place, perhaps even developing some of the symptoms that appeared during the illness is considered to be potentially harmful and should be discouraged.

The way in which children react to the death of a parent will be influenced by three factors: the age of the child; their relationship to the parent who has died; and, the extent to which previous losses and separations in their lives have been resolved.

Death of a sibling

The death of a child is a profound loss, as it runs against the natural order of events and therefore challenges people's fundamental assumptions about the universe which can leave children feeling vulnerable and afraid for their own future and that of other family members. Parental grief following the loss of a child is typically intense, debilitating and long-lasting. Since very few parents avail themselves of counselling most of them are likely to be struggling to cope with their own grief for months or even years and may be unable to provide sufficient help to their remaining children in coping with their reactions to the bereavement. Morgan (1985) suggests that, when parent's own grief prevents them from maintaining healthy relationships, surviving children are placed at risk of developing psychological problems. For example, younger children can react to the death of an older sibling by regressing to babyish behaviour in an attempt to prevent them growing to an age when death could occur. Alternatively, older children may become pre-occupied with their own future, anxious about whether they too will soon die.

Aware of their parents' grief, some children attempt to take the place of their dead sibling, perhaps by acting like them, even when this behaviour is not appropriate for their age. Children can experience considerable guilt, either about things done to or not done for dead siblings when they were alive, or about enjoying the feeling of having parents to themselves. If not recognised and dealt with during childhood these guilt feelings can lead to depression which can carry on into adult life and in extreme cases become a precursor to suicide (Morgan, 1985). Another possible problem occurs when parents displace their negative emotions onto siblings. As parents attempt to adapt to their loss, the anger and other intense emotions they experience may be displaced onto the surviving children who then sense their parents' hostility and feel that they are being punished for the death of their sibling.

Death of other significant people

The death of other family members such as grandparents, cousins, aunts or uncles can have a significant impact on children. This is especially so when there has been a particularly close relationship with the deceased. Also, the death of friends, classmates or teachers can be traumatic for children, as suggested in the case described above. Incidents, which involve the death of several school children, usually due to road accidents, tend to have a high profile because they are widely reported in the media. They actually happen quite infrequently but their impact when they do occur is devastating to the families involved, the children's school friends and the whole school community. The impact is greatest on those children who survived the accident who commonly experience such reactions as depression, sleep disturbances, bed-wetting, stomach problems, concentration difficulties, fear of hospitals, being hurt or of dying (Morgan, 1985).

The teacher's role

There are several reasons why teachers are in the ideal position to provide help in coping with bereavement, both directly to the children concerned and indirectly through their parents (Thornton and Krajewski, 1993). First, teachers have knowledge of child development and are therefore aware of the different levels of understanding of death which children have at different ages. Second, they see children five days a week so are in an excellent position to notice any behavioural changes which may indicate difficulties they are having in coping with a bereavement. Third, teachers may have access to information on death and grieving through Personal and Social Education curriculum material in their schools. Fourth, teachers may know of, or can find out about, the professional and voluntary help for the bereaved, which is available in the local community. Finally, teachers can provide a vital link between school and home. They can work closely with parents to ensure that children's emotional needs are met.

However, although teachers are well placed to help children and their parents cope with bereavement this frequently does not happen because death education has such a low profile in most schools. There has been a lack of training on the topic so most teachers simply do not know enough about the grieving process and how to help children cope with it. Therefore, the following sections provide a summary of the knowledge teachers need to have in order to help children directly or to be able to provide guidance to parents so they can enable children to cope more effectively with bereavement.

Children's understanding of death

Children's understanding of death progresses from a complete lack of awareness through phases of increased comprehension until an adult view is attained as follows

(Morgan, 1985):

- From birth to approximately two years of age children have no concept of death as such. They may experience grief due to separation from people they have developed close relationships with but have no realisation of the finality of death.
- Three to five year old children tend to view death as being similar to sleep. They do not see it as a permanent state, nor do they understand that all living things must eventually die.
- Between the ages of five and nine years children come to realise the finality of death but still are not aware that it is universal. This usually happens from about nine years of age when children may become upset at the idea of death in general and in particular about the possibility of their parents dying.
- From nine to twelve years children become aware of the finality, inevitability and universality of death and because of this often experience some anxiety associated with such thoughts.
- Teenagers tend to become defiant of death, almost daring death to occur by playing games such as 'chicken', in which they run across the road in front of cars.

Grief in children

Children are generally thought to go through similar stages of grief as adults so their reactions are illustrated by the model of adaptation to loss and trauma which is described above. Some writers, however, think that children's grieving is different, as suggested by the three-phase model proposed by Morgan (1985). The first phase is one of *protest*, when the child refuses to accept that the person is dead and, for some children, involves angry attempts to get them back. In the second phase children experience *hurt, despair* and *disorganisation* as they begin to accept the fact that the person has really gone. The third phase is one in which *hope* develops as children begin to reorganise their lives without the deceased.

Grief counselling

The ways in which teachers react to and deal with death is vitally important since they act as models for their pupils. It is important for them to develop preventative approaches rather than waiting for problems to occur. In order to do this, teachers need to understand the tasks involved in the process of mourning and to be familiar with the principles of grief counselling.

According to Worden (1991) there are ten major principles of grief counselling. The application of these principles to children who have suffered a bereavement is outlined below:

1. *Helping the child actualise the loss.* The first task of grieving is to accept that the loss has occurred, that the person is dead and will not return. Encouraging children to talk about the person who has died and how the death happened can facilitate this. Children may need to talk about the death over and over again to someone who has the patience and compassion to listen. It may also be useful to suggest that children visit the grave, or the place where the ashes have been scattered, thereby encouraging the expression of feeling.

2. *Helping the child to identify and express feelings.* Helping children to become aware of and express their feelings about the loss is the most important task of grief counselling.

For younger children drawing can be used both to identify hidden feelings and as a trigger for getting them to talk about how they feel. For older children getting them to write about the deceased can have a similar effect (Allan, 1988). Older children may feel guilty about how they behaved towards the deceased. Younger children may feel guilty because they believe that they were in some way responsible for the death. Angry feelings are generally projected onto other members of the family, doctors, other children or even teachers. Sometimes the anger is turned inward and experienced as depression or guilt. Sadness is a natural reaction to a major loss but the expression of sadness is often problematic.

3. *Helping the child to live life without the deceased.* As well as coping with their grief, bereaved children also need to be able to deal with the practical difficulties, which result from their loss. A child who has lost a parent or an older sibling will probably be expected to take on more responsibility around the home. A child who has lost a close friend will need to seek out other friendships.

4. *Helping the child to re-invest emotional energy.* Children need to be helped to find ways of maintaining the memory of the person who has died while re-investing their energy in other relationships so that their lives can continue. For example, they can be showed how to keep a journal of their thoughts about the deceased while at the same time being encouraged to develop new friendships.

5. *Providing time to grieve.* Most experts in grief counselling agree that it generally takes at least two years for a child or an adult to adjust to any major loss. Also, that this only applies if people are grieving during this time and not avoiding expressing their feelings, in which case it may take much longer.

6. *Providing ongoing support.* Children need continuing support for at least a year following the death and probably longer. Certain times may be particularly difficult for them, such as birthdays, Christmas and the anniversary of the death. Bereavement support groups can be very helpful (Hopmeyer and Werk, 1993), so parents and children should be made aware of their existence in the local community. Recommending books to parents, on helping children cope with grief, such as that by Dyregrov (1991), is also important.

7. *Interpreting normal behaviour.* Their thoughts and feelings following the death of someone close can frighten children. It is helpful to be able to explain the grieving process to them, including a discussion of typical reactions, in order to reassure them about the normality of what they are experiencing.

8. *Allowing for individual differences.* It is also important to explain to children that the reactions triggered by grief will be different for each person. Their surviving siblings, parents and friends will all be grieving in different ways.

9. *Examining defences and coping style.* Some of the ways in which children cope with a bereavement are not healthy because they involve using defences to avoid experiencing the pain of grieving. For example, children who withdraw from contact with friends and family or refuse to talk about or look at photographs of the deceased are using defence mechanisms to avoid facing up to their grief and need help in order to develop more effective coping strategies.

10. *Identifying pathology and referring.* The listening and counselling skills discussed earlier in this book are sufficient for teachers to be able to help the majority of children to cope with bereavement. However, these will not be sufficient for a minority of children who are experiencing severe difficulties coping with their loss and who will, therefore, need more intensive help. Also, some teachers will feel that they do not have the expertise, time or patience to counsel children who have been bereaved. It is important to recognise personal limitations and be prepared to suggest to the head teacher or to parents that professional counselling is required.

Dealing with trauma and loss at the school level

Some traumatic experiences or losses demand a response at the school level. The most obvious situation is when several members of the school community die as a result of an accident. In the news in the last few years there have been reports of multiple deaths of students and teachers from both road accidents and also from various outdoor experiences. In recent years there have also been several shocking incidents of children and their teachers being killed and injured deliberately while at school. In these cases it is obvious that there must be a response at the school level but in cases when a particular student or teacher dies it is less obvious and often is overlooked. In any of the above situations the whole school community need to be involved in a mourning process (Wagner, 1995). The school will need to work closely with the families of the dead to respect their wishes over the school's involvement in the funeral and in commemoration of the dead. The key issues which need to be addressed are outlined below in considering what schools should do when a student dies.

1. *Inform members of school community.* The first issue is one of how the entire school community will be informed about the student's death. It is usually best done by calling a special assembly of all staff and students. Sufficient details should be provided about how the student died to allay the spread of rumours.

2. *Provide opportunities for mourning.* The students can then be broken up into house, year or tutor groups in order to allow them to express their thoughts and feelings with the teachers who they know the best. Teachers can meet in year or departmental groups to share their feelings with colleagues. In these ways the school community can begin the grieving process. When the initial shock is over, many children particularly those who were close to the deceased, will benefit from further activities designed to help them work through their grief. For example, reading books about death, making a life-storybook, writing stories, acting out plays, doing drawings, paintings or writing a letter to the deceased (Lendrum and Syme, 1992). The use of strategies such as 'circle time' and developmental group work in facilitating mourning is discussed in Chapter 6.

3. *Arrangements for attending funeral.* It is important that all staff and students who wish to attend the funeral are allowed to do so. The school may need to be closed for part of the day to facilitate this.

4. *Memorials for the dead.* Following the funeral the school should mark the death in some way. This can be anything from a special prayer for the deceased at a normal school assembly to a full memorial service. Other memorials such as making a book about the deceased or the planting of a tree should also be considered. Exactly what is done needs to be in keeping with the wishes of the family as well as other students and staff.

5. *Continued close contact with families.* The school should remain in contact with the family of the deceased after the funeral otherwise they may feel that their child has been forgotten. One way of keeping in contact and also keeping the memory of the deceased alive is for the family to sponsor a sporting or academic trophy in the name of the student.

Children coping with their parents' separation or divorce

It has been estimated that, before they reach the age of sixteen, one in five children will experience the divorce of their parents, while an unknown number are affected by parental separation (Cox and Desforges, 1987). Around two-thirds of children will exhibit noticeable changes in behaviour at school, similar to the reactions to other losses already discussed, following parental separation.

Children who experience the separation or divorce of their parents are therefore at risk of developing emotional and behavioural difficulties (Hodges, 1991). The likelihood that such difficulties will result depends partly on the extent to which their special needs are met within the school. In order for teachers to provide for the special needs of these children they need to know about the family difficulties which they are likely to experience and about the reactions to parental separation common to children of different ages.

Family disruption is often a serious problem in the first year after a separation. Parents tend to be so involved with their own feelings and concerns in adjusting to their new situation that they overlook the needs of their children. Discipline in the home can be inconsistent and parents may not notice the pain which children are experiencing. So at the very time when children need most support their parents are least able to provide it because they are overwhelmed by their own problems. Studies of families where there has been a divorce, conducted in the USA (Morgan, 1985), have shown that at least one member of each family has exhibited disruptive behaviour or serious distress. In most cases the most seriously affected family members are the children. However, it must not be forgotten that parental divorce has an impact on all family members, including the extended family, especially grandparents, who face the possibility of being denied access to their grandchildren (Myers and Perrin, 1993).

A variety of factors contribute to a child's ability to cope with parental separation (Morgan, 1985). These include: the age and gender of the child; the maturity of the child; the financial situation of the parents; the degree of discord before and after the divorce; the child's relationship with each parent and siblings; the child's ability to cope with stress; and the availability of emotional support. The effects of these factors will depend on the age of the child.

Pre-school age children have difficulty fully understanding the situation and tend to react by either attempting to deny the reality of the separation or by regressing to more immature behaviour. Pre-school children often fear the loss of the other parent when one has left the family home, so they may cling more closely to the remaining parent and tend to get very upset at routine separations (Cox and Desforges, 1987).

Children of primary school age tend to find it particularly difficult to adjust to parental separation since they understand enough about the situation to make denial a less useful option. At the same time they have not developed the coping strategies which older children typically use (Morgan, 1985). They may feel guilty believing that in some way they have caused the separation, or they may become anxious about the possibility of the other parent leaving them. They may experience feelings of intense sadness or depression or be highly emotional with aggressive behaviour alternating wildly with episodes of crying (Hodges, 1991).

Children of secondary school age tend to experience either anger or depression. Their academic work may be seriously affected or they may participate in delinquent acts (Morgan, 1985). They often experience embarrassment about the family break-up and try to keep it a secret from their friends. They are much less likely than younger children to use denial or to regress in their behaviour. They have the ability to express their opinions and feelings, including their anger, towards the parent they blame for the separation.

What teachers can do to help

Teachers are in an excellent position to help children cope with effects of divorce and to provide support for parents. They are in a good position to identify changes in children's behaviour, which are indicative of their difficulties in adjusting to parental separation. Teachers are in regular contact with children and have the opportunity to develop sufficient rapport for them to feel comfortable enough to open up and talk about the things that are bothering them. Also, when teachers develop two-way communication with parents they are in an ideal position to provide guidance to parents and to collaborate with them in dealing with children's difficulties.

Many children whose parents have separated or divorced report that they would have liked someone at the school to encourage them to talk about their feelings and reactions to their situation and suggested relevant books for them to read (Morgan, 1985). A range of specific strategies which teachers can employ to help children cope with the separation of their parents have been suggested by Cox and Desforges (1987). These are outlined below:

1. *Develop a school policy.* Teachers need to acquaint themselves with the school policy for dealing with separation or divorce involving pupils attending the school. They need to know what is expected of teachers and of parents in the event of a separation. A school's expectations of parents in this situation should be written in the handbook which parents receive when their child enters the school. The statement needs to say that the school should be informed about any disruptions in home circumstances, including parental separation, which may affect a child's behaviour or progress at school.

2. *Organise support at school.* For children who are experiencing disruption and unhappiness at home, the school can provide a haven of calm and security which itself is very therapeutic. In addition, having a well-organised system of pastoral care is very important so that pupils have the opportunity to develop a rapport with a caring adult. Teachers acting in their pastoral capacity can thereby provide children with extra attention and support in order to help them cope with their parents' separation. Other members of the school staff, such as teaching assistants and dinner staff, can also provide emotional support since pupils often form close relationships with them. Teachers can also ensure that the Personal and Social Education curriculum used in the school includes sessions on coping with parental separation and divorce. Alternatively, the topic can be made the subject of class discussions held during form tutor periods, using a developmental strategy such as that outlined in Chapter 4.

3. *Keep records.* Schools should ensure that records of the family circumstances are kept updated. Teachers need to have the names and addresses of both natural parents and any step or foster parents. They need to record when separations and divorces have occurred and have a record of custody and access arrangements for each child whose parents have divorced. For example, is custody shared or does the child live mainly with one parent and see the other only at weekends? Teachers also need to record any legal restrictions placed on contacts between children and one or other of their parents. In addition, it is useful to keep a record of the problems which children have experienced at school since the separation.

4. *Providing opportunities for support.* Teachers are in an excellent position to provide supportive counselling for children whose parents have separated. Pupils are more likely to open up and talk about their problems with teachers or other school staff with whom they have developed a good rapport than with outside specialists such as educational psychologists or education welfare officers. The same applies to parents. They are much more likely to talk about their concerns to their children's teacher than to a professional counsellor.

5. *Involving both parents.* When teachers continue to involve both parents following a separation or divorce it sends an important message to both children and parents. Children need both parents to be interested in their education and welfare despite the fact that they are now living apart. It is, therefore, important for teachers to send letters of invitation and copies of school reports to each of the parents. Divorced parents should be given the opportunity to decide whether they will attend parents' evenings together or separately. If they are able to attend together then the school can provide a neutral setting for parents to discuss their children's education.

6. *Providing practical help.* Teachers can provide help to divorced parents whose children live with them on a number of practical matters. First, since many families experience financial difficulties following a separation or divorce, teachers can check whether children are eligible for free or subsidised school meals. Receiving free school meals not only eases the financial burden on parents but also communicates to other members of staff that parents may find it difficult to provide money for school trips and the like. Second, at times of family disruption children may not be able to find a calm place to do their homework so the provision of a homework centre at the school can be a tremendous help. Third, practical considerations, such as providing a safe place for pupils to leave bags packed ready for weekend access visits can make life easier for children and also reinforce the acceptability of their situation.

7. *Provide relevant reading material.* Teachers can help children adjust to their new situation by ensuring they have access to books which deal with separation and divorce such as that by Mitchell (1982). Teachers can also suggest books to parents which will help them to gain a better understanding of their children's needs following a separation such as that by Burgoyne (1984).

References

Allan, J. (1988) *Inscapes of the Child's World: Jungian Counseling in Schools and Clinics.* Dallas, TX: Spring.

Branwhite, T. (1994) Bullying and student distress: beneath the tip of the iceberg. *Educational Psychology,* 14(1): 59–71.

Burgoyne, J. (1984) *Breaking Even: Divorce, Your Children and You.* Harmondsworth: Penguin.

Cowie, H. and Pecherek, A. (1994) *Counselling: Approaches and Issues in Education.* London: David Fulton.

Cox, K. M. and Desforges, M. (1987) *Divorce and the School.* London: Methuen.

Dyregrov, A. (1991) *Grief in Children: A Handbook for Adults.* London: Jessica Kingsley.

Hodges, W. F. (1991) *Interventions for Children of Divorce* (2nd edn). New York: Wiley.

Hopmeyer, E. and Werk, A. (1993) A comparative study of four family bereavement groups. *Groupwork,* 6(2): 107–21.

Hornby, G. (1994) *Counselling in Child Disability.* London: Chapman and Hall.

Kubler-Ross, E. (1969) *On Death and Dying.* New York: Macmillan.

Lendrum, S. and Syme, G. (1992) *Gift of Tears.* London: Routledge.

Mitchell, A. (1982) *When Parents Split Up: Divorce Explained to Young People.* Edinburgh: MacDonald.

Morgan, S. R. (1985) *Children in Crisis: A Team Approach in the Schools.* London: Taylor & Francis.

Mulder, V. (1994) Words can make it better. *Times Educational Supplement* (Review Section), March 25, p. 5.

Myers, J. E. and Perrin, N. (1993) Grandparents affected by parental divorce: a population at risk? *Journal of Counseling and Develoment,* 72(1): 62–6.

Thornton, C. and Krajewski, J. (1993) Death education for teachers. *Intervention in School and Clinic*, 29(1): 31–5.

Rutter, M. (1975) *Helping Troubled Children*. Harmondswoth: Penguin.

Wagner, P. (1995) Schools and pupils: developing their responses to bereavement. In R. Lang, P. Best, C. Lodge and C. Watkins (eds), *Pastoral Care and Personal and Social Education: Entitlement and Provision*. London: Cassell.

Webb, N. B. (1993) *Helping Bereaved Children: A Handbook for Practitioners*. New York: Guilford.

Worden, J. W. (1991) *Grief Counselling and Grief Therapy* (2nd edn). London: Routledge.

11 Counselling for sensitive issues

Max Biddulph

In the midst of winter, I finally learned that there was in me an invincible summer.

(Camus)

Schools are interesting places of contradiction. Many readers of this book will no doubt have first hand experience of working in schools and the particular experience that this brings. An observer of a lively play ground or busy staff room will see the public business of the school being acted out in countless day-to-day interactions between members of the school community. What may be less obvious is what lies below the surface in terms of the private worlds of individuals. The dynamic that pushes individuals to categorise aspects of their experience into either the public or the private domain is at the heart of sensitive issues in school contexts. Rowling (1996) provides a useful overview of the elements that constitute sensitive issues in schools, noting the central role of values as criteria for defining 'sensitivity'. Each day, schools communicate a particular set of messages in terms of institutional values on a whole range of matters. There is a kind of expectation from many stakeholders in the enterprise ranging from parents to 'the state', that schools should be proactive in this function as being moral/spiritual arbiters in society.

However, the statements made in the public forum about how life 'should be', may contrast with the back home world of individuals and families. As a result, individuals may find themselves at odds with the public persona of schools and this can trigger powerful feelings of shame with its resultant silence. For young people, the tension between personal difficulties and public shame may surface under the guise of other presenting problems such as truancy, poor academic achievement or behaviour problems. It is easy to see why counselling people with sensitive issues can become challenging for teachers. The aim of this chapter is to explore the nature of these challenges within the context of a particular sensitive issue, namely sexuality.

Sexuality in school contexts

The use of the word 'sexuality' is revealing in itself in terms of its status as a sensitive issue within school contexts. In UK schools, 'sexuality' is often used as a euphemism meaning sexual orientation, that is, heterosexual, lesbian, gay or bisexual. Although the scenario of young people questioning their sexual orientation is one way in which sexuality manifests itself in school contexts, the use of the term 'sexuality' is intended to be much broader than the sexual orientation issue. The use of the term sexuality here is intended to be much less specific – simply meaning 'the experience of being sexual'.

An important question to ask is 'how do schools deal with sexuality?' Neil Duncan suggests that the line schools take is one of disavowal when it comes to sexuality:

> Schools openly control and order, manage and measure just about every other aspect of their pupils' experience but sexuality. Any human quality can be qualified and commended by praise from the assembly-hall podium: honesty, diligence; sporting and academic success but not sexuality. The official silence surrounding the topic is deathly with curricular remit halting at procreation and AIDS awareness; 'relationships' being discussed only fleetingly in PSE lessons.
>
> (Duncan, 1999, p. 135)

It is interesting to speculate on the causes of this avoidance. Epstein and Johnson (1998) attribute it to the nature of discourses that relate to schooling and sexuality. A particularly powerful one is the notion of children as being pre or asexual beings who are innocent and need protection from the outside world. Recent instances throughout the world of children being sexually abused by adults inevitably make this a highly charged, emotive and controversial issue. Whilst this is an understandable response, avoidance is questionable as a strategy for supporting young people who may be wrestling with issues relating to sexuality. A more effective response with young people, as will be argued later in this chapter, is for adult supporters in a school is to confront the issues with sensitivity.

The teacher as a supporter

Teachers occupy a significant place in the lives of young people when they are in school. The aspect of this relationship that is most potent is the fact that their presence is a constant. The cycle of the daily routine puts students and teachers together in each other's company with predictable regularity. I have frequently heard teachers underestimating their skill and effectiveness in supporting young people, discounting the effect that a consistent presence has. In conversing with one teacher in the preparation of this chapter, I was told that a student engaged the teacher in small talk every lunchtime for two years before disclosing that she was being sexually abused. This anecdote not only illustrates the potential support of a continuing presence but also the importance of the establishment of trust in relationships. The role of teachers sometimes presents a challenge in the establishment of trust in student–teacher relations. It is a fact that most teachers are authority figures in the eyes of young people – so can they be trusted? The proponents of the person-centred tradition (see Maslow, 1968; Rogers and Freiburg, 1994) in education would strongly argue that teachers can be trusted. The use of Rogers' core conditions of non-judgementalism, positive regard and authenticity form a sound starting point for the construction of a persona for helping and supporting. The teacher that remains a remote, judgemental, non-disclosing authority figure is unlikely to be approached. The challenge is to find a way of creating a teacher persona that is respectful, authentic and giving, whilst retaining the authority that the role requires.

A paradigm for helping and supporting

Blake and Laxton (1998) provide a useful model for providing support to young people who present with issues relating to sexuality. Whilst addressing some aspects of the model could be interpreted as guidance, for example, the provision of information relating to sexual health services, there is potential for counselling young people in other aspects. At least three opportunities are present. The first relates to the presence of self-esteem at the heart of the model. Providing young people with a space to explore who they are and how they feel about themselves is an obvious opportunity. The second opportunity relates to the emotional component of the model. Time constraints necessarily mean that much of the sex education taught in schools is primarily factual, with little opportunity to discuss feelings about sexuality, especially in a one-to-one situation. For young people who present with particular issues, it often is the exploration of feelings that enables a clarification of their situation to take place. It is this greater sense of clarity, which can provide a subsequent lead on future actions that may help to resolve the problem.

The notion of future actions is related to the third opportunity for providing support to young people via the use of counselling skills. Implicit in the model is the notion of personal agency. This means evolving a process of independence over a period of time in which young people take control over their sexuality. This ability to manage and take control requires thought-through actions that are positive choices made by the individual. The challenge for teachers who are present in the role of supporters, is how to foster this independence – the skill lies in achieving a balance of direction and facilitation. One scenario of course, is that this goal may lie beyond the remit of what teachers can realistically provide by way of support in schools. A knowledge of outside agencies may not just be useful in providing a referral for more specialist support, but enable teachers to delineate realistic boundaries in terms of the time that they can offer for support.

The role of values

Davies and Neal (1996) argue that to merely model the person-centred conditions in supportive interactions that relate to sexuality may not be sufficient. This challenging work inevitably means that teachers are forced to review their own values in the process. In making this statement, I would suggest that teachers need to get off the fence and work with their personal and school values in an assertive way. Given the complexity of the issues which are both geographically and culturally specific to individual schools, the skill will lie with practitioners who will adapt the various suggestions to the conditions on the ground at the time. This means being sensitive not only to the ethos and cultural context of the school but also to the relationship with the person being supported.

A case study: working with child sexual abuse

In this section I will explore some of the challenges of working with young people who may seek support from teachers focussing on the particular presenting problem of child sexual abuse. In presenting this case study it would be easy to problematise young people who may be wrestling with this issue. Instead, in the spirit of person-centredness, I want to be clear that it is the issue that I see as problematic, not the young people. In researching the case study I have reviewed a selection of the contemporary literature as well as conversing with a number of key informants who are either practitioners in the field or work with agencies who support teachers in this work.

Background

The problem of child sexual abuse has been publicly debated for at least twenty years. Briggs and Hawkins (1995) provide a useful overview of the evolution of this process identifying the key role of women in putting this issue on the agenda and in the development of subsequent child protection programmes. Plummer (1986), Daro *et al.* (1988) noted the comprehensive development of such programmes in the US whilst Briggs (1991) and Briggs and Hawkins (1994) describe similar developments in Australia and New Zealand. In the UK, the role of gender has been foregrounded recently by Chamberlain (1993) and Skinner (1999b). Julie Skinner describes how persons experiencing child sexual abuse were initially referred to as 'victims' (Kempe and Kempe, 1978) and then as 'survivors' (Kelly, 1988). Some sense of the heat that emanates from the debate can be gleaned from analyses that problematised the families in which the sexual abuse took place (Furniss, 1984) and then the 'bad mothers' (Furniss, 1984) who presumably colluded with it. It is easy to see how child sexual abuse is a potentially highly charged issue that is fuelled by feelings related to macro systems of power that exist in society. One aspect of these power relations is gender and Chamberlain (1993) and New (1993) point out that men perpetrate the vast majority of child sexual abuse. Additional levels of complexity are now beginning to emerge, Briggs and Hawkins (1995) note the under-reporting of child sexual abuse amongst males and a key informant claims that abuse perpetrated by a small number of women is also currently being debated in professional circles.

Definitions and presenting symptoms

A key question that needs to be asked when dealing with cases of child sexual abuse that are disclosed in school contexts is 'what constitutes sexual abuse?' Chamberlain points out that:

> The ways in which a text defines sexual abuse, and suggests its causes and effects, are of key importance in shaping teachers' perceptions of child sexual abuse, and can ulti-mately affect their response and management of any disclosure .... One cannot, there-fore, underestimate the power of these messages. It is vital that they are critically inspected.
>
> (Chamberlain, 1993, p. 29)

Chamberlain goes on to argue that the problem with some definitions is that they exclude certain scenarios that constitute child sexual abuse. Examples of such definitions are:

> The involvement of developmentally immature children and adolescents in sexual actions which they cannot fully comprehend, to which they cannot give informed con-sent, and which violate social roles.
>
> (Kempe and Kempe, 1984, p. 9)

and

> Sexual abuse is any exploitation of children under the age of sixteen for the sexual pleasure, gratification or profit of an adult or significantly older person.
>
> (Elliott, 1990, p. 118)

Ash (1984) in a critique of the widely used Kempe and Kempe (1984) definition points out that it does not acknowledge the potential use of force in interactions between the par-ties; MacLeod and Saraga (1988) question the possible limitations on abusive activity as being only that which 'violates social roles'. Chamberlain (1993) takes issue with the notion that abusers are necessarily adult in the Elliott definition. This she argues, excludes the possibility of abuse by peers which is a significant issue (see Kelly *et al.*, 1991 who estimate that peer abuse accounts for 25 per cent of all reported abuse).

A second area of concern centres on the issue of producing lists for professionals of 'presenting symptoms' that those survivors of sexual abuse will exhibit. Chamberlain (1993) argues that lists of symptoms can be misleading in that teachers may have an expectation that individuals must demonstrate some form of negative or undesirable behaviour. She points out that:

> abused children can be docile and well behaved, and excel at school – it might be the only place of safety where they feel that they can apply themselves. There is also the worry that children who disclose and do not display 'negative symptoms' are less likely to be believed or taken seriously.
>
> (Chamberlain, 1993, p. 33)

Skinner (1999b) also alerts us to the dangers of stereotyping. In her study of the experiences of teachers who had supported young people who had been sexually abused she reports that there is evidence that certain children were more likely to be believed than others and that certain cases provoked more surprise than others. There was also evidence that teachers assumed that children from 'deprived' families may be more prone to abuse than children in families in other social classes. Skinner concludes that teachers' expectations of sexual abuse incidence could colour the picture of the likelihood of sexual abuse in the school population and operate both for and against its identification.

Some key points to note at this stage are:

- Defining what constitutes sexual abuse is problematic. I would suggest that teachers will be guided by issues relating to age, consent, context and feelings of the person disclosing. The last suggestion puts the individual at the centre of the process, and puts an onus on the teacher to listen carefully to the individual's account in making their assessment of the situation.
- Teachers need to be aware of the dangers of stereotyping children, parents and families – this could negatively influence an evolving perception of a situation.
- Intuition can be helpful in bringing into consciousness suspicions of abuse. It is important, however, to keep an open mind until any disclosure is forthcoming.
- Where abuse is suspected, informal conversations with the person who has responsibility for child protection issues are important. This highlights the importance of the professional relationship that exists between colleagues in terms of openness and an ability to sustain an on-going dialogue. Skinner (1999b) reports that some of the teachers in her study were reluctant to have these conversations for fear of not being believed.
- Many schools have clearly laid down procedural guidelines with regard to sexual abuse – these need to acknowledge on-going vigilance in relation to this issue and highlight it as a responsibility for the whole school community. Kirkland et al. (1996) illustrate how this works in the UK context by providing a useful flow chart of potential actions that can be taken. The influence of local education authority procedures and national legislation, for example, UK Children Act 1989 are apparent here; similar influences will no doubt direct teachers' actions in other parts of the world.

Working with disclosure

The disclosure of child sexual abuse by a young person will always be a watershed type of event after which a difficult situation should change. Sadly, it is the experience of some young people that they are neither 'heard' nor believed by the person that they are disclosing to. Skinner (1999b) notes the effect that this may have in deterring the young person from taking the same risk again in a similar situation. Skinner also notes that in her research with abused young people, that a factor that had stopped them from disclosing to teachers in school was a worry about being judged culpable themselves in the situation. Despite this New (1993) points out that a high percentage of the children who are known to have been sexually abused, first made the disclosure either to a teacher or to some other professional in the school context, for example, a school nurse. Kirkland *et al.* (1996) acknowledge that:

> There is no knowing how or when a child will disclose, nor to whom. Sometimes it is the first 'friendly' adult face; at other times it is a 'neutral one'; at other times it is a 'safe' person. Everyone, therefore, within the school community needs to have some basic training and awareness raising in how to respond appropriately both in terms of the procedures and in the context of the child.
>
> (Kirkland *et al.*, 1996, p. 32)

Clearly a priority in a situation in which a child begins to disclose is to recognise the significance of the interaction and to acknowledge this to the young person through skilled, attentive and intensive listening. This requires the establishment of a quiet, safe space. Key counselling skills that are to be used in this situation are:

- Non-invasive eye contact and active listening
- Non-judgemental, non-interpretative stance
- Reflection of content
- Clarification of content
- Use of silence to enable further reflection
- Acknowledging feelings if appropriate
- Supportive statement which acknowledges the inappropriateness of the abuse and the courage of making the disclosure
- Discussion of subsequent actions that need to be taken including the limits of confidentiality and to whom this information will be passed on to.

The physical proximity of the teacher in relation to the young person may also be significant. Skinner (1999b) cites Draucker (1992) and Hall and Lloyd (1993) in recognising the need on the part of survivors for physical space and the distracting effect that sudden movements made by the supporter can have on them. Clearly there is a need to acknowledge what has been disclosed on several levels, namely the factual significance, the emotional significance and the social significance, all of which should contribute to the effect of feeling 'heard'. The cognitive understanding of events on the part of the supporter may be particularly important, given that many procedures in this eventuality require a written statement to be made after such disclosures. It is difficult to predict how a young person may respond in the process of disclosure personally, a fact that underlines the notion that sexual abuse is a very individual experience. Skinner (1999b) reports that emotional responses are complex, noting the role of defence mechanisms as one response in which 'emotional deadness' is apparent. She also cites Herman (1992) in noting that trauma can also disconnect normal function whereby survivors can be highly emotional with little memory of events to having detailed memories but with no emotional reaction. However distress manifests itself in these interactions, it would be extremely callous not to acknowledge it.

In an ideal world children will be aware of the limits of confidentiality when it comes to disclosing sexual abuse to teachers. However, events tend not to follow this preferred scenario. Young children may not understand the finer points of child protection procedures and older young people may disclose on the spur of the moment. Kirkland *et al.* (1996) note that most young people disclose with an expectation that the information will be passed on so that actions will be taken to change their situation. It is important that the young person is made aware of the fact that this information must be passed on. This needs to be phrased sensitively and a clear notion of what happens next needs to be communicated.

When a disclosure is made, the key issues that teachers need to address are:

- An assessment of the immediate physical safety of the child. Any doubts about this need to be expressed and appropriate actions taken by agencies outside the school to remove the child to a place of physical safety. If the abuse is taking place within school then similar immediate action needs to be undertaken and an investigation begun.
- The content of the case must be reported to the person in the school who has responsibility for child protection issues.
- A monitoring process needs to be instigated focussed on the individual concerned.
- Support systems need to be activated for the teacher to whom the disclosure has been made. Ideally this should take the form of a space for such individuals to process their own responses to the disclosure.
- The school needs to be prepared for possible difficult responses from parents – the importance of teachers being supported by the system is highlighted by Skinner (1999a) in this respect.

Providing and receiving on-going support

Skinner (1999b) acknowledges that child sexual abuse is a messy and complex business and that there is no 'right way' to deal with it. Each case will be different in terms of the response of the survivor both to the experience of the abuse and the events that follow the disclosure of it. New (1993) points out that the subsequent investigation and current court case will in themselves be the source of additional trauma, during which time the young person will need considerable support both inside and outside of school. In a moving account told to her by a survivor of child sexual abuse, Skinner (1999a) communicates a sense of the long-term effects which she describes as the aftermath of abuse, which in this case manifested itself as a pattern of self-harming behaviour that continued long into adulthood. This illustrates the fact that working through the experience will often be a lifetime's work for most individuals. In an ideal situation much of this will be done outside of the school context where specialist agencies are able to provide the long-term support that is required. Schools can have a complementary role in this situation, being in a unique position to have an overview of the young person on a day-to-day basis. New (1993) offers a useful insight into the factors that are most effective in moving these difficult situations forward when she points out that the best outcomes materialise if the child:

1. can tell a trusted adult about the abuse;
2. tells early on;
3. is believed by the parent/trusted adult;
4. receives long term support from the non-abusing parent;
5. receives therapeutic help;
6. remains at home (with the abuser removed from the home).

(New, 1993, p. 22)

Clearly the issue of trust is a central theme in the above scenario. Teachers can help rebuild that in their relationships with young people. This will not only need to take place over a period of time, but also may involve confronting difficult feelings in the process. For the child this may mean confronting feelings of stigma, shame, loss, guilt and anger. In some cases the response from the surrounding community in the child's life may not be all supportive, neighbours and other pupils in school alleging that they have lied or have a problematic sexuality. In the need to find someone or something to blame a range of other issues may be imported such as racism and homophobia. A key informant also instanced situations where, in some cases young people may have to continue attending the same school as the perpetrator or may experience flashbacks triggered by certain sights, sounds or smells in the environment. New (1993) raises the question as to how far teachers should make allowances when experiencing challenging behaviour from abused young people. What is clear is that the path to recovery may be arduous. One strategy might be for teachers to give pupils some time out in a quiet space. In such situations supporters can offer a listening ear and an opportunity to clarify the confusion and distress that the child may be experiencing. Chamberlain (1993) again reminds us of the dangers of stereotyping abused young people as being emotionally volatile. Skinner (1999b) discusses the concept of resilience as an apparent coping mechanism displayed by survivors. In actual fact, this may be deceptive, defences hiding a set of unprocessed responses to the abuse which present a different kind of challenging behaviour to be confronted. Whatever the situation, in the immediate aftermath, stability, routine and a sense of normality will be important building blocks to have in place.

Young people of course are not be the only people who are confronting difficult feelings in the period after a disclosure is made. Skinner (1999b) noted, in her research with teachers who had experience of supporting children who had been sexually abused, that they were very keen to talk about their experiences. Although supervision is a facility that is more likely to be used by practising counsellors, teachers could initiate a similar support mechanism for themselves. Listening to the harrowing details of abuse can be extraordinarily distressing for those who are in the role of a supporter – and there is of course the possibility that the supporter may have experienced abuse himself or herself. Skinner (1999a,b) and New (1993) both point to the procedural emphasis of in-service training programmes, with an absence of training on how to manage the feelings aspect of child sexual abuse cases. Clearly, supporters will not be in any position to offer effective support to young people if they are not acknowledging and processing their own feelings themselves. In terms of actions this means:

- Setting aside time for reflection.
- Reflecting on their own position in terms of life experience in relation to the issues that have been raised.
- Acknowledging the emotional response that they have in relation to the issues raised.
- Establishing a support facility with a friend/colleague to discuss specifically their emotional responses in the process of helping and supporting.
- Discussing strategies in future interactions with the young person.

The role of colleagues is important here as well as the teacher's support systems outside of school, which must operate within the boundaries of confidentiality.

Strategies for support

In terms of future strategies for on-going support, New (1993) argues that to merely adopt a background role in monitoring and 'being there if needed' for the young person may not be sufficient. She cites Maher (1989) who advocates the setting up of an in-school team that can coordinate the support of the young person in this situation. If this worked effectively, it would not only keep staff in school appraised of progress in the case but could also have a useful role in liaising with other outside agencies who may be involved with the case, including schools involved in the child's next phase of education. An additional role that the team could adopt could be to monitor interactions with other key players such as parents in the case. Skinner (1999a) offers the testimony of a lone parent who worked in the school and overheard the headteacher making derisory and derogatory comments about families of her acquaintance and did not want her own children labelled in this way. As a result the alleged details of abuse were kept from the school and the mother had to struggle on for a considerable time before seeking help. This anecdote serves to illustrate the kinds of discourse identified earlier in this chapter that may be in operation in schools. The result is that the effects of hearing such a judgemental sub-text are powerful in maintaining a silence on these matters in some quarters.

On a more positive note, there is now evidence to suggest that a point may be reached in supporting young people where a more proactive approach can be used to move them forward. Moon (1992) notes that targeting self-esteem may be a major factor in preventing future abuse and promoting protection. The model of sex education discussed earlier also has self-esteem integral to it and it is here that teachers may enable young people to explore what personal agency might mean for them in terms of future relationships with adults. Sometimes, teachers have an unrealistic expectation about improving the self-esteem of an individual. There are no quick fixes and it can be argued that the key lies in developing the nature of the relationship over a long period of time that exists between teachers and young people. In concretising her suggestions, Moon (1992) quotes as an example a resource developed by the UK Alcohol and Drugs Agency TACADE (The Advisory Council on Alcohol and Drugs Education).

Skills for the Primary School (SPSC) suggest that adults might like to use the CARING principle when children need to talk:

C : creating a warm, supportive atmosphere
A : allowing children to express strong feelings, accepting children, believing what they say
R : reflecting back and responding appropriately
I : investigating the situation and asking questions sensitively
N : negotiating a way forward – 'What do you want to do?' 'What would you like me to do?'
G : going forward, learning from mistakes, planning action, acting responsibly.

(Moon, 1992, p. 22)

Counselling skills clearly have potential in exploring the agenda itemised above. Conversations with young people on matters relating to sexuality will always need to be age-appropriate; for older young people a proactive approach might be to elicit what they want and do not want in future relationships. A useful piece of work might be to explore the principles of assertiveness in terms of rights and responsibilities – the facts that they have rights would be a major step forward on the road to a more empowered life. This realisation would help in terms of moving on from events in the past.

In conclusion, despite the magnitude of the experience of child sexual abuse, Chamberlain (1993) offers an optimistic perspective when she asserts that:

the fact is that sexually abused children are from every strata of society; many do very well at school, overcome the psychological trauma (often despite limited support and counselling facilities), care for children, and become productive members of society, professionals, teachers ... .

(Chamberlain, 1993, p. 33)

References

Ash, A. (1984) *Father–Daughter Sexual Abuse: The Abuse of Paternal Authority*. Bangor: University College of North Wales.

Blake, S. and Laxton, J. (1998) *Strides: A Practical Guide to Sex and Relationships Education with Young Men*. London: FPA.

Briggs, F. (1991) Child protection programmes: can they protect young children? *Early Child Development and Care*, 67: 61–72.

Briggs, F. and Hawkins, R. (1994) Follow-up study of children of 5–8 years using child protection programmes in Australia and New Zealand. *Early Child Development and Care*, 10: 111–17.

Briggs, F. and Hawkins, R. (1995) Protecting boys from the risk of sexual abuse. *Early Child Development and Care*, 11: 19–32.

Chamberlain, R. (1993) Critique of the definitions and ideologies of child sexual abuse that underpin current educational texts for teachers. *Pastoral Care in Education*, June, 29–35.

Daro, D., Abrahams, N. and Robson, K. (1988) *Reducing Child Abuse By 20% By 1990: 1986 Baseline Data*. Chicago: National Committee for the Protection of Child Abuse.

Davies, D. and Neal, C. (1996) *Pink Therapy: A Guide for Counsellors and Therapists Working with Lesbian, Gay and Bisexual Clients*. Buckingham: Open University Press.

Draucker, C. (1992) *Counselling Survivors of Child Sexual Abuse*. London: Sage.

Duncan, N. (1999) *Sexual Bullying: Gender Conflict and Pupil Culture in Secondary Schools*. London: Routledge.

Elliot, M. (1990) *Teenscape: a Personal Safety Programme for Teenagers*. London: Health Education Authority.

Epstein, D. and Johnson, R. (1998) *Schooling Sexualities*. Buckingham: Open University Press.

Furniss, T. (1984) Conflict-avoiding and conflict-regulating patterns in incest and child sexual abuse, *Acta Paedopsychiatrica*, 50: 299–313.

Hall, L. and Lloyd, S. (1993) *Surviving Child Sexual Abuse*. London: Falmer.

Herman, J. (1992) *Trauma and Recovery: From Domestic Abuse to Political Terror*. London: Pandora.

Kelly, L. (1988) *Surviving Sexual Violence*. Cambridge: Policy Press.

Kelly, L., Regan, L. and Burton, S. (1991) *An Exploratory Study of The Prevalence of Sexual Abuse in a Sample of 16–20 Year Olds*. University of North London, Child Abuse Studies Unit.

Kempe, R. and Kempe, C. (1978) *Child Abuse*. London: Fontana.

Kirkland, J. P., Field, B. and Hazel, A. (1996) Child protection: the continuing need for training and policies in schools. *Pastoral Care in Education*, March, 31–6.

MacLeod, M. and Saraga, E. (1988) Challenging the orthodoxy. *Feminist Review*, No. 28.

Maher, P. (ed) (1988) *Child Abuse: The Educational Perspective*. Oxford: Basil Blackwell.

Maslow, A. (1968) *Toward a Psychology of Being*. New York: Van Nostrand Reingold.

Moon, A. (1992) Child protection programmes in schools. *Pastoral Care in Education*, March, 18–22.

New, A. (1993) Sexually abused children: the importance of the school's role in providing on-going support. *Pastoral Care in Education*, June, 21–7.

Plummer, C. (1986) Prevention education in perspective. In M. Nelson and K. Clarke (eds), *The Educator's Guide to Preventing Child Sexual Abuse*. Santa Cruz: Network Publications.

Rogers, C. and Freiburg, H. (1994) *Freedom to Learn*. New York: Macmillan.

Rowling, L. (1996) A comprehensive approach to handling sensitive issues in schools, with special reference to loss and grief. *Pastoral Care in Education*, March, 17–21.

Skinner, J. (1999a) Dealing with the aftermath of child sexual abuse: a reflection on three case examples. *Pastoral Care in Education*, March, 32–6.

Skinner, J. (1999b) Teachers coping with sexual abuse issues. *Educational Research*, 41(3): 329–39.

12 Counselling and guidance of parents

Garry Hornby

> Widespread support for involving parents in their children's learning grows out of convincing evidence suggesting that family involvement has positive effects on children's academic achievement, social competence and school quality.
>
> (Webster-Stratton, 1999, p. 6)

Providing counselling and guidance for parents is a key element of meeting the social and emotional needs of all children, but it is particularly important for those children with behavioural difficulties or mental health problems. This is because parents of children with these difficulties are likely to require greater support and guidance than many other parents. There are many ways in which teachers can work with such parents in order to provide the most effective help for their children. This chapter will consider what teachers need to know and do in order to provide effective counselling and guidance to parents. First, the attitudes, knowledge and skills which teachers need in order to provide guidance and counselling to parents are outlined. Then, a model for understanding different aspects of working with parents is presented and various strategies which teachers can use to establish and maintain effective communication with parents are described. This is followed by some suggestions for working with parents in groups and the organisation of parent workshops. The final section of the chapter focuses on working with challenging parents.

Attitudes, knowledge and skills needed by teachers

Attitudes
The attitudes which teachers need in order to provide effective counselling and guidance to parents are ones which will help them develop collaborative working relationships. To bring this about teachers need to communicate to parents the attitudes of *genuineness*, *respect* and *empathy* which were discussed in Chapter 2. Parents need teachers to be people of integrity who will not shy away from being open and honest with them, but will do this with sensitivity.

Knowledge
In order to provide effective counselling and guidance to parents, teachers need to have certain knowledge which is over and above that which they require for effectively teaching children. There are several aspects of this additional knowledge. First and foremost, teachers need to have a good knowledge of the strategies for working effectively with parents

which are discussed in this chapter. Teachers also need to have a good understanding of parents' perspectives, that is, they must be able to see and appreciate the parents' point of view. Teachers must also be aware of family dynamics and be able to view all children within the context of their families (see Chapter 8). In addition, teachers need to know specifically what they can do to help parents of children with various types of difficulties, such as children affected by bereavement and family breakdown (see Chapter 10) as well as those with disabilities (see Hornby, 1994). Teachers need to be knowledgeable about the range of services and other resources which are available to parents. They need to be sufficiently aware of the beliefs and customs of the ethnic groups with which they work to be able to adapt their interventions so that they are culturally appropriate. Teachers also need to have adequate knowledge of how to work effectively with challenging parents, as discussed later in this chapter.

Skills

In addition to communicating appropriate attitudes and possessing relevant knowledge, in order to work effectively with parents, teachers need to have good interpersonal skills. An essential part of this is the possession of basic listening skills (see Chapter 3). Other interpersonal skills required by teachers include the assertion skills needed for working with parents and for collaborating with colleagues (see Chapter 13). Teachers also need the organisational and communication skills necessary for maintaining contact with parents through meetings, home visits, letters and telephone calls. These forms of contact are discussed later in this chapter. In addition, teachers need the skills required for involving parents in their children's educational programmes such as home–school behaviour programmes. Finally, teachers need group leadership skills (see Chapter 5) so that they can organize workshops for parents, as discussed later in this chapter.

A model for working with parents

A model (adapted from Hornby, 2000) which illustrates various aspects of collaborating with parents in order to help children experiencing difficulties at school is presented in Figure 12.1. The model consists of two pyramids, one representing a hierarchy of parents' needs, the other a hierarchy of parents' possible contributions. Both pyramids demonstrate visually the different levels of needs and contributions of parents. Thus, while all parents have some needs and some potential contributions which can be utilised, a smaller number have an intense need for guidance, or the capability of making an extensive contribution. The model also shows that, for parents' needs at a higher level, more time and expertise is required by teachers in order to meet these needs. Each of the components of the model will now be outlined and the teachers' roles in each of these discussed.

Parents' needs

Communication

All parents need to have effective channels of communication with their children's teachers. Parents need to feel that they can contact the school any time they have a concern about their child. Some parents prefer to communicate by telephone, many would rather call in to see the teacher face to face, while others find that contact through a written note or letter suits them best. Therefore, teachers need to ensure that a wide range of communication options is open to parents.

PARENTAL NEEDS

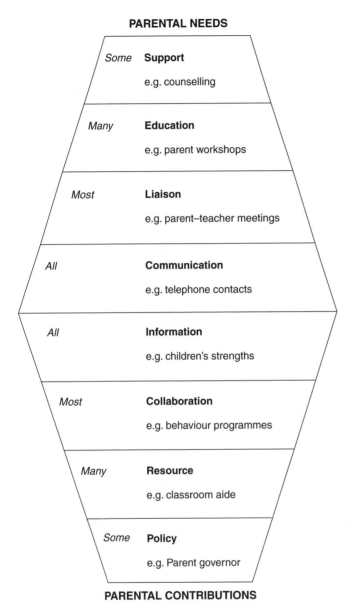

Figure 12.1 A model for working with parents.

Liaison

Most parents want to know how their children are getting on at school. They want to find out what their children have achieved and whether they are experiencing any difficulties. They regard teachers as the main source of information on their children's performance and behaviour at school and therefore need to have a good working partnership with them. Teachers can facilitate this by keeping in regular contact with parents through such means as telephone calls, home visits, letters and notes sent home, weekly report forms and by meeting with parents at school (Hornby, 2000).

Education

Many parents appreciate receiving guidance from teachers on dealing with their children's emotional or behavioural difficulties. In fact, they are much more likely to approach teachers, who are in daily contact with their children, than headteachers or educational psychologists, who they may see as less involved and more threatening. Class teachers are in an excellent position to provide parents with such guidance. They are knowledgeable about child development and see children on a daily basis, so have the chance to get to know them well and identify any changes in behaviour which occur. Therefore, opportunities for receiving such guidance should be freely available to all parents.

Support

Some parents of children with emotional or behavioural difficulties will be in need of supportive counselling, even though they may not actually request it. This support can be provided either individually by teachers, educational psychologists or social workers, or in groups such as self-help or support groups. Whereas most parents are reluctant to seek the help of professional counsellors, they will approach their children's teachers in search of guidance or counselling for the problems which concern them. Although such support should be available to all parents of children experiencing difficulties at school, if parents have good channels of communication and regular liaison with teachers, coupled with the opportunity to receive guidance about their children whenever they need it, then only a few of them will need extensive counselling at any particular time. Teachers should have a level of basic counselling skills sufficient to be good listeners and to help parents solve everyday problems. They should also be able to refer parents on to professional counsellors or support groups when problems raised are beyond their level of competence.

Parents' contributions

Information

All parents can contribute valuable information about their children because they have known them throughout their lives and have been the ones who have participated in previous contacts with professionals. Information concerning children's likes and dislikes, strengths and weaknesses, along with any relevant medical details can be gathered by teachers at parent–teacher meetings. Making full use of the parents' knowledge of their children not only enables teachers to provide more appropriate help, it also makes parents feel that they have been listened to and that an active interest has been taken in their children.

Collaboration

Most parents are willing and able to contribute more than just information. Most parents are willing and able to collaborate with teachers by reinforcing school-based behavioural programmes at home. However, while involvement in such schemes should always be offered to all parents, including those who have not collaborated in the past, it should be accepted that a small proportion of parents will not be able to participate for a variety of reasons. The class teacher's role is to optimize levels of collaboration for the maximum number of parents.

Resource

Many parents have the time and ability to act as voluntary teacher aides, either assisting in the classroom or on school trips. Others may have special skills which they can contribute such as in curriculum areas in which they have a special talent. In addition to the help which such parents provide their time at school helps cement collaborative relationships with teachers. Therefore, invitations for parents to help at the school need to be sent out regularly by such means as newsletters.

Policy

Some parents are able to contribute their expertise through membership of parent or professional organisations. This includes being a school governor, a member of the parent–teacher association (PTA), or being involved in a parent support or advocacy group. Others have the ability to provide a parent's perspective of children experiencing difficulties as a part of in-service training for teachers. Parents can influence policy on children with emotional or behavioural difficulties through their involvement as a governor or PTA member or through their involvement in parent support groups. Teachers should be on the look out for parents who can contribute in these ways so that their abilities can be used to the full.

Communicating with parents

There are five main methods for developing and maintaining effective communication between parents and teachers. These are informal contacts, various forms of written communication, telephone contacts, parent–teacher meetings and home visits. These are now discussed in turn, starting with informal contacts. Detailed guidelines for each of the five methods of communication with parents are described elsewhere (Hornby, 2000).

Informal contacts

Typical forms of informal contacts are school productions, open days, gala days and educational visits in the community. Such informal contacts are a useful way of 'breaking the ice' in most forms of human relationships and this is also the case in relationships with parents. These contacts provide a means whereby parents and teachers can meet each other as people with a mutual interest in building relationships on behalf of children, thereby helping to break down the barriers that often exist between school and home.

Written communication

Some parents prefer to communicate with teachers by means of letters. Other parents find that daily or weekly behaviour reports are the best means of keeping them in contact with the school when their child is experiencing difficulties. In addition, newsletters can keep parents in touch with what is happening at school. It is therefore clear that the written word provides an important means of communication between teachers and parents.

Telephone contacts

Some parents prefer to communicate with teachers by means of the telephone. Many parents appreciate the opportunity of being able to phone teachers directly either at school or at home. However, there are difficulties associated with both of these options. The main problem with parents calling up teachers at school is that teachers should have to leave their class to answer the telephone only in absolute emergencies. So it is best to get the school secretary to take messages and tell parents that the teacher will phone back as soon as possible. An alternative solution is to set a specified time during the week when parents know the teacher will be available to answer the phone.

Parent–teacher meetings

The form of contact with parents with which all teachers are familiar is that of parents' evenings or parent–teacher meetings. These meetings are a well-established method of involving parents and not without reason, as research has shown that they have an impact on both parent–teacher relationships and pupil progress. It has been found that children whose parents attend such meetings have higher attendance rates, fewer behavioural problems and improved academic achievement (Hornby, 2000). Of course experienced teachers would immediately suggest that this is because the parents of 'good kids' usually attend parents' evenings whereas parents of pupils with behavioural or learning difficulties tend not to turn up. However, it must not be assumed that parents who do not turn up to parents' evenings are not interested in their children's education. There are a variety of reasons why some parents do not attend such meetings, including transport and babysitting problems, as well as parents' negative feelings about their own school days. So additional forms of contact, such as home visits, telephone calls or written communication, need to be used.

Home visits

Many parents appreciate it when their children's teachers are prepared to come and visit them on their own territory. Such home visits can be pivotal in establishing close working relationships with parents. They enable teachers to see for themselves the circumstances in which the family is living. They also enable teachers to meet other members of the family such as siblings and fathers who they may not otherwise see. Knowledge of these factors can help teachers understand how their pupils may be affected by the home situation. Home visits also enable teachers to find out how their pupils spend their time at home, whether they have any hobbies, how much television they watch and what time they usually go to bed. It is also possible to find out how pupils behave at home and how their parents handle them. Finally, home visits provide an opportunity for teachers to answer parents' questions and provide any necessary guidance. This also provides an opportunity to learn about family circumstances and observe how parents manage their children at home.

Group guidance and counselling

Workshops and group parent education programmes can be very valuable for providing guidance and counselling to parents (Hornby, 1994). This section will consider the benefits of group work with parents and describe various types of parent education programmes so that teachers can learn how to provide group guidance and counselling for parents.

Benefits of group work with parents

The most important benefit of working with groups of parents is that, in talking with others, parents realise that they are not the only ones whose children are experiencing difficulties. In addition, parents can express their feelings regarding their children and discover that others have similar feelings, which often helps them come to terms with their own. Further, in a group with other parents, it is often easier for them to reveal concerns which they have not felt able to bring up individually.

Another benefit of group work is that parents experience mutual support from the other group members which helps them to become more confident in their own ability as parents. A further benefit of group work is that when parents participate in a group they learn together in a mutually supportive atmosphere and are often more responsive to changing their opinions and learning new strategies. Also, in a group, solutions for a particular parent's difficulties might be offered by other parents who may have experienced similar difficulties in the past. Parents tend to be more responsive to such potential solutions.

However, there are some negative aspects of doing group work with parents. Some parents do not feel comfortable being in a group with other parents and prefer to receive guidance individually. Also, in order to obtain maximum participation in group work with parents it is often necessary to hold sessions in evenings or at the weekend, which can cut into the teachers' leisure and preparation time. Finally, working with groups of parents requires skills and knowledge over and above that needed for individual work so these need to be acquired to a reasonable level before embarking on group work with parents. Group leadership skills and knowledge of group dynamics are described in detail in Chapter 5 and elsewhere (Hornby, 2000).

Parent guidance groups

Several programmes for providing guidance to groups of parents have been developed. The approaches described in this section are 'parent effectiveness training', 'parent behavioural training' and some other less widely used programmes.

Parent effectiveness training

Parent effectiveness training (PET) is the most widely disseminated parent education programme in the Western world with hundreds of thousands of parents having participated in it (Gordon, 1970). The aim of the programme is to facilitate communication and improve relationships between parents and their children. The programme consists of an eight-week course attended by ten to twelve parents with a leader who has been trained in leading PET groups. The methods used by leaders are a combination of demonstration and role-play of the skills being taught with open discussions conducted in a circle.

The programme focuses on four key aspects of parent–child relationships. First, parents are taught listening skills so that they can improve their ability to listen to their children. The most essential aspect of this is learning active listening, the skill which was discussed in Chapter 3. Second, parents are taught how to express their feelings using 'I' messages in order to avoid using 'you' messages which tend to put the blame on their children. Third, parents are taught how to analyse ownership of a problem so that they can decide which are their problems and which should be left with the child. The importance of allowing children to accept ownership of problems which belong to them is emphasised. Fourth, for problems whose ownership lies with both parents and children, parents are taught how to use a six-step method for resolving the conflict which is called 'no-lose problem solving'.

Behavioural group training

Behavioural group training (BGT) is a widely used approach to parent education with parents of children with behavioural problems and other kinds of special needs. The aim of

BGT is to teach parents the principles and practice of behavioural analysis in order to improve their management of their children's behavioural difficulties. BGT typically consists of an eight- to ten-week course attended by six to twelve parents and led by psychologists trained in behavioural methods. The training techniques used by the leaders include: lectures, modelling, role play, parent training manuals, discussion and homework assignments.

BGT programmes typically include the concept of positive reinforcement of appropriate behaviour, as well as discussion of the different types of reinforcers which parents can use and conditions for their effective use. Also covered are other techniques used to increase levels of appropriate behaviour such as stimulus control, contingency contracting and Premack's Principle. In addition, techniques used to decrease levels of inappropriate behaviour are taught, such as differential reinforcement, extinction, time out, response cost and over-correction (Graziano and Diament, 1992).

Other forms of group parent guidance

There are several other forms of group parent education programmes. Two of the better known of these will now be briefly described in order to demonstrate the wide range of approaches which are available. Systematic training for effective parenting (STEP) is a programme based on the ideas of Alfred Adler which have been developed into a parent education kit by Dinkmeyer and McKay (1976). The aim of STEP is to help parents develop a better understanding of their children's behaviour, improve communication with them and increase parents' influence over their children's behaviour. The STEP kit includes a leader's manual; charts which illustrate the main concepts to be taught; group discussion guideline cards; and cassette tapes with brief lectures and skill-building exercise for parents. Key aspects of the programme are study of the goals of children's behaviour and the application of natural consequences to deal with misbehaviour.

The Transactional Analysis approach to parent education is based on the ideas of Eric Berne which have been applied to children by Babcock and Keepers (1976). The aims of group parent education based on this approach are to increase parents' understanding of their relationships with their children and thereby to improve communication within the family. Key concepts in this approach are the 'ego states' of parent, adult and child which are highlighted in family communication and the complementary, crossed and ulterior transactions which occur within families. Also important are the 'basic life positions' adopted by individuals and the unconscious 'games' played by family members. Sessions include both didactic and experiential components. Relevant reading and practical homework assignments are used and specific problems brought to the group by participants are discussed and brainstormed within the group.

Combining different approaches

A particularly effective format for group parent guidance is one which combines guidance on children's development and behaviour with opportunities for parents to discuss their concerns. Parent guidance programmes which involve a group of parents, and employ a workshop format, easily lend themselves to providing a combination of guidance and sharing of concerns. This type of format enables parents to learn new skills and gain confidence through talking with other parents and teachers. A parent workshop model which uses this approach was developed in New Zealand in the 1980s and has been used since with a wide range of parent groups (see Hornby, 2000). The aim of this project was to develop the format for a parent workshop which combines group guidance in the form of brief presentations with group counselling conducted by means of small group discussions. It was considered that this format would provide a supportive environment in which parents could learn new skills and gain confidence through talking with other parents. The workshop can be used with groups of parents of children with a wide variety of difficulties including children with emotional or behavioural difficulties, those with disabilities or medical conditions, bereaved children and children from step-families.

Details of the parent workshop are presented below so that teachers can adapt it to suit the population of parents with whom they work.

PARENT WORKSHOPS: ORGANISATION

A summary of the main aspects of workshop organisation is presented below.

Recruitment. The best method of recruiting parents for workshops is by sending a letter of invitation to all parents likely to be concerned with the topic being addressed who are attending the school. Parents for whom workshops are not suitable tend not to participate from their own choice.

Venue. A venue which is familiar to the parents, comfortable and easy for parents to get to, is best. School staff-rooms are a popular choice of venue for smaller workshops.

Sessions. Between six and eight, weekly, two-hour evening sessions have been found to be the most satisfactory. Less than six sessions is too few for parents to benefit from the therapeutic process which the group will experience as the workshop progresses. More than eight sessions is often too great a commitment of time and too tiring for parents and teachers alike. Evening sessions are generally easier for both professionals and parents to attend but weekends can also be used. Two hours is considered to be the optimum time for the length of sessions.

Number of parents. Taking the group of parents as a whole can cater for a reasonably large number of parents during the introduction, presentation and final summary sections of the workshop and dividing them into small groups during the discussion section. About six to ten parents is generally the most satisfactory size for the small groups.

Group leaders. Small group discussions need to be led by professionals with previous experience of leading such groups. Teachers with no experience can be involved as co-leaders who work in tandem with the leader. In this way teachers can be trained to lead their own groups in subsequent parent workshops.

PARENT WORKSHOPS: FORMAT

Workshops are typically divided into four parts: introduction, presentation, small group discussion and summary. These are outlined next.

Introduction. The first fifteen minutes of workshops are used to help parents relax since many of them experience anxiety when they first come along to group sessions where they are expected to talk about their children. It provides an opportunity for parents to get to know other parents and teachers informally and also overcomes the problem of late arrivals interrupting the presentations.

Presentations. A maximum of twenty minutes is allowed for presentations to the whole group of parents, who are usually seated in a horseshoe arrangement around the speaker. The topics are best determined by sending out a list of potential topics beforehand and asking parents to suggest what they would like. Where necessary, relevant specialists can then be invited in to give some of the presentations. Clearly, the topics will depend on the needs of the children whose parents are involved in the workshops.

Small group discussions. The largest block of time in the workshop, of over an hour, is given over to discussion which is conducted in small groups. Discussions are conducted in separate rooms, with chairs arranged in a circle. Groups usually consist of a leader, a co-leader and six to ten parents. Leaders guide the discussions using the skills discussed in Chapter 5. Co-leaders work in tandem with leaders by focussing on the group dynamics and on the body language of group members so that they can draw the leader's attention to a parent who may want to say something but hasn't been noticed.

Summary. With all the parents present, a leader or co-leader from each small group reports back on the issues and concerns discussed in their group. Any handouts, such as a summary of the presentation for that session, are distributed and homework tasks, such as the completion of behaviour observation forms, are explained.

Working with challenging parents

Since parents, like teachers, have a range of personalities, some will be easy to work with and others will be more difficult. There will always be conflict caused by a small minority of parents. In fact, a certain amount of conflict has to be expected when parents and teachers work together because they have different perspectives. Since parents are advocating for their own children it is impossible for them to be totally objective in their judgements. Sometimes, their subjectivity leads to conflict with the teacher's views. Since some conflict between parents and teachers is inevitable teachers must be aware of the types of difficulties they are likely to encounter and need to know of appropriate techniques for dealing with them

The remainder of this chapter will focus on eight types of parents who are difficult for teachers to work with. For each type, the aspects of the parent's behaviour which are challenging are clarified and suggestions for how teachers can best approach working with such parents are outlined. These suggestions are discussed in more detail elsewhere (Hornby, 2000).

Unsupportive parents   It is particularly annoying to teachers when parents do not support their efforts in carrying out activities which are designed to involve them, such as in not attending parent–teacher meetings or not implementing behavioural programmes agreed with their child's teacher. It often appears to teachers that these parents just do not care enough about their children, but this is seldom the case. Some parents may be so over-whelmed by the demands of caring for their family that they have little time or energy left for involvement in their children's education. Teachers must attempt to get to know unsup-portive parents better and use listening and counselling skills in order to work toward a solution. It may well be that alternative forms of interaction need to be considered, for example, the teacher making occasional phone calls to parents, or notes sent home with children, instead of expecting parents to attend meetings at the school.

Uncooperative parents   Some parents are not just unsupportive, they are downright uncooperative. For example, some professional parents can be condescending, excessively critical or make unreasonable demands of teachers. Other parents give the impression of being too busy to devote time to activities such as listening to their children read at home. In contrast, some parents are so keen to become involved in activities, such as doing voluntary work in the school, that they can become too helpful and overstep their responsibilities or threaten to take over. Dealing effectively with uncooperative parents requires teachers to use the assertion skills which are discussed in Chapter 13. For example, they should be physically and vocally assertive and be prepared to use strategies such as the four-step process for responding to criticism, and the modified DESC script (see Chapter 13) for giving constructive feedback to parents.

Hostile parents, complaining parents, threatening parents   Some of the most difficult situations teachers have to deal with are when parents complain about something they see as the teacher's responsibility. Even worse are situations in which parents become aggressive or threaten teachers. Parents may have a genuine grievance with the teacher for which they are justifiably angry, or, more likely, another aspect of their lives has made them angry and they are inappropriately displacing this onto the teacher. Either way, it is important for teachers not to argue with parents but to stay calm and actively listen to what they have to say. By listening carefully, teachers can ensure that parents will calm down and can also determine whether parents' complaints are justified or not. If they may be justified then the four-stage process for dealing with criticism can be used (see Chapter 13). When parents' complaints are not justified, it is important to assertively refute them, but this can only be done when they are no longer being aggressive.

Abusing parents   The most frequently occurring form of abuse is neglect but teachers also have a role to play in identifying other types of mistreatment by parents, that is physical, sexual and emotional abuse. The key roles which teachers play in all types of abuse are: identifying potential cases of abuse; referring these on to the member of staff responsible for dealing with such cases; and, providing a supportive and caring environment for these children within the school. Therefore, teachers need to know how to identify the signs of the different forms of abuse children are subjected to. With *neglect* the child is often tired or hungry, dressed inappropriately, left unsupervised outside school hours or has medical needs which are not attended to. With *emotional abuse* children may exhibit antisocial or destructive behaviour. They may be withdrawn or aggressive and exhibit self-stimulatory behaviour such as rocking. With physical abuse there is evidence of non-accidental injuries such as bruises, burns, abrasions, bite marks, cuts and fractures. With *sexual abuse* children may be uncomfortable when sitting, reluctant to change for physical education, appear withdrawn or depressed, display precocious behaviour or demonstrate knowledge of sexual behaviour beyond their years.

Parents with personal, marital or family problems   Parents who are wrapped up in their own problems are a great concern to teachers because it is clear that they are unable to pay sufficient attention to their children's needs. Parents who are coping with the effects of traumatic events, such as a death in the family or separation or divorce, often become so overwhelmed by their own problems that children's needs are overlooked. When teachers suspect that parents' problems are affecting their children's behaviour they need to raise their concerns, tactfully, with the parents. This should be done in a face-to-face meeting with the parents, preferably at school but during a home visit if necessary. Most parents will appreciate the teacher bringing this to their attention. Teachers will need to use the listening skills presented in Chapter 3 in order to conduct this initial interview successfully. Once the problem has been acknowledged parents can be referred on to individuals and groups in the community who can provide the specialist personal, marital or family counselling that is needed.

Vulnerable parents   Some parents are vulnerable themselves and therefore need help in ensuring that their children's needs are addressed. Parents with their own health problems, or who are unemployed or poverty-stricken may not have the energy to attend to their children's emotional needs. Teachers need to reach out to these parents. If it is not possible to get them to come to the school then home visits will be necessary. In many cases, these parents will need guidance regarding their children's development and behaviour which, because of their experience with children, teachers are well able to give. Many of these parents will also benefit from the kinds of group parent guidance programmes discussed above.

Parents who expect too much or too little   Some parents are too perfectionist in their demands of their children's achievements. Other parents are overprotective of their children and expect too little. Teachers need to address the issue of expectations with such parents. They need to deal with them tactfully but assertively. It is counter-productive to get into an argument with parents about whether a child is capable of more or less. Teachers should keep the focus on an objective evaluation of what the child has achieved so far and on realistic suggestions of what should be tackled next.

Parents from different cultural backgrounds   Teachers often find it difficult working with parents who come from different cultural backgrounds to themselves and lower levels of parental involvement are usually in evidence for these parents. Parents who are from minority ethnic or cultural groups generally find it more difficult to interact with their children's teachers. Language difficulties may play a part in this, as does parents' apprehension about relating to teachers who are mainly from the mainstream cultural group. There are often also value differences as in many cultures collaboration between parents and teachers is not seen as something which is necessary or even desirable. Therefore, teachers need to learn more about the cultural norms and values of parents from different cultural groups so that they can work more effectively with them. They should be prepared to adapt their expectations and means of communication in order to optimise the effectiveness of their guidance for these parents.

References

Babcock, D. E. and Keepers, T. D. (1976) *Raising Kids O.K.* New York: Grove.

Dinkmeyer, D. C. and McKay, G. D. (1976) *Systematic Training for Effective Parenting*. Circle Pines, MN: American Guidance Service.

Gordon, T. (1970) *Parent Effectiveness Training*. New York: Wyden.

Graziano, A. M. and Diament, D. M. (1992) Parent behavioral training: an examination of the paradigm. *Behavior Modification*, 16(1): 3–38.

Hornby, G. (1994) *Counselling in Child Disability*. London: Chapman and Hall.

Hornby, G. (2000) *Improving Parental Involvement*. London: Cassell.

Webster-Stratton, C. (1999) *How to Promote Children's Social and Emotional Competence*. London: Paul Chapman.

13 Learning to collaborate

Working across the divide

Carol Hall and Garry Hornby

It takes a whole village to raise a child.

African proverb

In this chapter, we argue that the social, emotional and psychological health care needs of our most vulnerable students cannot always be met by teachers in schools single-handedly. Inter-agency and interprofessional collaboration are prerequisites for effective early intervention and service delivery for families and children at risk. Consultation frameworks with professional partners in the human services agencies can provide valuable opportunities for teacher as well as student learning and development, if managed effectively.

Personal limits to helping

A core competence for anyone who provides counselling is the ability to recognise and acknowledge the 'heart sink' moment when they no longer have the emotional capacity, knowledge or expertise to support someone's progress single-handed. The experienced counsellor will know that if the client is to be supported towards *long-term, competent self-management*, then they may need to discuss the possibility of appropriate consultation or referral to other support agencies. This can be a delicate and sensitive issue because it raises emotional as well as practical issues for both client and counsellor (Williams, 1993).

Similarly, even the most experienced of teachers will from time to time be confronted with a student whose disturbing behaviour or lack of academic progress is merely a symptom of a much more complex web of distress. Every teacher, at some time during their career, will experience this 'heart sink' moment. You can't help alone. Your resources are insufficient to scratch the surface of what is needed in terms of practical and emotional support.

Philip was a shy, excessively polite eleven-year-old, whose academic work was deteriorating steadily. His school attendance was erratic. His homework was always late. He was becoming increasingly withdrawn from his peer group and particularly unforthcoming with adults. His form tutor and other colleagues initially put down this behaviour to a painful and prolonged adjustment to secondary school life and tried the usual school sanctions to bring him into line. Reporting to the head of year with a report card and homework diary did little to change Philip's pattern of behaviour. Finally, Philip's friends from primary school began to drop hints to their tutor that something more sinister was going on. Patient and sensitive one-to-one work with Philip eventually revealed a story of marital breakdown, domestic violence, religious zealotry and physical and emotional abuse at home. The form tutor realised that if Philip was to get both the immediate and longer-term support he needed, within a family, as well as within a school context, then other agencies needed to be brought in.

The form tutor was experienced in counselling young people in her care but had reached the limits of what she could achieve with Philip alone. Despite the emotional closeness of the relationship, she had the experience and self-awareness to acknowledge this and that Philip needed the accumulated expertise and resources of other support services if he and his family were to be helped.

For novice teachers or teachers without basic training in counselling and helping skills, accurate diagnosis, consultation mechanisms or referral can be problematic processes. As a form tutor some twenty-five years ago, one of the authors was faced with a student who, as the months went by, literally appeared to be wasting away. As a young, inexperienced teacher, without any training, knowledge or personal experience of the signs of eating disorders, it was during an informal conversation with the head of year, that these concerns were raised. The head of year, alerted by the seriousness of the patterns of behaviour described, immediately contacted the school educational psychologist, who assisted in a systematic needs evaluation, finally leading to the engagement of the health and child psychiatric services.

How many more serious mental health issues such as depression, suicidal thoughts, substance abuse, self-harm, phobic disorders and so on, go similarly unrecognised by teachers unschooled in mental health issues, can be gauged by the claim that

> Between 10 and 20 per cent of children may require help at some time – that amounts to nearly two million children under the age of sixteen in England and Wales.
>
> (Young Minds, 1996, p. 11)

Evidence submitted to a Mental Health Foundation inquiry, was overwhelming in its conclusion that if specialist therapeutic or clinical interventions are to have a chance of success, young people at risk need to be recognised and assessed as early as possible (Atkinson and Hornby, 2002). The inquiry also reported the following key components of good practice in schools (The Mental Health Foundation, 1999, p. 60).

- early identification and assessment;
- work with the family as well as the child;
- inter-agency collaboration, particularly with health;
- flexible approach, including consultation as well as direct service from the educational psychology service;
- training for staff in schools on mental health issues.

This underlines the crucial role that pastoral teams have in the early recognition of troubled young people. Students may have the catch-all label 'emotional and behavioural difficulties' (EBD) attached to them, without necessarily having clear institutional policies for continuing the support process. Kottler and Kottler (1993, p. 13) provide teachers with a simple checklist to help assess whether further internal or external support is required for students who appear to be in difficulty.

- Is the behaviour unusual for the student?
- Is there a pattern to the behaviour?
- What further information do I need to make a judgement?

- Who can help me gather this information?
- Can I afford to wait?
- Is the student in danger?
- How can I improve my relationship with the student right now?
- Who do I need to consult?

However, one vital element of such a checklist is missing. At some stage in the diagnostic process, a teacher will need to undertake an honest and searching *self-assessment and self-appraisal.*

- Can I handle my own emotional reactions and responses to the student now and in the future?

Teachers who engage in helping and supporting relationships with vulnerable young people will inevitably find powerful feelings emerging within themselves, at some stage during the helping process. The strength of such unlooked for responses may catch even trained and experienced teachers by surprise and leave some confused and temporarily deskilled, while others may become evangelical in their determination to 'rescue' the child. Over-identification with the student's issue can render teachers incompetent to maintain the appropriate emotional distance for effective helping. In such cases, the management of the relationship should be handed to a colleague.

Even for experienced teachers, having the confidence to acknowledge that there are limits to their helping capacity may be an issue. But King (1999) reminds us that there may also be moral or ethical reasons why a teacher may not be appropriate to work with a student. For example, a teacher with strong views about abortion may not be the best person to work alongside a young girl who has just discovered she is pregnant. A teacher who has a religious objection or a strong negative reaction to a particular sexual orientation or behaviour, may rule themselves out of talking to a student who has anxieties about sexuality. Above all, teachers need the honesty and self-awareness to know when the problem a student brings may be too near their own emotional experience to be able to make professionally sound judgements. For example, a newly bereaved teacher may not have the emotional resources necessary to support a child going through a similar process.

Working in partnership: the new professionalism

Students, as their teachers are only too aware, do not come into school vacuum packed. They bring with them the 'lifespaces' which they inhabit for good or ill (Watkins, 1989) and as Corrigan (2000) observes, the impact of these lifespaces on school performance can be devastating. Life inside school has also become increasingly stressful for students. Regular testing, preparation for public examinations and the publication of national league tables for schools have forced teachers to concentrate their efforts on curriculum delivery rather than on student welfare and guidance. Wholesale educational reform, from professional cradle to grave, has taken place and the pace of this change agenda has to a large extent been driven externally, resulting in a fundamental redrawing of the map of teachers' working lives (Day *et al.*, 2000). Hargreaves and Fullan (1998) argue that in order to deliver on this standards agenda, both the pedagogical and relationship skills teachers need to carry out their professional roles have changed significantly. At the heart of the 'new professionalism' lies the ability to initiate, sustain and learn from collaborative, collegial relationships.

As teachers work more and more with people beyond their own schools, a whole gamut of new skills, relationships and orientations are fundamentally changing the orientation of their professionalism. This new professionalism is collaborative, not autonomous; open rather than closed; outward-looking rather than insular; and authoritative not controlling.

However, partnership, team work, collaboration, consultation, are all relatively new terms in the professional vocabulary of teachers, and while lip-service is paid to inter-group and inter-organisational co-operation, many teachers in leadership roles report that the day-to-day management of adult relationships can be more stressful, psychologically and socially, than relationships with students in the classroom (Day *et al.*, 1993). Fullan and Hargreaves (1992, p. 55) claim that there is still a long way to go before teachers are prepared to forego their traditional professional independence and autonomy,

However, the tendency to view isolation as autonomy can reveal the extent of the teachers' vulnerability when their traditional classroom management or emotional coping strategies fail if confronted with extremely challenging student behaviour.

Getting help

When teachers feel that they have exhausted their repertoire of strategies for dealing with individuals or groups of students, they need to know where they can turn for help and how to ask for it assertively. The ability to recognise the need for support and the assertiveness skills in requesting it, are at the heart of the new professionalism that Fullan and Hargreaves describe (1992). Alongside this competence must exist the institutional culture, enshrined in policies and procedures, which facilitate and validate the process of asking to consult colleagues when the going gets tough. Kottler and Kottler (1993) remind us that there are pragmatic reasons why teachers need to become more consciously competent at the process of consultation and collaboration. The spin-offs for teachers include:

- benefitting from the knowledge and expertise of other professionals;
- looking at issues or problems that students present from a different angle;
- hearing a detached perspective on critical incidents;
- benefitting from an extra pair of hands to handle demanding tasks;
- learning through having in-service training provided from outside 'experts'.

Glosoff and Korowicz (1990) add,

- helping to interpret student data, for example, standardised test results;
- designing and leading parenting programmes;
- participating in school committees that involve student guidance issues;
- providing relevant curriculum materials related to PSE;
- identifying and developing specialist programmes for students with special needs.

Successful collaboration in action

Schools are used to thinking of the educational psychology and other services as service deliverers. In fact, a no less important strand of their expertise is consultancy. Using expert colleagues as consultants can empower teachers by stretching their imagination and creativity about what it is possible to achieve. They also feel that they no longer have to struggle with intransigent problems alone. Miller's study (1994) provides examples of successful behaviour-support interventions in schools when educational psychologists and teachers got together to work jointly on strategies for managing challenging classroom behaviour. By training, educational psychologists are rigorous problem-solvers, who relish the opportunity to work collaboratively with teachers in order to solve seemingly insoluble dilemmas. Through the consultative process, they aim to develop the teachers' working repertoire of interventions with individuals or groups. Within the consultative relationship lies the opportunity for teacher, student and organisational learning. Miller's research describes and demonstrates the learning process which went on for teachers involved in his study. From the interview data, it emerged that teachers working with students with emotional and behavioural difficulties in their classrooms had commonly reported feeling overwhelmed, at a loss and with a reduced range of coping strategies. In other words nothing they tried with these students seemed to work. Coupled with this was a pervasive sense of having to cope alone, that student behaviour was their responsibility to manage and no one else would, could or wanted to help when things went wrong. This had the knock-on effect of lowering teacher self-esteem, producing feelings of incompetence and heightened their sense of being stressed and out of control.

When educational psychologists worked together with the teachers on positive intervention strategies with behaviourally challenging students, the results were impressive. Teachers in the study reported significant improvement in students' behaviour and were themselves startled at the efficacy of the planned interventions. Describing the problems and working with a supportive and trained professional had worked. Miller (1994) draws out valuable conclusions about the relationship dimension to these successful consultations. Key elements in the consultation process were, he claims:

- professional knowledge base – the psychologists had additional experience, information and insight that they were able to offer;
- skills – the communication skills of the consultant, for example, active listening and the ability to create a problem-solving dialogue with the teachers;
- personal qualities – the emotional intelligence of the consultant in being able to offer encouragement, empathic understanding and the ability to oil the wheels of social interactions;
- the role of the psychologist – authority and detachment were ascribed by the teachers to the consulting psychologist's role, so that their advice was taken seriously.

These findings are echoed by Day *et al.* (1998) who further argue that *both* partners in the relationship need to demonstrate a high level of skilful interpersonal behaviour if the relationship is to survive.

Relationship skills for successful collaboration

Working successfully in collaboration with, or consulting fellow professionals, whether it be fellow teachers, educational psychologists, social workers, Education Welfare Officers (EWO's), the police, Local Education Authorities (LEA) officers, health workers and the rest, takes more than simply agreeing to a common agenda and sticking to it. The Children Act requires agencies to work together in the best interests of the child (Working Together, Department of Health, 1991), but the 'best interests of the child' is still in practice all too often interpreted from an individual agency standpoint rather than negotiating agreed practices between agencies.

Cultural differences between organisations such as values, aims, policies, procedures, priorities, even working hours, abound, and can mean that durable collaboration, in the best interests of the child, is an elusive goal. Professional discourse gives voice to these organisational differences and it is perfectly possible to attend an inter-agency case conference where professionals appear to be using the same language but missing each others' meaning or emphasis entirely. Perceptions of organisational difference also can be picked up through the pervasive myths and stereotypes which exist to describe colleagues. Everyone knows that you can never get hold of an educational psychologist when you need one, social workers never answer the phone, teachers only care about their subject and don't understand the 'real' world that kids have to grow up in and doctors think they're god. Additionally, disagreements over the allocation or targeting of scarce human or financial resources can be compounded by over perceptions of power relations between agencies.

Fundamental disagreements, tensions, misunderstandings and frustration come with the emotional turf, so if teachers want their professional voices heard and understood in this climate, they will need to develop their assertiveness skills. Knowing how to build trust, maintain rapport and encourage co-operation in interpersonal relationships is therefore a prerequisite for any teacher involved in inter-agency partnership. The ability to employ these behaviours takes self-awareness, emotional stamina, interpersonal intelligence and flexibility of mind. However, few training courses are available for teachers who wish to develop these skills. The theory and practice of assertiveness provides a comprehensive repertoire of interpersonal strategies which can equip teachers to conduct themselves effectively in inter-agency dialogue.

Ironically, assertiveness is a term which is often poorly understood. Ask a group of teachers to describe an assertive person and they will often describe someone who is 'in your face', self-centred, and puts their own interests first. In fact nothing could be wider of the mark. Assertiveness is rooted in the notion that in relationships all of us enjoy basic rights but alongside these rights goes the responsibility to safeguard and promote the rights of others. In this sense it offers us a principled, humanistic view of interpersonal relationships as well as a set of communication skills to live out these values. Michelli (1998, p. 9) defines assertive communication as that which does not diminish or 'put down' another human being, it does not trespass on any human rights and it does not shy away from important issues. Rather, it encourages satisfactory communication where everyone's needs are being met in the best way.

Jakubowski and Lange (1978) present a 'bill of rights' that we can both expect from and offer to others, the right to:

- be treated with respect;
- self-fulfilment which does not violate the rights of others;
- experience and express feelings;
- take time to think about things;
- change your mind;
- ask for what you want;
- ask for information;
- do less than you are capable of;
- make mistakes;
- say 'no' without feeling guilty;
- feel good about yourself.

As a simple self-reflection exercise try reflecting on how many of these rights you feel entitled to claim and whether you feel confident enough to defend or maintain the rights of others in your relationships. The following strategies, taken from Hornby (1994), if practiced skilfully, can help to improve your communication with others.

Non-verbal assertion

It is important to start with an increased awareness of body posture. An upright, confident posture and expressive facial movements, with the ability to maintain good eye contact and no fidgeting or superfluous gestures all indicate an assertive personality, while invading people's space by finger pointing, getting too close or inappropriate touching will be interpreted as aggression. In order to enhance the effectiveness of what you want to say, use a firm, steady tone of voice. Take regular, deep breaths in order to stay relaxed and maintain calmness, especially if the conversation is becoming emotionally charged or overheated. A diffident, quiet voice will give the impression of passivity, while a loud, hectoring tone will be interpreted as intimidatory.

Asking for help and making requests

Teachers sometimes need to ask for help from colleagues and occasionally need to make requests of parents and other professionals. However, asking someone to do something for us is difficult for people, particularly so for those who lack confidence in themselves. Of course, it depends on variables such as how well we know the person, whether we have done something for them recently and how much of a nuisance we guess the request will cause them. However, whatever the situation, there are ways of increasing the chances of success without damaging your relationship with the other person. Manthei (1981) has provided some useful guidelines for making requests:

- state your request directly;
- say exactly what you want;
- focus on the positive;
- allow the person time to think about it;
- be prepared to compromise;
- recognise that the other person has the right to refuse your request.

Responding to verbal aggression

Teachers are occasionally subjected to verbal aggression by stressed or emotionally immature people around them. This might come from parents who feel aggrieved or have a sense of injustice, or through a disagreement with a colleague. Schools are emotional places and inevitably these emotions will spill over into anger and frustration which is expressed in negative or potentially destructive ways. It is vital to have coping strategies for these testing times. Techniques such as empathic assertion and selective ignoring can be learned and practiced to good effect (Bolton, 1979).

Empathic assertion

This is the best strategy for responding to someone who may be justifiably angry but is perhaps venting their aggression on the wrong person. It is clearly important that teachers can respond to anger or aggression in a way which defuses the tension and yet deals with the person's concerns. Empathic assertion involves using active listening skills. The person on the receiving end of the aggression identifies the feelings and the key message in what the aggressor is communicating and feeds it back to him or her. This confirms that you are not only listening but also that you understand the person's concern and feelings. For example, 'You object to what I did and you are angry about it'. Continue to listen attentively and calmly, occasionally reflecting back your understanding of the key issues, until the aggressor is convinced they have been understood, and have calmed down. Then you can assertively express your point of view. If the other person starts to become aggressive again, repeat the process.

Selective ignoring

This is a technique used mainly for dealing with verbal abuse such as sarcasm or comments intended as put downs. It involves telling the other person that you object to their comments and firmly requesting them to stop. If the abuse continues, make it clear that unless the put downs stop, you will not engage in further conversation. If the person continues to be abusive, then ignore them. If they ask why you're silent, simply repeat your condition for further dialogue. When the other person begins to speak without being abusive, resume the conversation and make a point of being particularly civil.

Responding to criticism

Holland and Ward (1990) have described a model which is useful in considering how to respond to criticism and turn it into useful feedback. The four steps of the model are described below.

Listening to the criticism

Use listening and responding skills to clarify what is being said. For example, 'That's an interesting perspective, it would be helpful if you could be more specific'. Asking for more feedback suggests that you are listening and are open to further dialogue. If additional feedback is given you may need to sort out priorities and deal with them one at a time.

Deciding on the truth

Before making a response, it is important to consider whether it is accurate. With honest reflection, you may consider it to be wholly or partially accurate or have no validity at all. The skill lies in putting your feelings on hold, while you decide which it is.

Responding assertively

If the feedback is fair, then it is best to acknowledge it. A brief apology may be helpful and an assurance that you will correct the situation. If the feedback is partially valid, then agree with the part considered to be valid. Again, briefly apologise, but at the same time correct the part which you consider to be an incorrect assessment. If the feedback is unjustified, it should be firmly but politely rejected, telling the other person exactly how you feel and perhaps seeking further explanation, followed by a positive self-evaluation. For example, 'I don't agree that I was wrong in that case and I'm offended by the suggestion. What grounds do you have for making such a comment? I believe my relationships with my students are generally very good'.

Letting go

It is important not to dwell on any perceived criticism you receive as it usually only represents the opinion of one person. Try to see all information you receive, intentionally or unintentionally, as an opportunity to learn more about how others perceive you and therefore as a vehicle for growth.

Giving constructive feedback

The ability to give as well as receive constructive feedback is an important skill for both our professional and personal lives. Giving constructive feedback aims to help relationships function more effectively through increasing the flow of information and therefore understanding. A model for providing constructive feedback which is extremely useful, is that adapted from the DESC script popularised by Bower and Bower (1976). DESC stands for:

Describe
Express or explain
Specify and
Consequences.

This is a valuable technique for use with young people as well as adults. The four steps involved in using the adapted DESC model for giving feedback are:

Describe. First, describe the behaviour giving concern in the most specific and objective terms possible. For example, 'when you change meeting times without consulting me I feel ...'

Express or Explain. Then you either express your feelings about this behaviour or explain the difficulties it causes for you, or sometimes include both in your statement. Your explanation or your feelings should be expressed calmly and positively without blaming or judging the other person, or 'putting them down.' For example, 'I feel annoyed (express) because decisions were made which affect me without my input' (explain).

Specify. Then you specify the exact change in behaviour you want from the other person. Suggest only one change and make sure that it is well within the other person's capability to make the change. For example, 'So, in future, will you make sure you consult me in advance if you need to change meeting times ...'

Consequences. The consequences which are likely to result from the other person complying with your request for the change in behaviour are stated. The benefits for both of you should be stated. For example, ' ... then, we will be able to maintain our excellent working relationship'.

The modified DESC script is simple enough to be delivered spontaneously but it may sometimes be worth rehearsing it beforehand. This gives you the opportunity to make sure the wording is assertive. You then need to decide when, where and how you are going to deliver it most appropriately (Hornby, 1994).

Expressing feelings

Many societies do not encourage the expression of feelings so people tend to suppress them. This method of emotional coping may work reasonably well for some time until the feelings become too intense and burst out in the form of angry, aggressive or exaggerated behaviour. What we need to learn are assertive ways of expressing emotion which enable us to communicate feelings without violating the rights of others and enable a dialogue to ensue.

Gordon (1970) made a useful contribution to improving this situation when he proposed using 'I' messages to express feelings. The simplest form of 'I' message includes the words, '*I feel*', for example, 'When you do that, I feel angry.' This is in preference to, 'You make me angry when you do that,' which conveys a strong element of blame and tends to make the other person react defensively. 'I' messages take responsibility for and own feelings. 'I' messages therefore enable the expression of feelings directly to another person without prompting a negative or defensive reaction from them. In fact 'I' messages tend to facilitate empathic responses in the other person.

The following are guidelines which specifically focus on the expression of anger. However, they can be used to facilitate the assertive expression of any emotion (Hornby, 1994).

- Recognise that anger should be expressed assertively not aggressively;
- Remember you are responsible for your own feelings;
- Learn to recognise the things that trigger your anger;
- Realise that feeling angry does not make you right;
- Remember that people don't have to change just because you're angry;
- Learn to relax and apply this when you're angry;
- Deal with issues spontaneously when they arise and don't stew.

In conclusion: can consultation be a cop-out?

McNamara and Moreton (1995: 31) argue strongly that reliance on the external expert or consultant to 'solve' or manage the students' (or teachers') problems can result in a dependency culture which may eventually lead to the deskilling or learned helplessness of the teacher. They comment that, 'It is our view that reliance on external sources of help tends to increase the problem rather than solve it'.

The key word here seems to be 'reliance'. We would share McNamara and Moreton's concern about an over-reliance or dependence on external support. It is crucial that schools first own the responsibility for existing problems and then map out a strategic plan for resolving them with external support when necessary.

Teachers live with the professional responsibility and the day-to-day reality of teaching *all* students in their care, valuing the cultural, physical and intellectual diversity and difference that each of them brings with them to the classroom. The professional imperative for inclusive practice, means that teachers will need to become more skilled at pulling together and holding in place resources – human, technical and economic – which can support vulnerable students and their carers. The process of consultation in its best and broadest sense, can serve to test and retest teachers' mental models, assumptions and habitual patterns of perception, so that schools develop into learning communities.

References

Atkinson, M. and Hornby, G. (2002) *Mental Health Handbook for Schools*. London: Routledge/Falmer.

Bolton, R. (1979) *People Skills*. Englewood Cliffs, NJ: Prentice-Hall.

Bower, S. A. and Bower, G. H. (1976) *Asserting Yourself*. Reading, MA: Addison-Wesley.

Corrigan, D. (2000) The changing role of schools and higher education institutions with respect to community-based interagency collaboration and interprofessional partnerships. *Peabody Journal of Education*, 75(3): 176–195.

Day, C., Fernandez, A., Hauge, T. E. and Miller, J. (2000) *The Life and Work of Teachers*. London: Falmer Press.

Day, C., Hall, C., Coles, M. and Gammage, P. (1993) *Leadership and Curriculum in the Primary School*. London: Paul Chapman.

Day, C., Hall, C. and Whitaker, P. (1998) *Developing Leadership in Primary Schools*. London: Paul Chapman.

Department of Health (1991) *Working Together (under The Children Act)*. London: HMSO.

Fullan, M. and Hargreaves, A. (1992) *What's Worth Fighting for in Your School?* Buckingham: Open University Press.

Glosoff, H. and Koprowicz, C. (1990) *Children Achieving Potential: An Introduction to Elementary School Counseling and State-level Policies*. Washington, DC: National Conference of State Legislatures and American Association for Counseling and Development.

Gordon, T. (1970) *Parent Effectiveness Training*. New York: Wyden.

Hargreaves, A. and Fullan, M. (1998) *What's Worth Fighting for in Education?* Buckingham: Open University Press.

Holland, S. and Ward, C. (1990) *Assertiveness: A Practical Approach*. Bicester: Winslow Press.

Hornby, G. (1994) *Counselling in Child Disability*. London: Chapman and Hall.

Jakubowski, P. and Lange, A. J. (1978) *The Assertive Option*. Champaign, Ill: Research Press.

King, G. (1999) *Counselling Skills for Teacher*. Buckingham: Open University Press.

Kottler, J. A. and Kottler, E. (1993) *Teacher as Counselor*. California: Corwin Press.

Manthei, M. (1981) *Positively Me: A Guide to Assertive Behaviour*. Auckland: Methuen.

McNamara, S. and Moreton, G. (1995) *Changing Behaviour*. London: David Fulton.

Mental Health Foundation (1999) *Bright Futures: Promoting Children and Young People's Mental Health*. London: Mental Health Foundation.

Miller, A. (1994) Mainstream teachers talking about successful behaviour support. In P. Gray A. Miller and J. Noakes (eds) *Challenging Behaviour in Schools*. London: Routledge.

Watkins, C. (1989) Parental involvement in the upper school. *Pastoral Care in Education*, June, pp. 77–85.

Williams, S. (1993) *Referral Issues for Counsellors*. Manchester: PCS Books.

Young Minds (1996) *Mental Health in Your School: A Guide for Teachers and Schools*. London: Jessica Kingsley.

14 Coping with stress and avoiding burn-out

Garry Hornby and Carol Hall

> Never before have teachers been so vulnerable and important at the same time.
>
> (Hargreaves and Fullan, 1998, p. xii)

The purpose of this chapter is to provide teachers with the necessary tools to enable them to be proactive managers of their personal and professional levels of stress, thereby avoiding the possibility of occupational 'burn out'. We will also encourage teachers to use the knowledge, skills and strategies we outline to inform debate about whole school approaches to coping with organisational stressors and to pass on basic stress management techniques to their students, parents and colleagues. In the first part of the chapter, theories of stress and burn-out are discussed and the importance of identifying the symptoms of stress over-load is emphasised. A comprehensive model for stress management is presented which can be used as the basis for whole school development planning. The model includes strategies which focus on personal, interpersonal, task related and organisational factors, all of which need to be addressed in order to manage stress effectively. Finally, the application of stress management techniques to common student stressors such as test anxiety, is discussed.

Teacher stress

Stress is an intrinsic element of human biology, psychology, social relationships and organisational structures. Stress is therefore an inevitable consequence of being human and alive. In order to reflect on how we might wish to safeguard ourselves from the more deleterious effects of stress, it is first necessary to accommodate this fact psychologically and emotionally. However, not all stress results in a negative outcome. Stress that motivates us to push against the limits of our human experience or learning, that we perceive as challenging rather than debilitating, is called 'eustress'. Eustress stimulates teachers to develop their professional competence and perform their roles more effectively.

However, when an individual perceives that the degree of stress they experience is too high, this can tip them into 'distress'. The subsequent loss of confidence and prediction of negative outcomes may lead to deterioration in performance or relationships. One of the writers, as a newly qualified teacher noticed that while other colleagues looked forward to Friday afternoons because the weekend beckoned, the hostile class of fourteen-year-old boys who lay in wait for double English, made her wish Friday would never come. Generally, though, it has come to be accepted that when we talk of teacher stress, we are referring to what Kyriacou (1997) defines as,

> ... the experience by a teacher of unpleasant emotions such as tension, frustration, anxiety, anger and depression resulting from aspects of his or her work as a teacher.
>
> (p. 156)

Ostell (1998) reminds us that the individual's 'experience' of stress is mediated by his or her own perceptual framework, helpfully adding to Kyriacou's definition:

> *A person is in a state of psychological stress when that person perceives and reacts to circumstances and events, whether real or imagined, internal or external, in such a way as to tax unduly or exceed, their resources for coping.*
>
> (p. 77, Italics author's own)

In a survey, Kyriacou (1989) found that 25 per cent of teachers in the UK rated their job as either 'very stressful' or 'extremely stressful' which clearly indicates that they judge their 'resources for coping' are being exceeded. Similar results were obtained from an international study of teachers in New Zealand (Galloway *et al.*, 1987). There can be little doubt that a substantial proportion of teachers experience their job as more than just professionally demanding and as actually stressful. In the last decade or so, the tidal wave of education legislation and its associated bureaucratic frameworks, has sometimes appeared to drown teachers' enthusiasm for change in a sea of paper. While the negative effects of this clerical overload have finally been acknowledged, it has undoubtedly added to the widespread perception of teaching as a stressful occupation. The unrealistic time scales given for the implementation of major educational initiatives such as the literacy and numeracy hours, threshold payments for teachers and so on have also been criticised for leaving teachers feeling ill-prepared and under-resourced to manage a centrally determined change agenda effectively (Kyriacou, 1998).

Walsh (1998) describes how research has shown that in occupations where high work demands are coupled with low job control or power of discretion, feelings of alienation such as anxiety, frustration or apathy result. All too easily the on-going experience of such feelings can result in a lowering of self-confidence, self-esteem and self-efficacy (Bandura, 1997). The pervasively low morale of teachers is inextricably linked to the systematic loss of professional discretion and autonomy which has been experienced over the last decade, particularly for those teachers trained before the Education Reform Act and the introduction of the National Curriculum.

Causes of teacher stress

Teaching is an emotionally as well as intellectually demanding profession. This is exemplified by Kyriacou (1998) in a review of studies of teacher stress. He argues that they have consistently shown the following five broad categories to be the most common sources of stress:

- poor pupil behaviour, ranging from low levels of pupil motivation to overt indiscipline;
- time pressure and work overload;
- poor school ethos, including poor relationships with the headteacher and with colleagues;

- poor working conditions, including a lack of resources and poor physical features of the school;
- poor prospects concerning pay, promotion and career development.

Undoubtedly, such a list will be culturally specific. One of the writers worked with a Zimbabwean student who reported that a major stressor for teachers in Zimbabwean schools was working with the human consequences of the AIDS/HIV crisis. A survey carried out in the Mwenezi District of Masvingo Province revealed that one in five school-aged children had lost a parent to the disease. Grief and loss were a constant emotional backdrop to the educational experience of young people, served by teachers emotionally ill-equipped or trained to cope with tragedy on such a grand scale (Machakata, 2000).

In the UK, although the cultural, social and economic context may be very different, what is similar is the experience of teachers who report that they feel incompetent to carry out a demanding pastoral role with confidence. This can lead to what Clarkson (1994) has termed the 'imposter syndrome'. By expecting teachers to undertake pastoral roles without specialised training or supervision or even providing real opportunities for 'talk time' during the week, further demands are placed on teachers which they may feel are impossible to comply with conscientiously. Most teachers will at some time have had the experience of feeling that they have let down a young person obviously in need of time to talk, because they are rushing off to teach their next lesson. The sensitive and compassionate management of situations such as this with students, colleagues or parents, means that there is a real need for teachers to learn effective time, as well as stress, management strategies as part of their professional development repertoire. By taking an active developmental approach they will be better equipped to fulfil both their teaching and pastoral duties effectively without damaging their own or others' physical or mental health.

Effects of stress

As we have already outlined, the experience of stress will be different for each individual. What one teacher finds stressful another does not. Similarly, the ways which teachers seek to control the stress they experience differs from person to person. What works for one teacher may not work for another. Stress can manifest itself in a wide variety of ways; physical, emotional, psychological or spiritual. When we are under constant unpleasant and unwelcome pressure it tends to first affect any areas of existing physical or psychological vulnerability. For example, one of the writers notices that the first sign of stress building up, is when he begins to re-experience a mild form of a childhood stammer. For others the bodily warning sign of too much stress may be problems with digestion, bowel dysfunction or difficulty in sleeping at night. Hinton and Rotheiler (1998, p. 104) summarised the research on teachers' physiological responses to stress and found that the most commonly reported symptoms were:

- physical exhaustion/fatigue and tiredness;
- skeleto-muscular tension/pains;
- heart symptoms and high blood pressure;
- headaches;
- digestive disorders;
- respiratory difficulties and complaints;
- sleep disturbances;
- voice loss.

Some teachers report experiencing unusual and sometimes frightening physical symptoms such as numbness in a limb or a sensation that they have suddenly become heavier and fatter. A sense of depression, feeling trapped, weighed down or powerless can induce a loss of meaning or purpose to life. An important preventative skill for teachers, therefore, is to develop the ability to pay close attention to their own physical and emotional states. We need to be sufficiently self-aware so that we are able to read and interpret accurately such warning signs at a sufficiently early stage in their onset in order to be able to take active measures to ameliorate their effects. Failure to recognise these early signs of stress and make appropriate lifestyle changes can result in teacher burn-out.

Burn-out

Teacher burn-out refers to the mental, emotional and attitudinal exhaustion which results from prolonged or uninterrupted exposure to high levels of stress (Kyriacou, 1998). The symptoms of burn-out include feeling chronically tense, exhausted or depressed. Teachers at risk of burning out may develop negative attitudes towards students and colleagues, become generally cynical or turned off and experience little feeling of value or accomplishment in their personal and professional lives. They may frequently be ill, absent from work for repeated or extended periods and increasingly depend upon the use of comforters such as chocolate, alcohol, caffeine and cigarettes to make life bearable. They are also likely to be involved in increased conflict at school and with family and friends either because of a psychological withdrawal from the effort of maintaining relationships or because of a loss of emotional self-control leading to them having a short fuse. Experiencing these symptoms of burn-out can have serious consequences for a person's long-term psychological and physiological health.

There are also substantial negative effects on organisations where staff suffer the effects of burn-out. High rates of staff absenteeism, increased numbers of accidental injuries, low overall morale among staff and less effective service delivery are all signs of organisational overload. Apart from the personal impact, the implications for the profession are profound. Early retirement due to ill-health, resignations, high staff turnover and the inability to recruit and retain senior staff are all symptomatic of a profession under strain. The Financial Times (1990) reported that the Health and Safety Commission was urging all LEAs to draw up policies for dealing with stress in schools. They calculated the cost to the nation in millions of pounds annually. By itself this is an impressive figure but what was not calculated was the cost in terms of impoverished teacher–student relationships and academic achievement in classrooms. For example, teachers experiencing the symptoms of burn-out are more likely to be impatient, irritable and less likely to regulate their emotional responses to stressful situations appropriately. This leads to poor judgement or hasty decision-making so that they may describe students who cause them difficulties in the classroom as having EBD (educational and behavioural difficulties) with the negative knock-on effects for that student. It is vital both for schools and their staff to learn to manage stress appropriately and thereby avoid the debilitating effects of burn-out. The first step in this is for everyone to recognise the early signs of burn-out and to employ suitable strategies to manage the stress in their lives.

Stress management model

People are very different in the ways they cope with high levels of stress. What works for some people will have no impact on others. Being told to develop interests outside work in order to get the job in perspective might mean gardening for some, bungy jumping for others. The model of stress management presented here, outlines a wide range of coping strategies from which individuals can choose the specific techniques most suited to them. The coping strategies are those that address the interpersonal, emotional, cognitive, physical, task-related and organisational aspects of stress. It is important to address each of these aspects of stress management in order to avoid the cumulative effects which stress can have on our lives.

Interpersonal responses

For many of us, much of the stress we experience results from our relationships, particularly with colleagues and family members. Therefore, it is essential that teachers develop the skills of communicating assertively in order to reduce the stress levels in their interpersonal relationships. Full use should be made of the assertion skills discussed in Chapter 13 (and Hornby, 1994), including: saying 'no' when you need to; expressing feelings constructively using 'I' messages; being able to both give and receive helpful feedback; and developing behavioural strategies for dealing with criticism or aggression. Assertive behaviour can enable us to develop mutually satisfying relationships with the significant people in our lives and as such is a key survival strategy.

Another important self-help strategy is the ability to be prepared to talk through personal concerns with an empathetic listener. Discussing problems with other people can enable us to hear our own stories and make sense of them. If we are lucky and have a skilful listener, they might even challenge us to take back a sense of control by working on strategies for dealing with the situation in a more assertive manner. Sharing your concerns with someone who has experienced similar problems can in itself be calming, since this generates a feeling of 'being in the same boat' which is widely acknowledged to be therapeutic (Rinpoche, 1992). Having a network of colleagues, friends and family members who can provide a listening ear and support when stress levels rise is invaluable. Try to stay aware of maintaining, and if possible expanding, personal support networks, so that during the tough times there will be people available to share concerns and fears as suggested by Rinpoche (1992, p. 180),

> Usually when you feel fear, you feel isolated and alone, and without company. But when somebody keeps company with you and talks of his or her own fears, then you realise fear is universal and the edge, the personal pain, is taken off. Your fears are brought back to the human and universal context. Then you are able to understand, be more compassionate, and deal with your own fears in a much more positive and inspiring way.

Another key survival skill is the ability to ask for help. When it becomes really difficult to cope with the vicissitudes of daily life, it is vital for teachers to be able to ask for help from colleagues or friends. For many this is easier said than done. Asking for help can make us feel vulnerable, exactly the opposite image that teachers often feel required to present to the world at large. *They* are the helpers, not the one's requiring help. There is also a pervasive myth that to ask for organisational support or help – or even be absent from school with a stress-related condition will have negative repercussions for career prospects. There are fears that owning up to being unable to cope with the stress created by disruptive pupils or massive amounts of paper work will be interpreted as a sign of inadequacy. Consequently, teachers may find it very difficult to ask colleagues for help, even when they are finding it almost impossible to cope.

There is still a reluctance to consider counselling as an appropriate form of professional support – you might have to be 'dangling from the light-shade' before admitting that professional counselling might be the answer. An example of the beneficial effects of counselling comes from a teacher who was a student on a counselling course, led by one of the writers. When she came to class on Monday evening, Meg reported that she was having frightening sensations of feeling heavier and fatter. A friend had told her that she looked different and when she looked in the mirror she agreed. When we explored how these sensations began, it emerged that she had been insulted by a year eleven boy in front of the class on Friday afternoon. To make matters worse, when she spoke to colleagues about the incident in the staff room after school, they just laughed at her distress. She was still upset about the incident on Saturday morning and crashed into the back of another car while driving her five-year-old to the local sports centre. Luckily, only the cars were damaged, but she was distressed that she had endangered her son's life because she was distracted by thoughts of the incident at school. Over the weekend she had not shed tears or expressed her feelings in any way. However, she did become aware of feeling fatter and heavier, as if a great weight was pressing down on her.

After exploring these events and Meg's reactions, it was suggested that we try an intervention based on a simple technique called 'focusing' (Gendlin, 1981). Meg was asked to close her eyes and to focus on the strange sensations she was having and describe them aloud. She talked of feeling physically sick and giddy, with a pounding in her head. She was asked to focus on the feelings and describe them. She focused on the pounding sensation and soon reported it to be moving to a different part of her head and then to disappear altogether. At this point she also experienced a lifting of the heavy weight she had felt pushing down upon her. She reported that the strange sensations had disappeared and felt she was returning to normal. This had all happened within two or three minutes. In talking through the process, it was explained that the sensations had come on because, in order to handle them, she had bottled up feelings of anger, fear and frustration rather than letting herself fully experience them. If the strange sensations recurred, she could get rid of them again by finding somewhere private where she could close her eyes and focus on the sensations as she had just done. Meg was learning a palliative technique to deal with the after-effects of a highly stressful, but unavoidable incident. The simple, self-help technique demonstrated induces feelings of relaxation and just as importantly gives the teacher a sense of increased power over his or her own emotional states.

Emotional responses

Useful strategies for coping with stress are those which are based on centring (Laurie and Tucker, 1982), breathing (Madders, 1979) and relaxation techniques (Cautela and Groden, 1978). Hypnotism, massage and various forms of meditation and yoga all involve combinations of these three types of technique and have been used for centuries to help people cope with the stress of living. Techniques which have become popular more recently for facilitating relaxation are guided fantasy and progressive relaxation.

During a guided fantasy, people are encouraged to close their eyes and imagine themselves in a relaxing situation such as having a long hot bath, lying on a beach, drifting down the river or going for a stroll in the countryside (Hall *et al.*, 1990). Progressive relaxation teaches us to recognise the difference between muscular tension and relaxation by inviting us to concentrate our awareness on the body. The instruction to tense a muscle and then let go of the tension and relax is repeated systematically around the various muscle groups throughout the body, from head to toe. More details of these techniques are provided in Chapter 6. There are a wide variety of commercially made audio tapes and CDs on the market, designed for people who wish to use relaxation exercises in the privacy of their own home (Naparstek, 1995). On the other hand, yoga or meditation classes, which invariably begin and end with a relaxation exercise, may be more suitable for those who need the stimulation of a group to keep them motivated. Relaxation (King and Ollendick, 1998) and meditation (Mclean, 2001) have been developed as classroom activities and the effects on students inevitably have a positive influence on the teachers involved. Ideally, meditation and relaxation techniques should be tailored to fit the needs of the individual and be built into daily routines (Chopra, 1990).

Cognitive responses

It has been shown that our emotional and physiological reactions to events are affected by the way we perceive those events (Meichenbaum, 1985). More specifically, it is the things we tell ourselves about the way we and others should act that often creates unnecessary stress – the should, must and ought messages. Mills (1982) points out that people tend to have unconscious rules about the way they and others ought to behave. For example:

- I must never make a mistake.
- I must do my best work at all times.
- Other people should always think highly of me.
- Other people should never disappoint me.

These unspoken rules create high levels of stress when we try to live up to them, or expect others to. Therefore, as Mills suggests, we need to make ourselves aware of our unconscious rules, challenge the thinking that accompanies them and revise them to produce less stressful messages. For example:

- I would rather not make any mistakes but if I do it just shows that I'm human.
- Although I always aim to produce my best work, sometimes this is not possible due to lack of time or energy, so it's acceptable to produce average work at these times.
- I like others to think well of me but realise that some won't and I can live with that.
- I would like everyone I have to deal with to be honest and reliable but unfortunately the world just isn't like that, so it's something I must accept.

In addition to identifying and re-evaluating the appropriateness of your 'should, must and ought' messages, it is also useful to learn the skill of reframing, that is, changing negative, stress producing thoughts to positive, calming ones (Mills, 1982). For example:

- Stay calm. You can handle this well as long as you don't lose your temper.
- Worrying about it will do no good. Whatever happens you can handle it when the time comes.
- It has been a difficult experience but there are things you have learnt from it.

By using positive self-talk in a systematic and disciplined way to counteract any negative thoughts you experience, your stress level can be made more manageable as you increase a sense of personal control.

Another way to reduce stress is through visualisation (Gawain, 1982). Developing the art of positive visualisation has been shown to have therapeutic effects in both personal and professional situations (Shaw *et al.*, 1981). Visualising feeling relaxed in situations where you might normally expect to feel tense, for example, giving a presentation to a large group of colleagues, can be helpful as can visualising yourself achieving a desired goal.

Finally, keeping a healthy sense of humour and sense of fun is a powerful strategy for managing stress. It is interesting to note that a first sign that stress is becoming unmanageable for some is when their sense of humour, their ability to laugh at themselves and the absurdity of situations, diminishes.

Physical responses

Taking care of yourself physically is an essential aspect of stress management. Getting adequate exercise, nutrition, sleep and rest is very important in managing professional and personal demands healthily (Hall, 1998). Both writers notice that when it becomes impossible to take a mid-day break because of work pressures, it increases the likelihood of making mistakes in the afternoon as well as returning home, shattered and unable to shake off the tension of the day.

Having a healthy diet, eating regular meals and avoiding the abuse of drugs such as alcohol, tobacco, tea and coffee are other important aspects of effective stress management (Madders, 1979; Hanson, 1987). A common response to high levels of stress is to eat more than we need. When food is used as a comforter, a buffer against the tribulations of daily life, then this is a sign that the real sources of stress are being avoided or not dealt with. One of the writers notices that increased chocolate consumption is the first sign of stress building up.

Participating in vigorous exercise at least three times a week is one of the best ways to counteract the negative effects of stress. Some people like to join a gym or health club and have an organised, exercise programme. Others prefer regular involvement in social sports such as tennis, badminton, bowling or golf. However, the best exercises for the whole body are considered to be swimming, cycling and brisk walking. Ideally, exercise should be built into your daily routine, for example, by walking to work, using the stairs instead of the lift or having a daily lunchtime jog. While schools have the facilities to provide teachers with regular exercise opportunities, it is surprising how few actually organise events for staff. This would not only be beneficial to the teachers themselves, but provide a positive role model for students whose own lifestyle may be relatively inactive. Interestingly, Aspy and Roebuck's research (1977) demonstrated that physical fitness and interpersonal stamina were linked. They demonstrated that physically fit school principals were better able to maintain their levels of interpersonal functioning over the course of a school week than their relatively unfit colleagues.

Another important aspect of stress management is to develop a healthy sense of perspective by having a change of scene from time to time. Mills (1982) suggests getting completely away from home and work environments on holiday, at least once a year, and also taking some weekends off to 'get away from it all'. It is also important to have changes of scene built into your weekly routine. Many people find that involvement in social sports such as golf, tennis or badminton enables them to meet up with people from a wide range of occupations and backgrounds which gives a whole new outlook. Others fulfil this function through hobbies, clubs or voluntary service. The risk is that it is these regenerative activities that are the first to disappear if work demands become excessive.

When people consider that they cannot justify taking the time needed for a regular sporting, hobby or social involvement it is important to realise that a few minutes a day devoted to nurturing themselves, can achieve a similar end. Covey (1992) calls this 'sharpening the saw' and uses a story to illustrate the message that we need to renew ourselves mentally, socially and emotionally, spiritually and physically in order to stay alive to realising our full human potential.

Suppose you were to come upon someone in the woods working feverishly to saw down a tree.

> 'What are you doing?' you ask.
> 'Can't you see?' comes the impatient reply. 'I'm sawing down this tree.'
> 'You look exhausted,' you exclaim. 'How long have you been at it?'
> 'Over five hours,' he returns, 'and I'm beat! This is hard work.'
> 'Well, why don't you take a break for a few moments to sharpen the saw?' you inquire.
> 'I'm sure it would go a lot faster.'
> 'I don't have time to sharpen the saw, the man says emphatically, 'I'm too busy sawing'.
>
> (p. 287)

One of the writers uses the concept of 'nurturing yourself' in working with parents of children with special needs. Many parents are so heavily involved in caring for their children that they tend to put their own needs on the back burner, which puts them at greater risk of experiencing the negative effects of stress. Typically, parents (particularly mothers) are shocked when they are asked to spend time during the week to do something that is just for themselves; something which they really want to do (not which they think they ought to do). Activities chosen include soaking in the bath, reclaiming a lost interest, taking long countryside walks or chilling out with friends. Feedback from parents on this suggests that it is a revelation to many of them to take time to nurture themselves in order to be better carers. Teachers react similarly and also report initial feelings of guilt when they begin to practise 'sharpening the saw'.

Task-related responses

A key component of coping with stress for busy people is managing time as efficiently as possible and much has been written about this topic (Black, 1987; Fontana, 1993). According to this literature the essential elements of time management are establishing priorities and careful planning. Covey (1992) has produced a useful weekly worksheet for doing just this. He suggests that we first analyse the roles which we fill, such as partner, son or daughter, parent, teacher, colleague, friend, neighbour. Next we should consider the goals we have in each of these areas and work out our priorities for these for the following week. Then we need to allot time on the weekly worksheet (or in our diaries) to work on our prioritised goals.

Other important aspects of time management include: delegating appropriately; refusing new roles you don't feel happy or competent to take on; and making a daily job list. A useful strategy is to handle each item which comes to you on paper only once, if at all possible. Another is not to waste unnecessary time in meetings. Teachers can get caught up in meetings for several hours each week and much of this time could be used more efficiently. Learning chairing and membership skills are essential if meetings are to be productive. Clear time boundaries, the purpose of the meeting and what needs to be achieved should all be clarified in advance. Important issues which need more discussion need to be delegated to a sub-committee or working party.

Another important aspect of time management is to ensure that whenever possible the most intellectually demanding tasks are done at the time of day when personal energy levels are at their highest. Also try 'Grandma's Rule'. Promise yourself a break or healthy snack after a particularly demanding piece of work. Students similarly can be advised to spend an hour on study and then take a short break with a reward as part of their exam preparation. A common problem is that people often procrastinate because of the volume of work which piles up. In this situation, it is generally useful to do a simple 'task analysis', that is, break the tasks down into manageable components and tackle them step by step. Focusing on one step at a time helps prevent being overwhelmed by the apparent enormity of the undertaking.

Organisational responses

Much of the stress which professionals experience is caused by organisational factors, such as poor communication between staff, an incompetent head of department or an ill-disciplined, self-orientated core of staff. The most effective long-term strategy to deal with such difficulties can be to bring about constructive change by becoming as involved as possible in the management of your workplace. However, such organisational factors are often ones which individuals can do little to change without expending enormous amounts of energy, so instead, it is frequently best to adopt specific strategies to manage these work related stressors.

One way of reducing stress at work is to develop collaborative working alliances with colleagues. As Covey (1992) suggests, initiating co-operative ventures with individuals or small groups of colleagues encourages teamwork and tends to increase everyone's effectiveness. Additionally, it is sometimes possible to get together a small group of colleagues into a support group. This can be a fairly formal group which could perhaps meet at lunch times, or it can be quite informal with a few people getting together over a drink once a week. Either way, this can be very supportive and is a useful strategy for reducing stress levels. One of the writers has experience of an intra-organisational support group of four, which met once a month to share experiences, and an inter-organisational group of three, meeting to discuss commonalities and differences in the workplace. The common denominator for both groups was that they were problem-solving, learning-orientated groups aiming to challenge each others' frames of reference in a supportive, constructive way. While they provided an opportunity to share feelings, they were not 'moan shops'.

Another useful strategy is to keep a clear distinction between work and home by leaving all incomplete work at school rather than bringing it home. It is usually better, if something has to be finished, to stay a little longer at school to get it finished, rather than bringing it home and having it ruin your evening or weekend. Many teachers experience the 'briefcase as albatross' syndrome. Lugging home an enormous briefcase and carrier bags of marking which sit menacingly in the hall, casting accusing glances each time you pass, can ruin an evening or weekend – your 'sharpening the saw' time.

An important strategy to control work related stress is not to lose sight of your long-term life or career aspirations. Covey (1992) calls this 'beginning with the end in mind'. Ensuring that you never lose sight of your life goals and what it is you want to be remembered for, the inheritance you would like to leave behind. Seeing your job in this way, as a step on the way to where you want to be in a few years time, is a way of keeping current concerns in perspective. Losoncy (1982) suggests that we should continually attend to self-promotion activities. That is, we should always allocate some of our work time to develop something that will help us move towards our career goals.

Finally, a last resort strategy, to use when stress at work has become so severe that you are struggling to cope, is to take a 'mental health day' (Shaw *et al.*, 1981). It is clearly better to take one day off and re-charge your batteries than to wait until your physical or psychological health breaks down, at which time you could need to take much longer off. You might want to remind yourself that no-one is indispensable and that, 'death is nature's way of telling you to slow down'.

Application of stress management model

The stress management model can be used by teachers as a source of guidance to ensure that they effectively manage the high levels of stress involved in teaching. In addition, the model can also be used to identify strategies which can be used to teach students how to manage specific stressors, such as test anxiety. In order to illustrate the application of the stress management model to common student stressors, an outline of the strategies is presented below. Those listed are selected from each of the different areas of the stress management model previously discussed.

Interpersonal: Teachers can

- encourage students to share their concerns with friends or family members;
- teach assertiveness skills, such as expressing feelings using 'I' messages;
- encourage students to talk with their form tutor or head of year about worries they experience.

Emotional: Teachers can

- use guided or scripted fantasy in PSE and in relevant subject areas;
- teach relaxation techniques, including breathing and awareness of muscle tension.

Cognitive: Teachers can

- help students to identify and change stress-producing unconscious rules;
- teach students to use positive self-statements to affirm their ability to cope;
- demonstrate how creative visualisation can be used to improve relaxation and achieve goals.

Physical: Teachers can

- teach students the importance of 'sharpening the saw';
- teach students the importance of a healthy diet and adequate sleep;
- emphasise the need to avoid the abuse of drugs such as alcohol, tobacco and coffee;
- reinforce the importance of regular exercise.

Task-related: Teachers can

- teach the importance of managing time efficiently;
- teach the use of effective work habits and study skills.

Organisational: Teachers can:

- help students understand and learn how to function effectively in school;
- encourage students to co-operate with their peers in order to learn most effectively.

Conclusion

Stress is one of the major undiscussed factors which currently hinders the school improvement agenda. Teachers are all too aware of the responsibility they carry for the education of the nation's youth. Commitment to public service, conscientiousness and a belief in the power of education to transform lives for the better are hallmarks of the profession. Teachers are at the very heart of the government's drive to raise educational standards in our schools (DfEE, 1997). However, this profound sense of moral and ethical purpose can paradoxically lead to increased levels of stress when teachers measure themselves against the combined demands and expectations of parents, students, colleagues, communities, the media and government. Teachers are too valuable a resource to the nation to lose their hearts and minds to the debilitating effects of stress. In this chapter, we have argued that for teachers and schools to take back control over the stress they experience they will need to be determined and confident actors in their own self and organisational management programmes.

References

Aspy, D. N. and Roebuck, F. N. (1977) *Kids Don't Learn From People They Don't Like*. Amhurst, Mass: Human Resource Development Press.

Bandura, A. (1997) *Self-Efficacy: The Exercise of Control*. New York: W. H. Freeman.

Black, R. (1987) *Getting Things Done*. London: Michael Joseph.

Cautela, J. R. and Groden, J. (1978) *Relaxation*. Champaign, Ill: Research Press.

Chopra, D. (1990) *Perfect Health*. London: Bantam Books.

Clarkson, P. (1994) *The Achilles Syndrome: Overcoming the Secret Fear of Failure*. Shaftsbury, Dorset: Element Press.

Covey, S. (1992) *The Seven Habits of Highly Effective People*. London: Simon and Schuster.

DfEE (Department for Education and Employment) (1997) *Excellence in Schools*. London: HMSO.

Financial Times (17th November, 1990) Policies Urged to Combat Teacher Stress.

Fontana, D. (1993) *Managing Time*. Leicester: British Psychological Society.

Galloway, D., Panckhurst, F., Boswell, K., Boswell, C. and Green, K. (1987) Sources of stress for class teachers in New Zealand. *Pastoral Care in Education*, 5: 28–36.

Gawain, S. (1982) *Creative Visualization*. New York: Bantam.

Gendlin, E. T. (1981) *Focusing*. London: Bantam.

Hall, C. (1998) Fitness for purpose: self-care and the pastoral tutor. In M. Calvert and J. Henderson (eds) *Managing Pastoral Care*. London: Cassell.

Hall, E., Hall, C. and Leech, A. (1990) *Scripted Fantasy in the Classroom*. London: Routledge.

Hanson, P. (1987) *The Joy of Stress*. London: Pan.

Hargreaves, A. and Fullan, M. (1998) *What's Worth Fighting for in Education?* Buckingham: Open University Press.

Hinton, J. W. and Rotheiler, E. (1998) The psychophysiology of stress in teachers. In J. Dunham and V. Varma (eds) *Stress in Teachers*. London: Whurr.

Hornby, G. (1994) *Counselling in Child Disability*. London: Chapman and Hall.

King, J. K. and Ollendick, T. H. (1998) Utility of relaxation training with children in school settings: a plea for realistic goal setting and evaluation. *British Journal of Educational Psychology*, 68: 53–66.

Kyriacou, C. (1989) The nature and prevalence of teacher stress. In M. Cole and S. Walker (eds) *Teaching and Stress*. Milton Keynes: Open University Press, pp. 27–34.

Kyriacou, C. (1997) *Effective Teaching in Schools*. (2nd edn) Cheltenham: Stanley Thornes.

Kyriacou, C. (1998) Teacher stress: past and present. In J. Dunham and V. Varma (eds) *Stress in Teachers: Past Present and Future*. London: Whurr, pp. 1–13.

Laurie, S. G. and Tucker, M. J. (1982) *Centering*. Wellingborough: Excalibur.

Losoncy, L. (1982) *Think Your Way To Success*. Hollywood, CA: Wiltshire.

Machakata, I. (2000) *Learning Alone?: Counselling Adolescents in Secondary Schools in Zimbabwe*. Unpublished BEd Dissertation, University of Nottingham.

Madders, J. (1979) *Stress and Relaxation*. Sydney: Collins.

Mclean, P. (2001) Perceptions of the impact of meditation on learning. *Pastoral Care in Education*, 19(1): 31–5.

Meichenbaum, D. (1985) *Stress Inoculation Training*. New York: Pergamon.

Mills, J. W. (1982) *Coping with Stress*. New York: Wiley.

Naparstek, B. (1995) *Staying Well with Guided Imagery*. London: Thorsons.

Ostell, A. (1998) Stress, anger and headteachers. In J. Dunham and V. Varma (eds) *Stress in Teachers*. London: Whurr.

Rinpoche, S. (1992) *The Tibetan Book of Living and Dying*. London: Rider.

Shaw, S. F., Bensky, J. M. and Dixon, B. (1981) *Stress and Burnout*. Reston, VA: Council for Exceptional Children.

Walsh, B. (1998) Workplace stress: some findings and strategies. In J. Dunham and V. Varma (eds) *Stress in Teachers: Past, Present and Future*. London: Whurr, pp. 14–36.

15 Ethical issues in counselling for teachers

Margaret Nelson Agee

You will be called on daily, if not hourly, to wear a number of different hats and to function in a variety of diverse roles for which you may not be adequately prepared. What will you do when a child confides in you that she is pregnant? How will you handle the student who is emotionally falling apart before your eyes? What will you do when you suspect that a child is abusing drugs or is suffering from an eating disorder? What will you say to the child who approaches you for understanding because he feels lonely? What will you do when a student solicits your promise to keep a secret, but then tells you that she is breaking the law and intends to continue doing so?

(Kottler and Kottler, 1993, p. 2)

Introduction

Throughout this book teachers have been encouraged to recognise and develop the potential of their counselling role with students. However, there are a number of possible pitfalls. In this chapter, guidelines for professional practice in counselling are outlined, potential dangers for both teachers and students are highlighted, and various practical and ethical issues are considered.

Why are practical and ethical guidelines needed?

Regardless of positive intentions inherent in any helping relationship there is the potential for both benefit and harm. It is essential that helpers work within frameworks of understanding and guidelines for practice that safeguard both the well-being and safety of those whom they are attempting to help, as well as the helper. A recent New Zealand study demonstrated that, even in schools where there are designated counsellors, a number of school staff besides counsellors become involved in counselling situations (Miller *et al.*, 1993). Similar findings have also been reported from the United Kingdom (Mabey and Sorensen, 1995).

The involvement of a wide range of staff members in the counselling process may reflect an increasing need for counselling services in schools, arising out of existing economic and social pressures such as poverty, neglect, violence, abuse, family disruption and substance abuse. As a senior staff member in a large secondary school with several counsellors reported

Counsellors are now dealing with life and death matters, and others are now picking up what 5 years ago the counsellor would have dealt with.

Counselling opportunities often arise most naturally in classroom situations, sometimes in conjunction with a topic being studied, and other times because of the relationship of trust that has developed between teacher and student. Students may also develop close relationships with non-teaching staff in a school, such as nurses or caretakers.

Questions must be asked about the extent to which administrators, teachers and other staff operate from a common understanding of what counselling means, their training and skill for engaging in this role, and the monitoring of their practice to ensure the safety of students. There are administrative responsibilities that must be considered when a number of staff are involved in counselling relationships, including legal issues, the possibility of parental complaints, communication and privacy issues. Policies and procedures need to be developed to address such concerns.

An essential aspect of the training of counsellors involves developing their understanding of professional ethics and legal guidelines and providing supervised practice in dealing with ethical dilemmas through engaging in processes of ethical decision-making. This framework needs to be extended to teachers who find themselves involved in counselling within their tutoring and other roles. This is especially true for those whose counselling role is formally recognised within the structures of the school, such as heads of year or senior teachers who have pastoral responsibilities. Otherwise, the current situation will continue, in which staff work in influential positions, largely unguided and unguarded, potentially placing not only students but themselves and school administrators in compromising situations.

No matter how well trained, competent and experienced the teacher, there is often insufficient preparation for the ethical complexities that can arise in counselling situations. This may not be so evident when a teacher is facilitating developmental group work, offering peer support or providing educational or vocational guidance. However, there is more potential for ethical difficulty in personal counselling, whether formal or informal, when a student, colleague or parent has disclosed sensitive personal information.

Nevertheless, it has been the author's experience as a teacher and school counsellor that frequently a student will 'test the water' with a teacher or counsellor by discussing a seemingly straightforward, practical problem such as a career or educational issue. If the counsellor or teacher appears trustworthy, students may disclose the more sensitive issues that are troubling them. A major issue for a child or young person can also surface in a moment of despair in the classroom, or when being dealt with for a disciplinary issue.

Kottler and Kottler (1993) have described other typical scenarios that can occur for a teacher on a day-to-day basis, making the point that often students cry out for help in subtle ways and teachers need to be alert to these signs of distress. All such situations require not only skills in listening and responding appropriately in the moment but also knowledge of the potential professional responsibilities and ethical implications that might ensue, as well as knowledge of when and how to refer a matter to other sources of help.

Ethical dilemmas can be associated with some important issues that arise for teachers involved in counselling. These relate to the role of the teacher as counsellor, and also to the nature of young people as clients.

Role clarification

A fundamental requirement of counselling in schools is clarity of role and purpose. Teachers need to be clear about whether they are using counselling skills within the broad definition of their teaching role in order to enhance their ability to facilitate communication with students within their pastoral capacity, or whether they are taking on a more specific counselling role.

If it is the latter, teachers need to be sure that school management officially sanctions it, with appropriate safeguards and support. Otherwise, if it is a personal decision to engage in unofficial counselling relationships with students, teachers need to consider the position this places them in with regard to school management and possibly the law.

Many professionals use counselling skills to some extent in the delivery of services within their primary role and in these contexts the skills are used informally. Both parties, in this case teacher and student, remain clear that the teacher is primarily acting as a teacher and the expectations of one another remain consistent. When a contracted arrangement is made with a student or parent to meet at a scheduled time and place for an explicit counselling interview, formal counselling is taking place (Mabey and Sorensen, 1995). In such a situation, each party may experience uncertainty about roles and expectations, so conflicts could arise for each party between their normal roles and this new one.

Role conflict and ambiguity

Students may have difficulty making the adjustment from a classroom relationship to a counselling relationship with a teacher. As a member of a class, the student receives academic instruction, undergoes assessment processes and is expected to conform to well-established codes of behaviour. The primary focus is the acquisition of knowledge and skills, and the teacher is responsible for the facilitation of the teaching and learning process. Teachers are, of course, far more than conveyors of information. In their awareness of the physical, emotional, social and intellectual needs of their students, they get to know them as individuals, care about their welfare and attempt to have a positive influence on their lives. However, students may tend to perceive teachers primarily as purveyors of information which it is their job to learn.

Experiencing the same person in both the roles of teacher and counsellor can be confusing and hard to handle for a young person who is having adjustment or developmental difficulties. An example of this occurred when the counsellor in a secondary school also maintained some classroom teaching responsibilities. A fourteen-year-old girl became a counselling client when her teachers noticed some interpersonal difficulties she was having with peers, and she was seen to be exhibiting some immature, attention-seeking behaviour in the classroom. After a series of sessions in which a range of issues was addressed, the counsellor took the client's class for several social education lessons. Even though the counsellor talked through the implications of this with her ahead of time, the student had difficulty coping with the change from an intimate, one-to-one relationship. It was clear to the counsellor that the student was uncomfortable, both in the classroom and in subsequent counselling sessions, to the extent that rapport and progress in both contexts were adversely affected.

The teacher can also experience role conflict. In a study involving counsellors and teachers in guidance networks in secondary schools in New Zealand, it was found that a number of teachers who engaged in counselling activities as part of their role, experienced issues of role conflict and ambiguity (Miller *et al.*, 1993). Lack of time, training, role definition and reimbursement, difficulty in maintaining communication with others in the guidance network, as well as overlap between staff members' roles, conflict between their actual and perceived roles, and confusion about their roles, were some of the problems mentioned by participants.

Role overload can be a danger for caring teachers who see the barriers to learning which students' personal needs present. On a day-to-day basis a teacher wears a variety of hats with students in addition to instructive roles, including a model of interpersonal effective-ness, a compassionate listener and a skilled helper (Kottler and Kottler, 1993, p. 2). Pastoral care is part of the job of any teacher, but the demands of attempting to work holistically and provide pastoral care for students can at times become too heavy, and there is a danger of developing unrealistic expectations when teachers extend their counselling role further. This can be detrimental to the teacher's own health and well-being, possibly leading to burnout. Quite apart from this, it can also impair the teacher's ability to function effectively in the instructional role.

> What do I do when Jane acts up in class, when I know so much about what's going on at home? How can I come down on her or report her to the Dean when I know she's working through sexual abuse and has so much on her plate already? But if I don't, the others will think I'm playing favourites. It diminishes my authority with them.

This is typical of the dilemmas teachers face when they have provided pastoral support to students who have shared personal difficulties with them. Regardless of whether the coun-selling role is sought by teachers or not, as long as students perceive particular teachers as approachable, caring and supportive, they will inevitably find themselves confided in. There will, therefore, be times when it is hard to know how best to respond or what to do with sensitive information which is disclosed.

Multiple role relationships

Illustrated above are some of the potentially negative consequences of what are known as dual or multiple role relationships, when professionals assume two or more roles simultane-ously or sequentially with a person seeking their help (Herlihy and Corey, 1997). Although duality is inherent in many professional relationships and dual relationships are neither completely avoidable nor necessarily harmful they are nevertheless controversial. It has been suggested that the potential for harm is always present since errors of judgement are more likely to occur because of the likelihood of the counsellor's objectivity becoming impaired (St Germaine, 1993). In a number of situations in which a teacher is also counselling a student, it would be difficult not to allow perceptions, biases, loyalties or other priorities related to the teaching role to colour interpretations and responses to the student.

Conflict between a student and teacher, for example, is an issue that is often raised with school counsellors. Teachers sometimes feel uncomfortable listening to complaints against a colleague, so discounting, minimising or rationalising can be common reactions. The potential for divided loyalties has been identified by Kitchener and Harding (1990) as asso-ciated with one of the three factors counsellors should consider in assessing the potential for harm in a dual role relationship. Another common example is at-risk students, who fre-quently present as behaviour problems or underachievers. When a teacher has experienced such a student in class or has heard the complaints of colleagues, it may be difficult to per-ceive the student openly and with a non-judgmental and accepting stance. Further, in working with students who tend to violate school rules, teachers who are counselling students can experience conflict in terms of their responsibilities to the client and to the school. The greater the divergence in responsibilities associated with the different roles, the greater is the potential for harm through divided loyalties and loss of objectivity (Kitchener and Harding, 1990).

A second factor that should be considered in assessing the potential for harm in a dual role relationship is incompatibility of expectations on the part of the client (Kitchener and Harding, 1990). When a teacher assumes a supportive, counselling stance and encourages personal disclosure on the part of students, they are likely to develop expectations of trust-worthiness and personal support that may be at odds with their experience of the disciplinary or assessment roles the teacher may assume in other settings. Also, students may expect the teacher to give advice or provide a clear solution as is commonly expected in the classroom. In addition, students' expectations of privacy may be at odds with the teacher's evaluation of the needs of the student and the demands of the situation.

The third factor that Kitchener and Harding (1990) identified is the power differential between the parties involved in a dual relationship. This is associated with the influence, power and prestige of the counsellor in relation to the relative vulnerability and powerlessness of the client. The greater the power differential, the greater the risk of exploitation and harm. Since the power differential between teachers and students is substantial, this may be problematic. It is always the responsibility of the person in the more powerful position to guard against exploitation and monitor the situation for possible problems (Herlihy and Corey, 1997). Thus, teachers who act as counsellors need to be aware of the potential for harm in such relationships and take steps to prevent this from occurring.

It would appear that there is substantial risk of harm to students when teachers take on the dual role of counsellor. In many instances, however, dual or multiple role relationships are simply unavoidable in schools. In many countries this is the only way of providing essential support and guidance for students, given the lack of designated counsellors, the inadequacy of external services or the difficulty for students in accessing community services. Since this is the case the onus is not just upon individual teachers to recognise and seek to avoid the dangers, but also on school leaders to provide structural supports and safeguards for teachers fulfilling a counselling role.

Support structures and supervision

In providing structural support for pastoral care, guidance and counselling, a comprehensive school policy, tailored to the particular culture and needs of each school, is necessary. School administrators, by means of a consultation process, should develop this with staff at all levels. The policy should be reviewed and modified regularly to ensure that it remains appropriate to changing trends and needs within the school community. An essential part of this process is the need to develop clear definitions of the roles of all staff in the guidance network of the school, spelling out the type of pastoral care provided and the responsibilities of each person. This includes subject teachers, form teachers, heads of year or house, senior teachers, counsellors and non-teaching staff. Within the chain of responsibility, processes for effective communication and oversight need to be established so that, as far as possible, no staff member will feel isolated or unsupported. Staff members should be discouraged from working alone, acting without the sanction of management, or going beyond the boundaries of their competence. As well as a general policy, there needs to be specific policies and procedures developed to address such circumstances as trauma and sudden death, physical and sexual abuse, as well as violence and bullying. If there is no counsellor on staff, it is advisable to involve a counsellor or other specialist from the community as a consultant or facilitator in the development of such policies. Professional development opportunities in counselling and guidance need to be made as widely available as possible so that all staff members will be encouraged to develop helping skills appropriate to their roles. Opportunities should be provided for staff to work through some challenging situations as well as test out the effectiveness of the communication and referral processes within the school.

Supervision

An essential aspect of the professional practice of counselling is the process of supervision, a formal arrangement in which counsellors meet on a regular basis with one or more experienced colleagues to discuss issues that are arising in their work with clients and their own professional development. This is mandated by organisations such as the British Association of Counselling and Psychotherapy (BACP) and the New Zealand Association of Counsellors, and is a confidential relationship designed to monitor the safety and effectiveness of the counsellor's practice, and to provide personal support for the counsellor. It is a source of on-going professional development, where counsellors can monitor both the maintenance of objectivity and their personal involvement in counselling relationships. Supervision provides an important independent perspective to assess ethical issues and standards of practice (Bond, 1993). Counselling supervision is separate from management supervision, which deals with non-clinical, administrative issues, and may be offered by a senior staff member overseeing pastoral care and guidance within the school.

Anyone working as a counsellor in a school should be receiving regular professional supervision, preferably from an independent, experienced counsellor outside of the school. For staff members using counselling skills within their roles as teachers, this may not be feasible, but the possibility should be considered of making available periodic group or individual supervision, facilitated by a trained counsellor, who may be the leader of the pastoral care and counselling team. Day-to-day leadership of this team or network should ideally be provided by someone who is a trained counsellor and a member of a professional body, who understands ethical guidelines and can facilitate the analysis and handling of difficult issues that arise. Additionally a senior staff member with responsibility for pastoral care should act as mentor or adviser to staff involved in counselling, and take ultimate responsibility for decision-making in crises or organisationally sensitive situations. The effectiveness of a pastoral care system and the way in which counselling is regarded within a school are frequently dependent on the nature and quality of support provided by senior management.

Professional Codes of Ethics

It is expected that counsellors maintain membership in a professional organisation such as the BACP and that they practice according to the code of ethics of their organisation. This expectation is common to many professional groups, including teachers, which have developed systems of self-regulation or statutory accountability. In addition to the Code of Ethics and Practice for Counsellors (BAC, 1992), the BACP has also developed a Code of Ethics and Practice for Counselling Skills, which applies to members who do not regard themselves as counsellors but who use counselling skills to support other roles. Teachers involved in counselling may wish to seek membership of the BACP or a similar organisation and familiarise themselves with the professional codes of ethics. Membership of a professional organisation also has the advantage of providing exposure to current knowledge and debate as well as opportunities for professional development. It also has the advantage for clients that they have access to a complaints procedure. Although complaints against incompetent teachers can be laid with senior staff and governing bodies of schools, the provision of another avenue specific to counselling issues can be an added safeguard for consumers of counselling services.

Confidentiality

One of the most challenging ethical and practical issues for anyone involved in counselling in schools is that of privacy. An obvious problem with teachers acting as counsellors is the general informality of the settings in which this occurs. Professional counselling settings typically involve a location affording privacy, a mutually understood time frame and role clarity. These factors afford a greater degree of safety for both client and counsellor than the *ad hoc* nature of many informal counselling encounters between teachers and students or teachers and parents. It can compromise students' or parents' privacy and lead to embarrassment or more serious personal consequences to attempt to conduct discussions involving personal issues in a public place. Therefore, as soon as it appears that a discussion is likely to be of a personal nature, it is essential to arrange a place that affords protection from intrusion and sufficient time to address the issues.

The emphasis on the importance of confidentiality in counselling practice is based on the principle of respect for clients' capacity for self-determination (autonomy) and the principle of fidelity. Sensitive personal issues are discussed in counselling and a key element in the success of a therapeutic relationship is trust. It is regarded as vital that a counsellor honours the right of the client to expect that what is discussed will remain confidential. Corey *et al.* (1998) have listed circumstances in which it is ethically permitted to break confidentiality as including:

*   When a client poses a danger to self or others.
*   When a client discloses an intention to commit a crime.
*   When abuse or neglect of a child is suspected.
*   When a court orders a counsellor to make records available.

In addition, when counselling children, the younger the child, the greater the need to collaborate with the parent and, therefore, the greater the potential for a counsellor or teacher to break confidentiality. School policies can also require the disclosure of certain information to authorities in implementing policies and procedures laid down by management, for example, with regard to sexual abuse. Whilst on the one hand there is often a need for adults to share a certain amount of information, young people themselves often seek more control than they believe they will be given in counselling relationships (McGuire *et al.*, 1994).

Conflicts between considerations of autonomy and welfare are at the heart of many ethical dilemmas facing teachers in counselling and clearly, in the case of a young child or a suicidal adolescent, considerations of welfare would generally take precedence. Ethical and legal guidelines, however, do not provide clear-cut answers but whatever the age of a client, it is strongly recommended in the legal and professional literature, that as far as possible, the client is consulted about any disclosures and has control over them. Adolescents are regarded as having similar confidentiality rights to those of adults (Corey *et al.*, 1998). Regardless of the circumstances surrounding the initiation of a counselling relationship, the principles of informed consent and confidentiality about the nature of the counselling process and the disclosure of information must apply, including explanation of the limits to confidentiality.

If it becomes apparent to the teacher that others may need to be informed about or involved in working with the student to resolve the issues, a process developed from those proposed by Taylor and Adelman (1989) can be used:

- Explore with the student who else is involved in the situation at issue, and who might be concerned, might need to know, or want to help. Frequently the student is able to identify key people, and initiate the acknowledgement that information needs to be shared.
- If the student does not initially recognise the need for others to know or be involved, the teacher then needs to explain the perceived need for disclosure and discuss the reasons. The student may then acknowledge the necessity for the disclosure and take an active part in the process.
- Whether the need for disclosure is initiated by the student or teacher, explore with the student the likely consequences, both within the counselling relationship and beyond it.
- Discuss with the student the question of who will take responsibility for disclosing what information, to whom, and how and when to proceed, in order to minimise negative consequences and maximise any benefits.
- Discuss with the student what on-going support you are able to offer as the process of informing and possibly involving others develops.

Harm to self and others

Whenever a teacher detects any sign that a student might be suicidal or may pose a threat to the safety of others it is imperative that the teacher consults with senior colleagues, preferably a trained counsellor. All counselling codes of ethics contain clauses exempting counsellors from responsibility for maintaining client confidentiality in situations of potential self-harm or harm to others. It has been recognised that in situations of potential danger to others from a client, counsellors have a duty to warn the potential victim (Corey *et al.*, 1998).

Whilst some suicidal young people feel relieved when they have confided in someone and are then willing to share with other key people how they are feeling and thereby accept help and support, others insist that a teacher keep their secret. To agree to this would be highly irresponsible, as it is an impossible task for anyone to take upon him or herself the sole responsibility for the survival of another. To retain the secret would be to deny the student the resources needed, which could possibly be life saving. A fundamental tenet of working with suicidal people is never to work alone, both for the sake of the client and for the helper's well-being. Whilst caring family members, friends, teachers and others in a student's social network can offer valuable support, any suicidal young person or adult requires the assistance of a skilled counsellor or other mental health professional.

Within the pastoral care networks in schools, guidelines need to be developed for responding to signs that a student might be suicidal. All teachers and non-teaching staff need to be educated in recognising these indications. This does not mean that every time a student discloses suicidal thoughts it should become widely known as this could be extremely damaging. Rather, each situation needs to be discreetly and carefully monitored and on-going counselling must be made available to students who are in any way at risk. If there is no professionally trained counsellor on the staff, a referral to outside professional help must be made. Ideally, this person could help others in the student's caring network, including teachers, to provide effective support for the student through the crisis and beyond.

Making referrals

In situations such as suicidal behaviour or for other kinds of specialist help, it is frequently necessary for teachers to refer a student, parent or sometimes a colleague, to other sources of help. Referral is sometimes experienced as a single event, that is an action which involves relinquishing of a responsibility that seemed beyond one's capacity to cope, handing it over to someone who can. But handling a referral well involves each party in a process which, although relatively brief, can determine the success or otherwise of the client's on-going care.

Beyond the issues of knowing when and when not to refer, key aspects of the referral process are the preparation of oneself, the preparation of the student or client, and liaison with other sources of support or counselling (Williams, 1993). In the author's experience, it is also advisable to monitor the process to ensure that a successful connection is made between a new helper and a student or adult client.

Most of these factors are self-evident but preparation of oneself needs explanation. It involves examining one's 'values, experiences and beliefs' about referral (Williams, 1993, p. 33). These can sometimes inhibit professionals from allowing themselves to feel vulnerable, accepting that they do not know the answers or have all the resources that their students need, and accepting that it is not a sign of failure to have to refer a student to someone else. 'To become aware of such pressures or such a culture in one's workplace may be a first step towards challenging such notions within yourself' (Williams, 1993, p. 34).

When a teacher is referring a student to another teacher or helper either within or outside the school, the most open and constructive process involves first discussing the issue of referral with the student, then contacting the person to whom the student is being referred. The circumstances and need for the referral can be explained, the viability of the referral can be confirmed, and the best way in which this might be managed can be explored. Ideally this will be done with the permission of the student, if possible in the student's presence if it is by telephone, or face-to-face, so that the student not only knows what has been said about the situation but can also take part in the process. If a letter of referral is being written this can be shown to the student for comment before being sent.

When the student is scheduled to meet the new helper or counsellor, it can ease the process of transition if the teacher accompanies and introduces the student. Although on many occasions this may simply be a matter of ensuring that the student finds the new helper's office and is safely delivered into other hands. In some situations it can be a real advantage to have a teacher who is a caring presence in the student's life at school taking some part in the student's on-going therapy. There are counsellors and other mental health professionals in community agencies that welcome the participation of teachers or school counsellors when appropriate.

Referrals do not always work for a range of reasons, and if this is the case, it may be necessary to find alternative sources of help. Therefore, if a teacher is not involved in an on-going role in a student's therapeutic care, it is advisable to check with the student a short time after making the referral to ensure that contact has been made successfully and the arrangements are meeting the student's needs.

Conclusion

This chapter has examined the principles of ethical counselling practice, and highlighted some key professional issues that need to be considered when counselling. In developing a counselling role with students, teachers will be faced with challenging situations and ethical dilemmas. Some principles and guidelines intended to help teachers think through key issues have been identified, and these can be applied to other ethical dilemmas and issues that may be encountered. In this way teachers can develop their own processes of ethical decision-making and reflection which will enrich their work with respect to both teaching and counselling in schools.

References

Bond, T. (1993) *Standards and Ethics for Counselling in Action*. London: Sage.

BAC (1992) *Code of Ethics and Practice for Counsellors*. Rugby: British Association of Counselling.

Corey, G., Corey, M. S. and Callanan, P. (1998) *Issues and Ethics in the Helping Professions* (5th edn). Pacific Grove, CA: Brooks/Cole.

Herlihy, B. and Corey, G. (1997) *Boundary Issues In Counseling: Multiple Roles And Responsibilities*. Alexandria, VA: American Counseling Association.

Kitchener, K. S. and Harding, S. S. (1990) Dual role relationships. In B. Herlihy and L. Golden (eds) *Ethical Standards Casebook* (4th edn, pp. 146–54). Alexandria, VA: American Counseling Association.

Kottler, J. A. and Kottler, E. (1993) *Teacher as counselor: developing the helping skills you need*. Newbury Park, CA: Corwin Press.

Mabey, J. and Sorenson, B. (1995) *Counselling for Young People*. Buckingham: Open University Press.

McGuire, J., Parnell, T., Blau, B. and Abbott, D. (1994) Demands for privacy among adolescents in multimodal alcohol and other drug abuse treatment. *Journal of Counseling and Development*, 73(1): 74–8.

Miller, J., Manthei, R. and Gilmore, A. (1993) School counsellors and guidance networks: roles revisited. *New Zealand Journal of Educational Studies*, 28(2): 105–24.

St Germaine, J. (1993) Dual relationships: what's wrong with them? *American Counselor*, 2(3): 25–30.

Taylor, L. and Adelman, H. (1989) Reframing the confidentiality dilemma to work in children's best interests. *Professional Psycholgy: Research and Practice*, 20(2): 79–83.

Williams, S. (1993) *An Incomplete Guide To Referral Issues For Counsellors*. Manchester: PCCS Books.

Index